Law and Society
Recent Scholarship

Edited by Melvin I. Urofsky

A Series from LFB Scholarly

Drug Laws and Institutional Racism

The Story Told by the Congressional Record

Cheryl L. Chambers

LFB Scholarly Publishing LLC
El Paso 2011

Library of Congress Cataloging-in-Publication Data

Chambers, Cheryl L., 1969-
Drug laws and institutional racism : the story told by the Congressional record / Cheryl L. Chambers.
p. cm. -- (Law & society: recent scholarship)
Includes bibliographical references and index.
ISBN 978-1-59332-410-0 (hbk. : alk. paper)
1. Drug control--Social aspects--United States--History. 2. Narcotic laws--Social aspects--United States--History. 3. Racism--United States--History. 4. Sociological jurisprudence--United States. I. Title.
HV5825.C433 2010
344.7304'460262--dc22
2010038567

ISBN 978-1-59332-410-0

Printed on acid-free 250-year-life paper.

Manufactured in the United States of America.

Table of Contents

CHAPTER 1

Introduction

I began this research questioning the difference between the laws for cocaine and crack[1]. They puzzled me because I could not understand why the sentences for crack were so extreme as compared to cocaine, when crack is a derivative of cocaine. While researching this line of questioning I found that the United States Sentencing Commission, which had assisted in writing the sentencing guidelines in the Anti Drug Abuse Act of 1986, was lobbying Congress to amend the guidelines by reducing the penalties for crack and bringing them closer to those for cocaine. In 1995, Congress rejected the U. S. Sentencing Commission's recommendation to reduce the penalties for crack; this marked the first time that Congress had rejected a Sentencing Commission recommendation[2]. Just days before Congress voted, African American men from all over the U.S. met in Washington for the Million Man March. Was this coincidence or did the African American men's ability to mobilize influence legislator's decision? The answer may never be ascertained definitively, but it did lead me to

[1] Possession of 5 grams of crack cocaine carried a 5 year sentence whereas 500 grams of cocaine were required for a 5 year sentence.
[2] On March 17, 2010 the Senate passed the Fairness in Sentencing Act of 2010 which reduces the 100 to 1 quantity ratio to 18 to 1, raising the quantity of crack cocaine from 5 grams to 28 grams (Sentencing Project, 2010).

question to what extent social context does affect legislation. Is there a connection between the social climate and the advent of legislation?

Law is one of the mechanisms we use to instigate social change and bring about equality, ironically, law is also the tool that has been and may still be used to institutionalize, legitimize and perpetuate inequality. Throughout history the U.S. has experienced periods of acknowledgement of racist laws. Has racism been institutionalized in our federal drug laws? Are we continuing to utilize laws to institutionalize racism? Has this changed over time? How do the political and/or economic contexts of the time-periods affect the drug laws? In order to answer these questions, historical research is required.

Throughout U.S. history, beginning with the Constitution, we have used the institution of law as a means for legitimizing inequality and racial subordination. At times, laws have been blatantly discriminatory in their wording, intent and outcome. Since the passage of the Civil Rights Act of 1964 it has become popular to assume that laws are no longer discriminatory (Bonilla-Silva, 2001; Ringer, 1983). This may be an accurate assumption or recent laws may have become subtler in their wording and intent, yet just as discriminatory in their outcome. Historically, racial discrimination has, at times, been present in naturalization, immigration, voting, family, and labor laws to name but a few. In the past, beliefs of racial inferiority, savagery, and inability have resulted in the passage of legislation designed to perpetuate the subordinate status of racial minorities. Utilization of law as a tool used to be overt and blatant; however, with the changing political climate and the passage of antidiscrimination laws, the question arises as to whether the law is still responsible for the perpetuation of inequality in ways that are covert and not easily recognized, regardless of whether or not these outcomes are intended.

Our drug laws may help to illustrate the misperception of the declining significance of race[3]. Race issues were at one time discussed

[3] Wilson (1978) contends that the significance of race is declining and it is more a matter of class.

openly in the political arena and were focused on during the era of the Civil Rights movement (James, 1998). Since then in the political arena, open discussions of race have been minimal and racism has become increasingly difficult to recognize, especially its structural character. President Clinton illustrated this in a 1995 speech stating that race "is not about government, but about the hearts of people" (James, 1998: 62). Failure to recognize or even to allow for the possibility of the structural nature of racism in our laws may contribute to normalizing the racial imbalance, increasing minority populations in prisons, and treating both as contingencies of poverty or proof of assumed black criminality. Tough on crime policies (e.g. three strikes laws) and structured drug sentencing laws have focused on the elements of a crime and prior criminal history, thus purporting to take race out of the equation since sentencing is predetermined by guidelines. In doing so, those establishing these guidelines may have ignored the racial implications of these laws.

Drug laws may also illustrate how the way in which law has fostered discrimination has changed over time. With the enactment of our first drug laws, racism was overtly present in the wording. For example, San Francisco's 1875 city ordinance outlawed the smoking of opium in dens only for people of Chinese decent, the American-Chinese treaty of 1880 prohibited only Chinese citizens residing in the United States from importing smoking opium, and an 1887 law prohibited the importation of opium and the smoking of opium only among the Chinese. After the first opium laws, although federal drug laws (e.g. the Marihuana Tax Act of 1937 and the Anti Drug Abuse Act of 1986) are no longer blatantly racist in their wording, they may still systematically generate disproportionate outcomes. For example, African Americans comprise approximately 12% of the United States population, 13% of drug users, 35% of drug arrests for possession[4],

---

[4] 1 out of 5 drug violations is for sales/trafficking (Bureau of Justice Statistics, 2003). In 1990, 57% of offenders convicted of trafficking were black (Bureau

55% of drug convictions and 74% of drug prison sentences (The Sentencing Project, 1993). If our drug laws represented equality, then African Americans would comprise approximately 12-13% of our drug sentences not 74%. Despite what these statistics may seem to indicate, the few studies conducted since the War on Drugs and the enactment of sentencing guidelines offer inconsistent findings in regard to racial differences in sentencing (Human Rights Watch, 2000; Spohn & Spears, 2002; Albonetti, 1997; Myers 1989; Chiricos & Bales, 1991). Although disproportionate arrest and incarceration rates are not necessarily proof of discrimination, they do indicate that the racial disparities related to drug laws need to be addressed. Additionally, with the War on Drugs, inmates incarcerated for drug offenses represent our fastest growing prison population (Tonry, 1995; Bureau of Justice Statistics, 2003; Bureau of Justice Statistics, 1994). In a fifteen year period (1980-1994) drug offense inmates increased from less that 25% of the federal prison population to approximately 60% (Bureau of Justice Statistics, 1994). With the majority of all prison (federal and state) drug offense inmates being African American (The Sentencing Project, 1993; Mauer, 2009), the racial implications of our drug laws needs to be examined (Uggen & Manza, 2002).

LAW AS AN INSTITUTION

Although the law has been utilized to institutionalize beliefs and practices, the fact that it is an institution in and of itself has often been overlooked by institutional racism theorists. Institutional racism is discussed in the context of prominent structures such as the economic and educational systems, yet institutional racism theorists seem to skirt

---

of Justice Statistics, 1994). Additional statistics for sales/trafficking by race are unavailable at this time. As of 2005, African Americans represented 14% of current drug users, 33.9% of drug offense arrests, and 53% of drug prison sentences (Mauer, 2009)

the issue of law being one of those institutions. Institutional racism theorists may argue that a law illustrates institutional racism, but within the context of economic institutions or the institutions of higher education rather than addressing law as an institution utilized to reproduce inequality. Historically, law was an institution utilized to maintain inequality (e.g. Jim Crow laws). But since the passage of the Civil Rights Acts law has been seen as a device for furthering equality. Since the end of the 1960's studies have found racism embedded in several institutions: housing (Oliver & Shapiro, 1995; Yinger, 1995; Massey & Denton, 1993; Feagin & Feagin, 1978), employment (Williams, 1987; Feagin & Feagin, 1978), education (Sedlacek & Brooks, 1976; Bourgois, 1995; Kozol, 1991; Feagin & Feagin, 1978), social services (Feagin & Feagin, 1978), and heath care (Feagin & McKinney, 2003; Feagin & Feagin, 1978). Given these findings, it is reasonable to ask why the institution of law would be an exception.

From a sociological perspective an institution "is an enduring set of ideas about how to accomplish goals generally recognized as important in a society" (Johnson, 1995: 142). Institutions are also plans for action that can simultaneously be taken for granted yet considered sacred (Sutton, 2001). They can also constrain yet be a source of power. In America law is considered an essential part of democracy (e.g. the rule of law). For many, law represents the basic values we idealize and strive for in our society and, thus, is sacred. Law does provide plans for how to do things, it can constrain us, and it can be a source of power; law is an institution (Sutton, 2001; Parsons, 1962).

Law is one of the major institutions of U.S. society; it governs (or at least attempts to govern) behavior. In a sense it is the ultimate institution in U.S. society, what better way to ensure racial stratification than to codify it into law. Once racial ideology becomes embodied in law, especially if it is not explicit in the wording, it would be easy to deny the injustice of racial subordination by rationalizing that it is not wrong, it is the law.

CHANGE OVER TIME AND CONTEXT

Law also changes over time; it is not static. The social conditions of our times aid in the shaping and defining of the legal structure. According to Pound (1959 – in Grana, 1999) law should be used as a tool of social change, the transformation of culture and other social institutions. Law has been both a cause and an effect of social change. It has been used to draw racial lines (Jim Crow laws) and as a remedy to change racial discrimination (Civil Rights Act) in this country. Consequently, laws and public policy are created within a historical and political context.

Legal theorists acknowledge that law adapts "to changing social circumstances," but few focus on how the law "is influenced by its social context" (Sutton, 2001: 7). Law does affect society, but it is also produced by society (Cotterrell, 1998; Grana, 1999). Legal ideas are the outcome of historical, cultural and political conditions. Thus, laws are created in a historical and political context. In order to understand why a law was created one needs to understand what was occurring prior to and during its creation (Cotterrell, 1998; Chambliss, 1964). Therefore, to understand why a law exists one must look at more than just its wording. Intention is difficult if not close to impossible in some cases to ascertain, but a plausible case concerning the motives behind a law may be built by assessing its social context, specifically the economic and political contexts, and by inferring motivation from the congressional discussions regarding the law.

To understand how laws may have been used to perpetuate racial inequality, it is necessary to look at the nature of law and its reciprocal relationship with society from a sociological perspective. Although laws can and have been viewed from both a conflict and functionalist perspective, since the U.S. is a democratic society there is a tendency by the general public to view our laws from a functionalist perspective, that is, if a law is enacted then it takes on an air of legitimacy and is widely assumed to be for the good of all (The Roper Center 2001a, 2001b; Robinson, 1999; McInturff & Weigel, 2001; Brodie, Parmelee,

Brackett & Altman, 2001). We also assume that through our electoral process (especially since the passage of the 1964 and 1965 Civil Rights Acts) that legal representation in our government is achieved, and thus, everyone has a voice. In essence, the majority of U.S. citizens believe, at least in the abstract, in "for the people, by the people" (The Roper Center 2001a, 2001b; Robinson, 1999; McInturff & Weigel, 2001; Brodie, Parmelee, Brackett & Altman, 2001).

From a functionalist perspective, law has many purposes but in its most basic form, law is the codification of dominant beliefs and values (Grana, 1999; Trevino, 1996; Tittle, 1994). Those beliefs held sacred and regarded as crucial to the solidarity of society are elevated to the level of law. Thus, laws are the foundation of a society and can be the ultimate form of institutionalism. From a conflict perspective, the law is an instrument used by those with power to maintain their status and/or privileges (Trevino, 1996; Tittle, 1994; Chambliss, 1964; Turk, 1976). Beliefs and practices that benefit those in power are codified, and thus, institutionalized. Both the functionalist and conflict perspectives view inequality as intrinsic in the administration of law (Tittle, 1994).

For the most part, in the United States law is viewed as legitimate authority. Because law is a legitimate authority it affects actions and attitudes (Grana, 1999). It is also viewed as sacrosanct and infallible, even though several Supreme Court cases and repealed laws illustrate that unjust laws have been enacted. Regardless of whether law makers were unbiased, the intent of the law can never equal its effect (Turk, 1976). At best laws may fail to exhibit their intended effects; at worst they may result in discriminatory consequences.

In the past, beliefs of racial inferiority, savagery, and inability have resulted in passage of legislation designed to perpetuate the subordinate status of racial minorities. Utilization of law as a tool used to be overt and blatant; however, with the changing political climate and the passage of antidiscrimination laws, the question arises as to whether the law is still responsible for the perpetuation of inequality in ways that are covert and not easily recognized, regardless of whether or not these outcomes are intended.

CONGRESSIONAL RECORD

For this research I focus on the motives behind some of our federal drug laws rather than their consequences. I chose to use the Congressional Record as my data source because it is the official record of the proceedings of both the House of Representatives and the Senate. Until CSPAN began televised coverage of the House in 1979 and the Senate in 1986 (McKinney, 2002), the Congressional Record was the only almost verbatim account of Congressional discussions and proceedings. Analyzing the latent content of the discussions prior to the enactment of drug legislation may develop a plausible case (actual intent is difficult to ascertain) concerning the motives behind the drug laws.

I chose to assess the first opium laws in the late 1800's and 1909, the Marihuana Tax Act of 1937 and the Anti Drug Abuse Act of 1986. Each of the laws or sets of laws were chosen due to their legal and historical significance. The opium laws were selected because the 1909 opium law is considered the United States first federal drug law. Additionally, prior to the opium legislation the United States experienced an influx of Chinese immigrants. This influx fostered the Chinese Exclusion Acts which were discussed and enacted during the same time period as the opium laws. Also of note, the early opium laws usually focused on one form of opium, smoking opium which was associated with Chinese users. Did the anti-Chinese sentiment during this time influence the opium legislation?

The Marihuana Tax Act of 1937 changed the legal standing of marijuana. The legislation seems to have emerged from Commissioner of Narcotics Harry Anslinger's public campaign to demonize marijuana. Anslinger's campaign was widespread, the anti-marijuana messages and salacious stories were available in a variety of media formats: radio, newspaper, magazine, and film. The classic example is the 1936 film Refer Madness that depicts the downward spiral of students smoking marijuana and commitment of one student to a mental hospital. Furthermore, during the same time period the United States was experiencing an increase in Mexican immigration and migration. Popular belief also associated Mexicans with marijuana and violent crime (Bonnie & Whitehead, 1999; Inciardi, 1992). Is there a connection between the social climate of anti-marijuana rhetoric and negative Mexican and marijuana association and the advent of Marihuana Tax Act?

The Anti Drug Abuse Act of 1986 is the law that established the mandatory sentencing guidelines penalizing possession of 5 grams of crack cocaine and 500 grams of cocaine with the same five year sentence. This Act and its consequences are what first sparked my interest in drug laws. Why is the amount of cocaine required for the 5 year sentence 100 times that of crack cocaine when crack cocaine is a derivative of cocaine? Is it because crack cocaine is usually associated with lower class minorities while cocaine use is associated with higher classes and whites? Prior to the enactment of the Anti Drug Abuse Act the United States was experiencing the backlash from the California v. Bakke (1978) decision that race should be an admission factor and claims of reverse discrimination (Pholmann, 1999). Coupled with the end of a recession and high unemployment, reverse discrimination gave the perception of economic threat pitting black against white for limited resources (Pholmann, 1999; Glazer, 1975). It also was during this time period that the term "welfare queen" used in reference to black women gave rise to the myth of lazy women who live well off welfare instead of getting a job and have child after child to supplement the benefits (Feagin & Vera, 1995). Did this social climate affect the legislation of the Anti Drug Abuse Act of 1986?

The early opium laws, the Marihuana Tax Act of 1937 and the Anti Drug Abuse Act of 1986 represent three different time periods allowing for the assessment of whether there has been a change over time in regard to the both the content of the discussions of the legislation and the wording of the laws. By analyzing the latent content of the discussions prior to the enactment of the drug legislation some of the aforementioned questions may be addressed. Do the discussions of opium contain anti-Chinese rhetoric? Similarly, do the discussions of the Marihuana Tax Act and the Anti Drug Abuse Act contain, respectively, anti-Mexican and anti-Black rhetoric? Has racism been institutionalized in our federal drug laws?

CHAPTER 2

Conflict Theory and Racial Inequality

Prior to the late 1960's racial inequality theories were dominated by structural functionalism and assimilation theories (Doob, 1996; Feagin & Feagin, 1978). The paradigm shifted in the late 1960's, when the adequacy of assimilation theory in analyzing discrimination was questioned, focusing more on conflict theories and addressing the role that wealth, power and competition for resources have in formulating and maintaining racial inequality. There was movement from the individual and attitudes to the structural features of society and institutional racism (e.g. Blalock, 1967; Wilson, 1973).

With the systematic rethinking of racial inequality, the interest group competition theory of discrimination, internal colonialism and institutional discrimination were more fully developed (Feagin & Feagin, 1978). Interest group theory[5] of discrimination posits that the

[5] Blalock (1967) contends that discrimination involves the fear of economic competition and the fear of a political power threat. As a minority population grows, the dominant group may fear an increase in competition and power resources of the minority group. This threat may be an inferred potential or a reality; in other words, perception of threat may be as critical if not more so than the reality. The resources for which the dominant group fears competition include but are not limited to money, property, prestige, authority, jobs, and

motivating force behind discrimination is the desire to protect one's own interests (competitive advantage), power, and/or privilege (Blalock, 1967; Feagin & Feagin, 1978). Groups compete for scarce resources (e.g. jobs, money, and prestige) and discrimination is a means of perpetuating the dominant group's current economic and political gains. A specific form of interest theory, internal colonialism theory[6],

---

membership in organizations. However, in order to represent an actual power threat, the minority group needs the ability to exercise power. This ability may be directly related to population size especially in regard to voting. Without resources or power potential, the dominant group cannot effectively discriminate against a minority group. The fear of competition for resources and power motivates the dominant group to maintain and perpetuate inequality by means of discrimination.

Wilson (1973) applied Blalock's theory and compared United States and South African race relations. He concluded that racial stratification is due to competition for scarce resources and the dominant group's efforts to maintain their position of control by neutralizing minority group members as competitors and by exploiting their labor. During times of economic growth both whites and blacks experience growth and race may become less of a factor. However, during an economic recession, minority group member's economic advancement becomes a threat.

[6] Internal colonialism posits that control imposed on indigenous and/or imported racial minorities passes from whites in the home country to whites within the new nation (Doob, 1996; Aguirre & Turner, 1995; Barrera, 1979; Blauner, 1972). Internal colonialism theorists analyze the establishment of racial stratification and the control processes that maintain white dominance and racism (Feagin & Feagin, 1993). Internal colonialism also attempts to address how an imbalance of privilege is incorporated into society in the first place (Feagin & Feagin, 1978). Thus, while whites may acknowledge historical inequities, they fail to comprehend the realities of racism for current minority groups (Doob, 1996). Internal colonialism attempts to address these realities and show how racism affects daily life. The four conditions of internal colonialism have existed in America: control over minority group governance, restriction of racial minority's freedom of movement, colonial-labor principle (racial minorities must serve white interests and needs and be kept in the lowest levels of the stratification system), and a belief in the inferiority of racial minorities' culture and social organization (Doob, 1996).

From an internal colonialism perspective, racial inequality is grounded in economic interests: the desire for cheap labor to maximize profits and control of desirable land (Feagin & Feagin, 1999; Aguirre & Turner, 1995). In order to create and maintain economic dominance, the government must participate by

attempts to explain the origins and development of economic and political power imbalances. Institutional racism theory[7] focuses our attention on the specific direct and indirect mechanisms (e.g. social institutions such as housing, employment and education) through which discrimination is reproduced (Feagin & Feagin, 1978). The development of these theories shifted the perspective to one grounded in conflicts and/or struggles over scarce resources. These theories help illustrate and delineate a historical pattern of the motivation, competition or fear of competition for economic and political resources and power.

A historical analysis of our drug laws may illustrate that competition and threat were present prior to the enactment of the laws. For the purposes of this research I focus on two types of competition/threat: economic and political.

POLITICAL COMPETITION

In terms of political resources and power, in the United States, whites have always had control over minority groups' governance, which is illustrated by looking at past and present political leaders. The power to create law (at the federal level) is vested in three "offices," the President, Congress and the Supreme Court, in which minorities have historically been underrepresented. The office of President until President Obama took office in 2009 had never been held by anyone

---

legitimating the exploitation through laws. Historically, the U.S. government has supported economic exploitation by legitimating slavery in the Constitution, the Fugitive Slave Act of 1793 and the Dred Scott decision (Pohlmann, 1999). Political exploitation is viewed as following and supplementing the economic exploitation (Feagin & Feagin, 1998). Therefore, the focus is usually on capitalistic economic exploitation rather than the political subordination.

[7] For a more in depth review of Feagin and Feagin's institutional racism theory see the first two pages of Chapter Three of this book.

other than a Protestant white male (with the exception of John F. Kennedy), only in the last fifty years have African Americans and women been represented on the Supreme Court with five Justices, and minority group representation in Congress is still lagging behind population representation (African Americans comprise approximately 8% of Congress specifically the House of Representatives yet approximately 12% of U.S. population[8]).

Prior to 1860, whites had complete control over federal governance in that no minorities held a federal office (Pohlmann, 1999; Lusane, 1996). However, African Americans did hold local and state offices: Alexander Lucius Twilight was elected to the Vermont state legislature in 1836, William A. Leisdesdorf to the San Francisco town council in 1847, and John Mercer Langston as Brownhelm, Ohio township clerk in 1855 (Lusane, 1996). The political participation of minority groups changed with the ratification of the Thirteenth Amendment in 1865 outlawing slavery, the Fourteenth Amendment in 1868 requiring state's to recognize the citizenship of "all persons born or naturalized in the United States" (United States Constitution), and the Fifteenth Amendment in 1868 prohibiting states from denying the right to vote based on race (Pohlmann, 1999). With the passage of these Amendments black political participation increased rapidly in voter registration, voter turnout, and election to office (Lusane, 1996).

During Reconstruction twenty-two African Americans served in Congress: two senators from Mississippi, Hiram Revels and Blanche K.

---

[8] Currently 8% of Congress is African American, less than 1% is American Indian, 1% is Asian, less than 1% is Pacific Islander, less than 1% is Vietnamese, 5% is Hispanic and 85% is Caucasian. The House of Representatives has more minority representation than the Senate with 83% of members Caucasian, 9% African American, 5% Hispanic, 1% Asian and less than 1% each American Indian, Pacific Islander, and Vietnamese. The Senate is 96% Caucasian, 1% African American, 2% Asian and 1% Hispanic (Congress.org, 2010). There have been only six African American Senators all of whom served their terms as the only African American in the Senate (Senate.gov, 2010).

Bruce, and twenty Members of the House of Representatives (Lusane, 1996; Pohlmann, 1999). The brief time of Reconstruction was the height of black political power given their representation in Congress as well as state and local government (Lusane, 1996). With the end of Reconstruction, southern states rewrote their constitutions nullifying the voting rights of blacks through poll taxes, literacy tests, grandfather clauses, felony disenfranchisement, and all white primaries, substantially eroding African American political power by approximately 1900 (Lusane, 1996; Pohlmann, 1999). It was almost 30 years before blacks were elected to the House of Representatives and approximately 60 years for the Senate (Pohlmann, 1999). Thus, for decades disenfranchisement laws bolstered and then maintained white political hegemony, especially in southern states and those with large minority populations.

From 1966 to 2002, only three African Americans were elected to prominent state offices (Hacker, 2003). Edward Brooke was elected senator from Massachusetts in 1966 and served two terms. Fourteen years after Senator Brooke, Carol Moseley-Braun was elected Illinois Senator in 1992 and served one term. They both served their terms as the only African American in the Senate. Douglas Wilder of Virginia became the first African American governor when he was elected in 1990 (he also served only one term due to Virginia's one-term limit). During this span of 36 years, 230 people served as U.S. senators of which two were African American, five Asian, one Hispanic, one Native American and 221 white. Of the 316 state governors four were Asian, four Hispanic, one African American and the remaining 307 were white. Thus, between 1966 and 2002 whites held 96.9 percent of the U.S. senate and state governor offices and maintained their political hegemony. The lack of representation in these two offices is significant not only in terms of minority group voice and legislation that makes it to the floor, but also in that U.S. senator and state governor are the two political offices that usually serve as stepping stones to the presidency.

Whites have maintained a political hegemony at the federal level and thus control over minority group governance. Nevertheless, minorities, especially African American, have increased their political power over the years, despite setbacks. Even so, minority political power has never come close to attaining that of whites. However, both during Reconstruction and after the Civil Rights movement, specifically the 1965 Voting Rights Act, the number of registered voters, voter turnout and elections to Congress may have given whites the perception that African Americans were threatening white political power. Especially, given that in terms of voting power, African Americans have played a key role in the election of most Democratic Presidents since World War II (Edsall & Edsall, 1992; Pohlmann, 1999). An increase in black support for the Democratic Party occurred in the 1964 presidential election due to the Democratic Party's strong support of civil and voting rights legislation. This increase marked a shift in black support for the Democratic and Republican Party's; black support shifted to the Democratic Party while working and middle class white support, especially in the south, increased in the Republican Party. Since the shift in 1964, the Democratic Presidential candidate has received 82-94% of the black vote. The power of the black vote was illustrated to an extent in the 2000 and 2004 elections (Bositis, 2004). In several states that Gore won or came close to winning the black vote was key; blacks represented 59% of Gore voters in Louisiana, 28% in Florida, 21% in Missouri and 20% in Michigan. In 2004, the increased black voter turnout aided Kerry's victory in Pennsylvania (7% to 13%) and Michigan (11 to 13%) while a more modest increase in Ohio (9 to 10%) resulted in a close loss for Kerry (Bositis, 2005). Although the vast majority of black voters still voted Democratic the percentage decreased from Gore's 90% to 88% and Bush won the 2004 election by a wider margin than he did in 2000. With a few Congressional and Presidential elections in the past few decades being decided by less than 1.1% shifts in the black vote can affect elections. Therefore, although whites have maintained a political hegemony, there is minority representation which at times has been to the degree that whites may have feared a loss of political power due to both perceived and actual increases in minority political power. However, in this country with African Americans representing approximately 12% of the population the likelihood of an actual political power threat in terms of representation in government is slight; rather it remains an implied threat.

In each of the three time periods of the drug laws, political threat may be more of a perceived than an actual threat. Per the Naturalization Act of 1870, the majority of Chinese immigrants were excluded from becoming citizens because they were not free (the majority of Chinese immigrants were indentured slaves) and thus could not have actual political power since they did not have the right to vote or run for public office. By the 1930's the Senate had only two Hispanic Americans both from New Mexico and only Dennis Chavez was a Senator during the legislation of the Marihuana Tax Act (Senate.com, 2008). Therefore, although Mexican immigrants could become citizens and then vote and hold public office, their level of actual federal political power was minimal. African Americans and Hispanic Americans had more potential for being a political threat in the 1980's due to increases in representation in public office and voting power. However, a likelihood of political power threat in each of these time periods is more likely to remain an implied threat. The reaction to the perceived political threat may potentially be seen in legislation such as drug laws enacted during or after an increase in minority population size.

ECONOMIC COMPETITION

In addition to competition for or threat of political power, a historical analysis of drug laws may illustrate that economic competition or threat was present prior to the enactment of the laws. Economic threats are driven by minority population size; an increase in minority population implies a threat to the dominant group. It is assumed that minority group members will work for less money than whites and will also upset the balance of economic power (Bonacich, 1972; Aguirre and Turner, 1995). This sense of threat due to population size can occur when a minority group's population is increasing due to an influx of immigrants, migrants, or when the group mobilizes such as the Civil Rights movement. As previously mentioned, economic threats are based on the assumption that minority group members will work for less money than whites thus depriving whites of jobs. More recently, with the enactment of Affirmative Action, there is a perceived economic threat that minorities, especially African Americans and Latinos, are being placed in jobs for which they are not qualified and are thus taking jobs away from "more qualified/deserving" whites.

Prior to the enactment of the early opium laws, the Chinese may have been perceived as an economic threat. In the mid to late 1800's there was an influx of Chinese immigrants who worked primarily on the railroads and in the mines (Fernandez, 1998; Kennedy, 1990; Musto, 1999). The railroads actively sought Chinese labor due to their work ethic and willingness to work for lower wages (Musto, 2002). As the railroad and mining booms subsided, America experienced an economic depression, and the supply of white labor increased creating more competition for jobs with the Chinese (Kennedy, 1990; Musto, 1999). Did this economic competition present prior to and perhaps during the enactment of the opium legislation influence members of Congress to focus more on Chinese opium usage?

Similar to Chinese immigrants and the opium laws, Mexican immigrants may have been perceived as an economic threat prior to the legislation of the Marihuana Tax Act. In the first three decades of the twentieth century there was an influx of Mexican immigrants who settled primarily in Texas and other border states and worked in agriculture (Musto, 2002; Bonnie & Whitehead, 1999). By 1930 significant numbers of Mexican immigrants had migrated to the Midwest's industrial region. With the advent of the Great Depression there were claims that Mexican immigrants had jobs that U.S. citizens should have resulting in the repatriation of more than 400,000 Mexicans (Katz, Stern & Fader, 2007; Alba & Nee, 2003). Did this wave of Mexican immigration and economic competition present prior to and perhaps during the Marihuana Tax Act legislation influence members' of Congress discourse about marijuana?

In the late 1970's and early 1980's the United States experienced a couple economic recessions as well as debates over Affirmative Action and reverse discrimination. Reverse discrimination discourse alluded to Blacks taking jobs away from more qualified whites due to Affirmative Action requirements. Did this economic competition affect the Congressional discussions and proceedings regarding the Anti Drug Abuse Act of 1986?

In summation, an analysis of the Congressional discussions surrounding some of our federal drug laws may illustrate that competition and threat were present prior to the enactment of the laws. Although this research focuses on both economic and political competition/threat, economic competition or threat is more likely to have occurred in all three sets of laws.

CHAPTER 3

Institutional Racism and the Use of the Congressional Record

INSTITUTIONAL RACISM

This research investigates whether there is a connection between the social climate and the advent of some federal drug laws. It examines the content of Congressional discussions to ascertain if we have and perhaps continue to institutionalize racism in our federal drug laws.

For the purposes of this research, institutional racism occurs when privilege based on race becomes institutionalized: when discriminatory practices are embedded in the norms and rules of society's social structures (e.g. laws), which then guide individual behavior (Doob, 1996). Institutional racism[9] can be direct or indirect (Feagin & Feagin, 1978). Direct institutionalized discrimination is actions and practices that are intentional and have a differential and negative impact on

[9] Since the end of the 1960's studies have found racism embedded in several institutions: housing (Oliver & Shapiro, 1995; Yinger, 1995; Massey & Denton, 1993; Feagin & Feagin, 1978), employment (Williams, 1987; Feagin & Feagin, 1978), education (Sedlacek & Brooks, 1976; Bourgois, 1995; Kozol, 1991; Feagin & Feagin, 1978), social services (Feagin & Feagin, 1978), and heath care (Feagin & McKinney, 2003; Feagin & Feagin, 1978).

members of a subordinate group[10]. The discrimination can come in the form of formal laws that are blatantly directed at subordinate groups. Indirect institutionalized discrimination also involves practices that have a negative impact on subordinated groups, however they lack intent. Therefore, institutional racism can and does involve the actions of people who have no intention of subordinating others (Downs, 1970; Feagin & Feagin, 1978). In terms of laws, direct institutionalized discrimination involves laws that intentionally discriminate against members of a subordinate group, whereas laws that constitute indirect institutionalized discrimination lack clear intent (Feagin and Feagin, 1978).

Institutionalized racism is sustained by the legitimacy that the organizational environment grants discriminatory actions. Institutionalizing racism provides a "shield" that enables individual discriminators to hide behind. Because the discriminatory practices have been institutionalized, individuals can defend their actions by referring to the organizational environment (in this case our legal system) that has legitimated it and in effect claim they are doing nothing wrong (there is no discrimination); they are merely following the rules.

This research investigates the extent to which racism is institutionalized in our federal drug laws, specifically opium laws in the late 1800's through 1909, the Marihuana Tax Act of 1937 and the Anti Drug Abuse Act of 1986. The research addresses the following:

1. Has racism been embedded and thus institutionalized in our drug laws?

---

[10] An example of direct institutionalized discrimination is the Home Owners Loan Corporation's appraisal system that categorized communities that were racially changing or were already black as undesirable and placed them in the lowest category, red, leading to decades of redlining central-city counties and negatively impacting African American's ability to attain loans and buy property (Oliver& Shapiro, 1997; Massey & Denton, 1993).

2. What is the content of these drug laws? Are the laws racially biased or race neutral in their wording? Has there been a change over time from the opium laws in the late 1800's to the Anti Drug Abuse Act of 1986 in the pattern of the wording of these laws?

3. What is the content of the political discussions surrounding the legislation? Does it appear that the rhetoric of the time-period impacted the discussions leading to the passage of the drug laws?

4. From what economic and/or political context did the drug laws emerge? How has competition for scarce resources, specifically economic and political, affected drug laws?

5. How are minority groups vilified during the period leading up to the enactment of drug legislation?

Although no work of the scope of this book can answer these questions definitively, the research may develop a plausible case concerning whether racism has been embedded in our drug laws that can contribute to the ongoing debate over the declining significance of race.

THE CONGRESSIONAL RECORD

Secondary sources and archival data were assessed to determine the economic and/or political contexts from which the drug laws emerged. The Congressional Record was used to analyze the discussions regarding the opium drug laws in the late 1800's, the Marihuana Tax Act of 1937 and the Anti Drug Abuse Act of 1986.

Pursuant to Article I, section 5 of the United States Constitution, both the Senate and the House of Representatives are required to keep a "Journal of its Proceedings and from time to time publish the same" (The United States Constitution). The proceedings of Congress are recorded in the Annals of Congress, the Register of Debates, the Congressional Globe and the Congressional Record[11].

Since the GPO began publishing the Congressional Record with the 43rd Congress, Congressional members have been able to revise their comments. Although they are not allowed to make substantive changes nor can they alter anything but their own comments, members can alter the wording of their comments. In essence they have the opportunity to remove or rewrite remarks, such as profanity and racially biased or any salacious comments that may be offensive to someone reading or reporting from the Record. Additionally, members of Congress have been able to make submissions for publication in the Appendix since the Register of Debates, this practice was continued with the Congressional Record. The Appendix contains the extension of remarks and insertions that were not delivered on the floor of Congress (McKinney, 2005). All revisions, extensions of remarks or insertions not delivered on the floor of Congress appear in capital letters. Submissions can be made for both the daily and bound versions, giving members ample time to alter their remarks. Although these remarks and insertions are included it does not necessarily mean that they were read by members of Congress. Therefore, although the extended remarks may provide more insight into individual Congressional member's motives or thoughts regarding the legislation, what is said on the floor is more important due to how it may influence other Congressional members.

---

[11] See the Appendix for a more in depth discussion of the Congressional Record.

Coding

The Congressional Record discussions were coded for latent content. This assesses the underlying meaning of the discussions providing a more in depth overall assessment rather than quantifying how many times specific words or phrases occurred.

One of the goals of this research is to build a plausible case that there is a connection between the social climate and legislation. The start codes[12] for each time period include codes for competition for resources as well as vilification which is one way for a dominant group to maintain power over a minority group. With the passage of opium laws, the Marihuana Tax Act and the mandatory drug sentencing guidelines following economic recessions, perceived or actual increased job competition, and vilification of one or more minority groups in reference to the drug, it is plausible that competition for scarce resources (the social climate) is connected to drug legislation.

Strengths and Weaknesses of the Congressional Record as Data

Few if any studies have analyzed the latent content of the discussions and legislative proceedings contained in the Congressional Record and assessed change over time. While these discussions may yield insight into the motives behind the legislation, there are some drawbacks. First, as previously mentioned, members of Congress have the opportunity to make non substantive changes to their remarks. Therefore if they made racially biased or salacious comments they can remove them either prior to the publication of the daily edition and/or the bound edition. Although the revisions are denoted in the Congressional Record, the original words are no longer available. In addition, there are references in the Congressional Record to reports from committees. These reports are usually not published in the Congressional Record and depending on the age some of them were never published or may no longer exist.

---

[12] See the Appendix for a more in depth discussion of coding and sampling.

Using the Congressional Record as the data source also limits the analysis to discussions on the floor of Congress. Members of Congress may have discussed the legislation more freely and in more depth outside of Congress. There is however, no record of these conversations and therefore no way of analyzing the legislative discussions that occur in the hallways or private offices. Despite these drawbacks the Congressional Record is the official and most complete written record of the proceedings of Congress.

CHAPTER 4

Opium Laws of the Late 1800s and 1909

Opium comes from the opium poppy, *Papaver somniferum* (Courtwright, 2001; Abadinsky, 2008; Liska, 2004). Historically the opium poppy was grown in the mountains of Turkey, Afghanistan, and Pakistan and the mountains of Myanmar, Thailand and parts of Laos[13], (Liska, 2004). Although the opium poppy could be grown in America in the South, Southwest and California, attempts to grow it were unsuccessful due to labor costs and low potency levels (Morgan, 1981). Thus the opium poppy is typically not grown in America and the vast majority of opium is imported (Courtwright, 2001).

Opium is the gum or latex fluid found in the partially ripened seed pod of the opium poppy (Courtwright, 2001; Abadinsky, 2008; Liska, 2004). The seed pods are scored to release the milky latex. Once released and exposed to air the latex fluid hardens and turns brown. It is then scrapped from the seed pod and formed into a ball of crude opium (dried preparation or extract containing multiple chemicals).

[13] Although not native to Columbia, the opium poppy is now grown in the Andes (Liska, 2004). It is also grown in some parts of Mexico.

The crude opium can be processed into smoking opium, used to extract morphine and codeine or used to manufacture heroin.

GENERAL HISTORY OF OPIUM

Although opium did not receive much public or governmental attention until the 1800's, according to some its existence dates back to approximately 4000 B.C. and the ancient Sumerians (Liska, 2004) while others claim it existed in the Stone Age (Abadinsky, 2008). However, the first undisputed reference to opium was recorded in the third century B.C. by Theophrastus. Art relics also depict the Egyptians using opium in their religious rituals as far back as 3500 B.C. and the Ebers Papyrus listed opium as a pain reliever indicating that the Egyptians had medical knowledge of opium as early 1500 B.C. (Abadinsky, 2008). Though the Egyptians knew of and used opium, it was introduced to China by Arab traders and used for dysentery (Abadinsky, 2008; Liska, 2004). With the spread of opium use in China, the British East India Company began trading Indian grown opium for tea. When the Chinese government attempted to control the importation of opium it resulted in the Opium Wars, the first in 1841 with Britain and the second in 1856 with France and Britain.

Prior to 1800 opium was available in its crude form in America and was an ingredient in many prescription and patent medicines (Musto, 1999). In 1803, 1832, and 1898 morphine (by Freidrich Serturner), codeine and heroin, respectively, were extracted from opium (Morgan, 1974; Abadinsky, 2008; Provine, 2007). The pharmaceutical company currently known as Merck began extracting morphine from opium in 1832 and became the largest morphine producing company in the 1800's (Musto, 1999). During this time, opium was widely available and considered a cure for just about everything which aided in creating addicts (Abadinsky, 2008). The late nineteenth century was also the height of patent medicine which had high opium contents (Musto, 1999). Many of these medicines that contained cocaine as well as opiates could be purchased at any store, by mail or from traveling salesmen (Musto, 1999). Although statistics on the prevalence of patent medicines are scarce one study indicated that in 1906, more than 50,000 patent medicines were available and sold (Liska, 2004). The medicines claimed to be cures for ailments such as tuberculosis, diabetes, cholera, malaria, bronchitis, gall stones, cancer and mental illness (Abadinsky, 2008; Liska, 2004). Some patent medicines also claimed to be remedies for problems with internal organs including the liver, kidneys and heart (Liska, 2004). Patent medicines containing opiates were marketed for all age groups including children, such as Mrs. Winslow's Soothing Syrup for teething (Liska, 2004; Provine, 2007). There were no restrictions or controls placed upon either the claims of patent medicines or any requirement to list the ingredients until after the passage of the 1906 Food and Drug Act (Abadinsky, 2008; Liska, 2004; Provine, 2007).

While opium was available in a variety of forms throughout most of the 1800's, the general public seemed unconcerned about its use or the possibility of addiction so long as it was confined to the lower echelons of society, i.e. the Chinese, prostitutes, gamblers or artists (Morgan, 1974). Public discussion of opium increased after the Civil War and opium addiction was often referred to as the soldiers disease due to the volume of soldiers given morphine for their injuries (Liska, 2004; Provine, 2007), but the press focused for the most part on opium smoking (Morgan, 1974). By 1870, opium addiction research indicated that opium use and addiction was not confined to the lower classes of society; opium addicts represented all levels of society. With the change in affected populations, governmental and public concern about opium escalated but still focused on smoking opium and the Chinese. Although the general public may have associated smoking opium with the Chinese, authorities on opium addiction stated that it was a national problem not restricted to the Chinese. Per an 1881 report on smoking opium, some claimed that smoking was less physically harmful, less addictive and easier to cure than the opiate morphine. Despite this report, most doctors in the 1880's did not believe that medicine, specifically morphine, was addictive when injected with a hypodermic.

Thus while smoking opium was considered harmful and morally wrong, the use of other opiates such as morphine was still socially acceptable. However, by 1900 many doctors had ceased proscribing opium because of addiction and popular magazines warned customers of the dangers of opium and opium containing medicines (Provine, 2007).

The exact number of addicts at any given time in the 1800's and early 1900's is difficult to ascertain due to the accuracy of the statistics and a person's ability to recognize addiction (Morgan, 1974). Horace Day estimated that there were 80,000 to 100,000 American opium addicts in 1868 while Dr. Keeley estimated 500,000 addicts in 1882. A medical group in 1902 estimated 200,000 addicts but an opium commission in 1908 estimated between 100,000 to 150,000. Thus, the contemporary estimates of addiction varied.

Since estimates of the number of addicts varied widely and were inaccurate at best, studies also focused on importation records and sales in an attempt to ascertain usage. The escalating use of opium was illustrated in import records beginning in 1840. There was a rapid rise in importation from the 1870's until opium importation peaked in 1896 and then gradually declined (Liska, 2004). One study claimed that by 1870 only 20% of the opium imported was used by legitimate medical doctors, implying that 80% of the imported opium was used in either patent medicines or for non medical purposes such as smoking opium (Morgan, 1974). Escalation of use was also determined by comparing population growth to importation statistics. The Committee on the Acquirement of the Drug Habit concluded that between 1898 and 1902 the United States population had only increased 10 percent, but the importation of cocaine had increased 50%, opium 500% and morphine 600% (Musto, 1999). Since the importation of opium outpaced population growth by a 50:1 ratio the use of opium had significantly increased. Escalation of use was also determined by comparing population growth to increases in the sale of medicines. According to Morgan (1974), the United States population increased 83% between 1880 and 1910 but the sale of patent medicines rose 700%. An escalation in sales that outpaced population growth by more than 600% indicated an increase in opium dependency given the high opium content in patent medicines. Although the available statistics for the time period vary in their estimation, a portion of the United States population was addicted to opium and it appeared to be a growing problem, but the exact extent is unknown.

The available statistics not only suggested that the United States had an escalating drug problem, but also indicated that the population most afflicted was white women (Fernandez, 1998; Gray 1998; Bonnie & Whitebread, 1999; Morgan, 1974). White women were prone to addiction due in part to doctors' willingness to prescribe opium and the availability of laudanum and patent medicines. Doctors often freely prescribed opium for menstrual and menopausal problems as well as non gendered ailments. In addition, women self-prescribed laudanum, the liquid form of opium (powder opium dissolved in alcohol), which was odorless and readily available at the local apothecary and later in patent medicines. Laudanum also became the drug of choice for women early in the 1800's, in part because women were not allowed in bars and it was socially unacceptable to drink, but women could drink laudanum in the privacy of their homes (Fernandez, 1998). By the 1850's America's opium-addicted population consisted mostly of white women who had the money to purchase laudanum or patent medicines regularly. Between 1878 and 1885 surveys indicate that 56 to 71 percent of opium addicts were middle to upper class white women. Even with the advent of Chinese immigration and the increase in smoking opium white women had the highest addiction rate. Moreover, the addiction rate was more than double that of today (4.59 per 1,000 as compared to 2.04 in the late 1990's).

Whereas white women took laudanum or patent medicines, some of the Chinese immigrants brought with them their habit of smoking opium (Fernandez, 1998; Liska, 2004; Abadinsky, 2008). Other Chinese immigrants started smoking opium once in America. Although opium dens were predominately Chinese domains, Americans did frequent the dens. By the 1870's and 1880's the stereotype of the "heathen Chinese" was widely reported in newspapers and magazines (Morgan, 1974). The numerous articles on opium dens in Chinatowns solidified public association between opium and the Chinese. By 1875, opium smoking was widespread among gamblers, prostitutes and men and women of the middle and upper classes (Inciardi, 1992) though it was generally associated with the Chinese (Musto, 1999). The general association and, to a certain extent, acceptance of the Chinese and smoking opium was illustrated by the railroads treatment of Chinese laborers. While working on the railroads, the Chinese smoked opium which was claimed to increase work productivity. The association with increased productivity was enough for the railroads to keep a supply of smoking opium to sell to their workers and in turn reinforcing the stereotype of a Chinese opium smoker.

Even though Chinese immigrants did smoke opium, the available statistics still indicated that white women had the highest addiction rates. Statistics also indicated that the age of opium addicts was between thirty and forty, even though patent medicines were marketed for people of all ages including children and doctors prescribed opiates regardless of age (Morgan, 1974). Despite what was known about opium addiction, public attention focused on what people wanted to believe. The largest addiction estimates garnered the most public attention, over estimating the opium problem and creating a stereotype of an opium addict that differed from reality. The images of the Chinese, gamblers and prostitutes smoking opium were the most prevalent rather than rural farmers injecting morphine or white women drinking laudanum. The public viewpoint also held that the opium addict lacked inhibitions, lacked responsibility, was deceitful, engaged in crime, and was promiscuous (Morgan, 1974). Some even believed that smokers used opium to "seduce innocent girls" (22). Thus, from the public's perception, it was smoking opium (and in turn the Chinese) which was most addictive, caused the most harm, and, therefore, should be the most feared and reviled rather than the much more commonly used and more addictive forms of opium available in medicines.

CHINESE IMMIGRATION AND LABOR

The first Chinese immigrants came to the United States to find gold in California mines (Dickerson, 2003; Coolidge, 1969). Within four years, from 1848 to 1852, the Chinese immigrant population in California increased from three to almost 20,000. Between 1852 and 1870, more than 70,000 Chinese came to America and settled on the West Coast to work in the mines and on the railroads (Fernandez, 1998). Although, it may have seemed, given the number of Chinese arriving, that their population was outpacing other immigrants, many Chinese immigrants returned to China after they had worked and accumulated enough money (Seward, 1970). Therefore, to obtain an accurate estimate of the number of Chinese custom reports listing arrivals and departures had to be assessed. According to Seward's 1881 analysis utilizing census and custom statistics the Chinese population in 1870 had increased to 62,674 residing primarily in the western and Pacific coast states as illustrated in Table 4.1 (Seward, 1970). Approximately, three decades (specifically 1876 to 1880) after the first Chinese had immigrated, their numbers did not exceed 100,000 in the United States with approximately 75,000 residing in California. Given Seward's calculations the ratio of Chinese to California's total population was 1:11 in 1860, 1:11.5 in 1870 and 1:13 in 1880. During this time, white immigration in 1870 and 1880 was 10 and 12 times, respectively, that of the Chinese. In addition to Seward's estimates, United States census reports indicate that the Chinese population was 775 in 1850, increased to 35,565 in 1860, 63,042 in 1880, 106,688 in 1890 and decreased to 81,827 in 1900 (Li, 1916). Though the census reports provided lower estimates than Seward's study for the majority of decades, there is agreement that the Chinese population did not exceed approximately 100,000 (give or take a few thousand). Despite the availability of this information, the general public as well as the public figures who advocated against Chinese immigration believed Chinese immigration was much higher such as 200,000 in the United States and that "the number of adult Chinese in California 'is as great as that of all the voters in the State.'" (12). Therefore, the public's perception of the extent of Chinese immigration greatly exceeded the reality leading some to think the issue was more pressing than perhaps it was.

Table 4.1 George Seward's Distribution of Chinese Immigrants by State in 1870*

State	Number of Chinese
California	48,790
Nevada	3,143
Oregon	3,326
Idaho	4,267
Montana	1,943
Utah	445
Washington	234
Wyoming	143
Other States and Territories	383

* (Seward, 1970: 9)

The building of the railroads and the "Gold Rush" of 1849 drove the importation of Chinese "coolie" labor (Kennedy, 1990; Musto, 1999). The Chinese laborers were brought to the United States to work in the gold mines, specifically in the most dangerous jobs such as "blasting shafts, placing beams, and laying track line in the mines" (Abadinsky, 2008: 40) that white workers would not do. In addition to the more dangerous labor, the Chinese also built mining roads and water flumes (Dickerson, 2003). Although Chinese laborers and white miners worked in close proximity, the Chinese laborers were prohibited from living near the white miners and in some locations they were also prohibited from filing claims on mines. Despite the restrictions, the Chinese flourished economically, establishing bathhouses, laundries and restaurants servicing white miners. With the increase in Chinese immigration and, thus, Chinese laborers in the mines, hostility towards the Chinese laborers increased and by 1850 had erupted in approximately a dozen riots resulting in death and destruction of Chinese miner's homes. When the mining boom ended in the late

1860's white and Chinese miners moved to the cities in search of employment.

Although mining was the initial lure for many Chinese immigrants (Kennedy, 1990; Musto, 1999; Li, 1916), they worked in many industries (e.g. farming, fishing, brick laying, cigar making, domestic servants, shoe making, etc.) and opened their own businesses. With their work ethic and business acumen, "by 1852, Chinese immigrants had over 2 million dollars invested in California" (Lusane, 1991:31). The growth of Chinese small businesses and manufacturing was seen as a threat to white businesses. The threat to white workers was heightened when railroad companies sought Chinese workers due to the quality of their work and willingness to work for lower wages (Musto, 2002).

With the lure of mining, the railroads had difficulty hiring white workers and hired some Chinese laborers in 1858 and 1860 to work on the California Central Railroad and the San Jose Railway, respectively (Chen, 1996; Li, 1916). Despite the positive reports of the Chinese work on these railroads, when the Central Pacific Railroad Company (CPRC) needed workers (at one point they had 600 men and were trying to hire 5,000) there was some initial hesitation to hire Chinese laborers due to Leland Stanford, one of the four owners, previous advocation for the exclusion of Chinese. The CPRC had hired Irish men to build the western half of the transcontinental railroad, but they refused to do the dangerous work of scaling mountains, setting explosives and living in tunnels (Dickerson, 2003). When the white workers threatened to strike in 1865, CPRC hired 50 Chinese laborers (The Chinese in California, 2008; Chen, 1996) and continued hiring them because they worked hard, seemed to be fearless and willing to do the most dangerous jobs and would work for less pay than white workers (Dickerson, 2003; Abadinsky, 2008). Thus, the Central Pacific Railroad Company was the first to hire Chinese contract laborers also known as coolies (Dickerson, 2003). By 1867, approximately 90% of CPRC's workers were Chinese (Dickerson, 2003; Chen, 1996). When the railroad was completed in 1869 approximately 15,000 Chinese had worked on it (Chen, 1996). With the completion of CPRC's railroad the California labor market was flooded with approximately 10,000 white and Chinese laborers looking for employment (Li, 1916). Some of the Chinese workers moved to the cities looking for work while others continued in the railroad industry (Chen, 1996). Most of the railroads that were built from then on benefited from the Chinese workers skill and lower wages including the Southern Pacific-Texas; the Atcheson, Topeka, and Santa Fe; the Northern Pacific; the Great Northern; and the Virginia and Truckee line. Railroad companies including Union Pacific not only hired Chinese laborers, but also stated that the railroads would not have been built without them.

As the railroad and mining booms subsided, America experienced an economic depression, and the supply of white labor increased while the demand for labor decreased creating more competition with the Chinese for jobs (Kennedy, 1990; Musto, 1999). When the Northern Pacific railroad company declared bankruptcy leading to the stock market crash of September 19, 1873 (Black Friday), California began its first economic depression and experienced record unemployment (Chen, 1996; Dickerson, 2003). With fewer jobs available, competition between Chinese and white workers increased as did the push for Chinese exclusion. During California's economic depression, Dennis Kearny helped organize the Workingman's Party, a labor organization opposed to Chinese laborers and advocated for the end of Chinese immigration, escalating the sense of competition among white workers (Dickerson, 2003; Li, 1916; The Chinese in California, 2008).

The anti-Chinese sentiment intensified over the years culminating in several riots. In 1867, after an Anti-Coolie Labor Association meeting several hundred men who were also associated with the Workingmen's Party attacked Chinese men and women and burned Chinese businesses in San Francisco (The Chinese in California, 2008; Dickerson, 2003). Four years later, 15 Chinese men were hanged during riots in Los Angeles. In total, 19 Chinese immigrants were killed and numerous homes and businesses were burned. During the Rock Springs riot in the Wyoming Territory on September 2, 1885 150 armed men killed 28 Chinese and injured another 15 (Li, 1916; Dickerson, 2003). The value of the property destroyed during the riot was estimated at $147,748.74, given that the average monthly wage was $28-$31, the damage was extensive (Li, 1916). The violence did not stop with Rock Springs; instead it spread, with whites attempting to drive the Chinese out of cities such as Bloomfield, Boulder Creek and Eureka. The repercussions of the Rock Springs riot were several indemnity discussions in Congress and payment of $276,619.75 for all loses and injuries to bolster the United States' relationship with China (Li, 1916; Congressional Record, 1887).

In addition to the violence and riots, the anti-Chinese sentiment also resulted in anti-Chinese legislation at both the state and federal level. From 1860 to 1876 California passed a series of anti-Chinese legislation attempting to exclude immigration from Asia and the Pacific in order to decrease labor competition between whites and Chinese (Kennedy, 1990). California passed a number of tax laws aimed at the Chinese including a mining tax for foreigners and a tax on Chinese passengers (Li, 1916). California's anti Chinese movement succeeded in creating a state constitution that restricted employment of aliens and prohibited alien land ownership and voting (Provine, 2007). California also successfully lobbied Congress for the Naturalization Act of 1870 to include blacks but limit all other eligible groups to "free white persons" (Kennedy, 1990: 38) and thus exclude Chinese immigrants. With the passage of the Chinese Exclusion Act of 1882 the United States prohibited the immigration of Chinese laborers for ten years as well as the naturalization of Chinese (Li, 1916). The Geary Act of 1892 extended Chinese exclusion for another ten years and increased the restrictions to no longer allow Chinese immigrants to travel home to China and return to the United States.

OPIUM LAWS

During this time our first federal drug laws were passed. These first federal drug laws involved opium, specifically smoking opium.

America's first drug law was the San Francisco opium ordinance of 1875 that prohibited opium dens for people of Chinese descent (Gray, 2000). By the passage of the first federal opium drug law several states had followed San Francisco's ordinance and passed opium legislation that targeted Chinese immigrants. The first federal opium law was the American-Chinese treaty of 1880, a commercial treaty, that prohibited Chinese citizens residing in the United States from importing smoking opium (anyone else could import smoking opium) (Wright, 2002). Although this treaty with China was concluded on November 17, 1880 and ratified on October 5, 1881, no legislation to enforce the treaty was passed for approximately 6 years. On February 23, 1887, Congress passed a law prohibiting the importation of opium and smoking opium among the Chinese, but not among white Americans (Szasz, 2003; Lusane, 1991). This law reiterated the provisions of the 1880 treaty and provided for its enforcement. Approximately three years later, on October 1, 1890, Congress passed another law that restricted the manufacture of smoking opium to American citizens only.

On February 9, 1909 Congress passed what it considered to be the first opium law, despite the fact that it had passed laws prohibiting opium importation and manufacturing in 1880, 1887 and 1890 (Musto, 1999). At the time the United States was preparing for the Shanghai Opium Commission and decided the lack of national narcotic legislation would be an embarrassment to the U.S. After almost three decades of immigration laws restricting Chinese immigration, the U.S. needed to demonstrate to China, which already had opium laws and was concerned about the opium trade, their support in the hopes of attaining a better stance for trade negotiations. Secretary of State Root proposed legislation with minimal prohibitions to hasten its passing. The 1909 law prohibited importation of smoking opium; medicinal opium (essentially all other forms of opium) could be imported.

The relevant text of the 1880, 1887, 1890 and 1909 laws are provided in Table 4.2. Due to the length of the treaty and acts, only the sections pertaining to opium are included. Per their text, the 1880 treaty and the 1887 law distinguish between United States citizens and

Chinese subjects. While the treaty and law enforcing the treaty made this distinction it was due to the nature of treaties and fostering relations between the two nations. Of note is that both nations agreed that citizens of each country would not import opium into the other nation. The treaty had no provisions regarding citizens importing opium into their own country. On its face the 1887 legislation enforcing the 1880 treaty made no substantive changes to the 1880 treaty. Thus, per these two laws the Chinese were the only people prohibited from importing opium into the United States, anyone else could still import opium.

Since these two laws only prevented the Chinese from importing opium into the United States it may seem that the Chinese were being discriminated against. However, the laws originated in the treaty between China and the United States in which both nations prohibited citizens of the other nation from importing opium into their country. If the treaty prohibited the Chinese from importing opium into America, yet allowed United States citizens to import opium into China, then the wording of the treaty and the question of the Chinese being discriminated against would bear more weight.

Although the wording of the 1880 treaty is not racially biased, the wording of the 1887 law is more questionable. It was designed to enforce the 1880 treaty and therefore contained the same provisions as the treaty as well as the punishments for the offenses. Per the 1887 law, Chinese who imported opium into the United States "shall be deemed guilty of a misdemeanor, and on conviction thereof shall be punished by a fine of not more than five hundred dollars nor less than fifty dollars or by an imprisonment for a period of not more than six months nor less than thirty days, or by both such fine and imprisonment, in the discretion of the court" (24 Stat. L. 409, 1887). The punishment for American's who imported opium into China

TABLE 4.2 Opium Laws

Title/Citation	Text of law
"Treaty as to commercial intercourse and judicial procedure" (treaty with China concluded on November 17, 1880 and ratified by President on October 5, 1881)	Art. II. The Governments of China and of the United States mutually agree and undertake that Chinese subjects shall not be permitted to import opium into any of the ports of the United States; and citizens of the United States shall not be permitted to import opium into any of the open ports of China, to transport it from one open port to any other open port, or to buy and sell opium in any of the open ports of China. This absolute prohibition, which extends to vessels owned by the citizens or subjects of either power, to foreign vessels employed by them, or to vessels owned by the citizens or subjects of either power, and employed by other personas for the transportation of opium, shall be enforced by appropriate legislation on the part of China and the Untied States; and the benefits of the favored-nation clause in existing treaties shall not be claimed by the citizens or subjects of either power as against the provisions of this article.
[Act of February 23, 1887, ch. 210, 24 Stat. L. 409.]	AN ACT to provide for the execution of the provisions of article two of the treaty concluded between the United States of America and the Emperor of China on the seventeenth day of November, eighteen hundred and eighty, and proclaimed by the President of the United States on the fifth day of October, eighteen hundred and eighty-one. SECTION 1. [Importation of opium by Chinese prohibited.] That the importation of opium into any of the ports of the United States by any subject of the Emperor of China is hereby prohibited. Every person guilty of a violation of the preceding provision shall be deemed guilty of a misdemeanor, and on conviction thereof shall be punished by a fine of not more than five hundred dollars nor less than fifty dollars or by an imprisonment for a period of not more than six months nor less than thirty days, or by both such fine and imprisonment, in the discretion of the court. SEC. 2. [Forfeiture.] That every package containing opium, either in whole or in part, imported into the United States by any subject of the Emperor of China, shall be deemed forfeited to the United States; and proceedings for the declaration and consequences of such forfeiture may be instituted in the courts of the United States as in other cases of the violation of the laws relating to other illegal importations.

TABLE 4.2 Opium Laws (continued)

Title/Citation	Text of law
[Act of February 23, 1887, ch. 210, 24 Stat. L. 409.] cont.	SEC. 3. [Citizens of United States prohibited from traffic in opium in China: Punishment, jurisdiction, forfeiture.] That no citizen of the United States shall import opium into any of the open ports of China, nor transport the same from one open port to any other open port, or buy or sell opium in any of such open ports of China, nor shall any vessel owned by citizens of the United States, or any vessel, whether foreign or otherwise, employed by any citizen of the United States, or owned by any citizen of the United States, either in whole or in part, and employed by persons not citizens of the United States, take or carry opium into any such open ports of China, or transport the same from one open port to any other open port, or be engaged in any traffic therein between or in such opens ports or any of them. Citizens of the United States offending against the provisions of this section shall be deemed guilty of a misdemeanor, and upon conviction thereof shall be punished by a fine not exceeding five hundred dollars nor less than fifty dollars, or by both such punishments in the discretion of the court. The consular courts of the United States in China, concurrently with any district court of the United States in the district in which any offender may be found, shall have jurisdiction to hear, try, and determine all cases arising under the foregoing provisions of this section, subject to the general regulations provided by law. Every package of opium or package containing opium, either in whole or in part, brought, taken, or transported, trafficked or dealt in contrary to the provisions of this section, shall be forfeited to the United States, for the benefit of the Emperor of China; and such forfeiture, and the declaration and consequences thereof, shall be made, had determined, and executed by the proper authorities of the United States exercising judicial powers within the Empire of China.
October 1, 1890 [26 Stat., 567]	SEC. 36. That an internal-revenue tax of ten dollars per pound shall be levied and collected upon all opium manufactured in the United States for smoking purposes; and no person shall engage in such manufacturing who is not a citizen of the United States and who has not given the bond required by the Commissioner of Internal Revenue.

TABLE 4.2 Opium Laws (continued)

Title/Citation	Text of law
[Public-No. 221; H.R. 27427] February 9, 1909	AN ACT To prohibit the importation and use of opium for other than medicinal purposes. *Be it enacted by the Senate and House of Representatives of the United Sates of America in Congress assembled,* That after the first day of April, nineteen hundred and nine, it shall be unlawful to import into the United States opium in any form or any preparation or derivative thereof: Provided, That opium and preparations and derivatives thereof, other than smoking opium or opium prepared for smoking, may be imported for medicinal purposes only, under regulations which the Secretary of the Treasury is hereby authorized to prescribe, and when so imported shall be subject to the duties which are now or may hereafter be imposed by law. SEC. 2. That if any person shall fraudulently or knowingly import of bring into the United States, or assist in so doing, any opium or any preparation or derivative thereof contrary to law, or shall receive, conceal, buy, sell, or in any manner facilitate the transportation, concealment, or sale of such opium or preparation or derivative thereof after importation, knowing the same to have been imported contrary to law, such opium or preparation or derivative thereof shall be forfeited and shall be destroyed, and the offender shall be fined in any sum not exceeding five thousand dollars nor less than fifty dollars, or be imprisonment for nay time not exceeding two years, or both. Whenever, on trial for a violation of this section, the defendant is shown to have, or to have had, possession of such opium or preparation or derivative thereof, such possession shall be deemed sufficient evidence to authorize conviction unless the defendant shall explain the possession to the satisfaction of the jury.

carried the same fine but no imprisonment, thus the Chinese received harsher penalties. In addition, with this legislation Congress could have placed more restrictions on the importation of opium into the United States, but only prohibited its importation by the Chinese. Thus, the 1887 law is not race neutral.

Unlike the two previous laws, the 1890 and 1909 laws did not mention the Chinese specifically. Rather than addressing opium and all its derivatives, these laws focused on smoking opium. The 1890 law levied a ten dollar per pound tax on all smoking opium manufactured in the United States and prohibited anyone who was not a United States citizen from manufacturing it. Although it may be assumed that this law refers to all non citizens, smoking opium was generally associated with the Chinese. This focus on smoking opium continued in the 1909 law. In its text this law is referred to as "an act to prohibit the importation and use of opium for other than medicinal purposes" (Public-No. 221; H.R. 27427) but it is commonly known as the Smoking Opium Exclusion Act. Although the wording is couched in "medical purposes," the only form of opium that is specifically prohibited is "smoking opium or opium prepared for smoking." Even though the Chinese are not specifically mentioned in the laws, through the focus on smoking opium the 1909 and 1890 laws did indirectly target Chinese immigrants.

CONGRESSIONAL DISCUSSIONS & POLITICAL/SOCIAL CONTEXT

As, if not more important, than the wording of the laws is the social context from which they emerged. Analysis of the latent content of the discussions occurring on or around the discussions of the opium laws illustrated common themes of anti-Chinese sentiment, labor competition, political competition, localization of issues and a focus on smoking opium, especially as a habit associated with the Chinese.

Anti-Chinese Sentiment

Due to the influx of Chinese immigrants and the anti-Chinese sentiment expressed in the newspapers and magazines, it was assumed that Congressional discussions would also include anti-Chinese sentiment. Of the Congressional discussions included in this analysis, anti-Chinese sentiment was most prevalent in discussions surrounding immigration and labor, respectively. Although references were made to the Chinese during the discussions of the opium legislation, it was in regard to their use of opium, specifically smoking opium, rather than the anti-Chinese remarks made in the context of immigration and labor. Despite the lack of overt anti-Chinese sentiment in the opium discussions, the anti-Chinese sentiment already expressed during the immigration and labor discussions may have influenced the Congressmen in that these discussions occurred before, during and after the opium discussions. In some instances the discussions occurred immediately before the discussion of the opium legislation.

Of the Congressional discussions searched and analyzed, those surrounding Chinese immigration were the most prevalent and were present in every Congress included in the analysis. As assumed, anti-Chinese sentiment was laced throughout the Chinese immigration speeches and discussions. The Chinese were occasionally referred to as a sickness from which the United States needed to be protected. According to Mr. Page of California, the Chinese represented a harmful threat to American citizens.

> **Mr. Page of California:** *We have the right to protect them [citizens] by shutting our borders to the entrance of pestilence and plague from foreign lands...to protect ourselves against the introduction of noxious immigration into this country...*(House of Representative, April 22, 1880)

More frequently during these discussions, the Chinese were referred to as the "curse" and an "evil." The allusion to evil was used in two ways: in reference to the Chinese themselves and in reference to what would befall the United States if Chinese immigration was not restricted. Due to the influx of Chinese immigration, the "evils" inherent in increased and/or continued immigration were more prevalent in the discussions. The Pacific coast Congressmen, especially the California Congressmen, dominated the immigration discussions remarking about the "incalculable evils of Chinese immigration" (Mr. Page, House of Representatives, February 10, 1875) and the "evil…this sudden and alarming influx of the Mongolian race is casting" (Mr. Mitchell, Senate, May 16, 1876). Mr. Sargent of California alluded to the grim future of the United States and its youth if Chinese immigration was allowed to continue.

> **Mr. Sargent of California**: *The Chinese curse is blighting the prospects of our youth, retarding the development of our country, and taking from our social being the very essence of its vitality, the manhood of the present and future generations.* (Senate, June 19, 1876)

In addition to the evils fostered by Chinese immigration, the Congressmen also referred to the Chinese themselves as being evil. Mr. Page, a Congressman from California, used the allusion of evil to refer to the general character of the Chinese. He quoted from an 1855 book by Bayard Taylor to support his assessment of the Chinese.

> **Mr. Page of California**: [quoting Bayard Taylor] *...the Chinese are, morally, the most debased people on the face of the earth.* (House of Representatives, April 22, 1880)

The Congressmen from California also bolstered their stance on the Chinese character by discussing the fact that the majority of Chinese immigrants were male and the few who were female usually were forced to engage in prostitution. Thus, not only were the Chinese morally bankrupt per the Congressmen's standards and a threat to the prosperity of the Nation they were also engaging in criminal activity.

Although the association between Chinese immigrants and criminality was not as prevalent, it did reinforce the allusion to evil. In his speeches on the floor of the Senate, Mr. Sargent of California used stories of Chinese violence as well as referencing newspaper articles regarding the violence.

> **Mr. Sargent of California**: *The Chinese, where numerous, so as to give each other countenance, are dangerous infractors of the peace and violators of law. They are divided into clans and fight savagely among themselves on some unknown cause of hatred. I have seen a hundred or two Chinese lining each side of a narrow street violently gesticulating...as if each party sought to provoke the other to the first blow....These feuds among the Chinese are frequent and notorious. My California and Nevada newspapers speak of deadly affairs of the kind that have just happened at San Jose and Virginia City.* (Senate, May 1, 1876)

Mr. Page of California used similar tactics in the House of Representatives when he referred to the Chinese as a "cesspool of corruption" and used the previously mentioned quote from the Bayard Taylor book to support his stance of the "forms of vice" and the "deeps of depravity" of the Chinese (House of Representatives April 22, 1880). In associating the Chinese with violence and criminality, the Congressmen buttressed their standpoint of the evilness of the Chinese and Chinese immigration.

Table 4.3 contains all of the above referenced quotes as well as some additional quotes that illustrate the anti-Chinese remarks made during the Congressional discussions. The table also illustrates another aspect of the anti-Chinese sentiment. The anti-Chinese rhetoric utilizing terminology such as "evil," "curse," and "plague" occurred most frequently in the early Congresses included in the analysis,

TABLE 4.3 Anti-Chinese Sentiment in Congressional Discussions

Congressman & State	Location & Date	Quote
Mr. Sargent of California	Senate, February 13, 1874	"they [the citizens of California]*as the Senate to pay attention to the condition of the treaty between the United States and China, and see if by some appropriate legislation, or by a modification of that treaty, the evils which they depict, of an influx of Chinese into this country, may be prevented……I ask whether a curse would not be inflicted upon Iowa by such a change"
Mr. Page of California	House, February 10, 1875	"That your petitioners would urge upon your honorable consideration the necessity of an immediate revision of our treaty relations with China to restrain this overwhelming evil……I have attempted to place before the House the incalculable evils of Chinese immigration…"
Mr. Sargent of California	Senate, May 1, 1876	"The Chinese, where numerous, so as to give each other countenance, are dangerous infractors of the peace and violators of law. They are divided into clans and fight savagely among themselves on some unknown cause of hatred. I have seen a hundred or two Chinese lining each side of a narrow street violently gesticulating…as if each party sought to provoke the other to the first blow….These feuds among the Chinese are frequent and notorious. My California and Nevada newspapers speak of deadly affairs of the kind that have just happened at San Jose and Virginia City."
Mr. Sargent of California	Senate, May 1, 1876	"…asked for the relief which the giant growth of the evil has now made unendurable to us and a near calamity for the whole nation."
Mr. Mitchell of Oregon	Senate, May 16, 1876	"The evil, Mr. President, which this sudden and alarming influx of the Mongolian race is casting upon our common country ….menaces to-day the stability and purity of our moral peace, the integrity of our social and political structure, and jeopardizes and disturbs the civilization of our

TABLE 4.3 Anti-Chinese Sentiment in Congressional Discussions (continued)

Congressman & State	Location & Date	Quote
		age….of the Chinese empire, of a people the dregs and the debased of whom are by the thousands upon thousands to-day flooding our country, is it at all strange that this people [people of the North Pacific coast]* should appeal to the Congress of the nation in terms of more than ordinary earnestness for some measure of relief against this great evil?...It is not a question as to obligation, or duty, or power with reference to our attitude toward our dealing with those inferior races and classes or people."
Mr. Sargent of California	Senate, June 19, 1876	"The Chinese curse is blighting the prospects of our youth, retarding the development of our country, and taking from our social being the very essence of its vitality, the manhood of the present and future generations."
Mr. Davis of California	House, April 22, 1880	[in reference to Chinese immigration]* "We have the right to protect them [citizens] by shutting our borders to the entrance of pestilence and plague from foreign lands...to protect ourselves against the introduction of noxious immigration into this country…"
Mr. Page of California	House, April 22, 1880	"The State of California, which I have the honor in part to represent, ahs been knocking at the door of the National Legislature for many years asking that the Congress of the United States should pass some bill to relive that State and the Pacific coast from the evils of Chinese immigration….The State of California has for the past thirty years been suffering from a flood-tide of Mongolian slaves, who have been and are a curse to the prosperity of that great State."
Mr. Page of California	House April 22, 1880	"But when California comes here and says this "home of the downtrodden and oppressed of all nations" is being overrun by the Chinese to whom you deny the right of citizenship and

TABLE 4.3 Anti-Chinese Sentiment in Congressional Discussions (continued)

Congressman & State	Location & Date	Quote
		naturalization, and tells you that three of our fairest States on the Pacific coast are being flooded from this cesspool of corruption…"
Mr. Page of California	House April 22, 1880	[In support of his stance on the Chinese, Mr. Page read a quote in Congress from a 1855 "book written by Bayard Taylor, entitled India, China, and Japan"]* "…the Chinese are, morally, the most debased people on the face of the earth. Forms of vice which in other countries are barely named are in China so common that they excite no comment among the natives. They constitute the surface level, and below them are deeps and deeps of depravity so shocking and horrible that their character cannot even be hinted….Their [Chinese]* is pollution, and harsh as the opinion may seem, justice to our own race demand that they should not be allowed to settle on our soil."

* Explanation added

specifically in the 43rd, 44th and 46th (1874-1877 and 1879-1881). The two most vociferous Congressmen on the subject during this time were Senator Sargent and Representative Page both California Republicans. Senator Sargent served from 1873-1879 while Representative Page served from 1873-1883. They were no longer representing their state during the later Congresses when the anti- Chinese sentiment was not as virulent indicating that they may have been the driving force behind the usage of terminology such as "curse," "evil," "plague" and other derogatory remarks in reference to the Chinese. Furthermore, the subsequent California Congressmen may not have felt the need to be as forceful since the Chinese Exclusion Act had been passed in 1882.

Despite the anti-Chinese rhetoric utilized by the California and other Pacific coast Congressmen; the sentiment was not shared by all

Congressmen. According to Mr. Townsend there was no ill will against China.

> **Mr. Townsend of Illinois**: *There is no sentiment of hostility in this country against China.* (February 3, 1887).

Although he said there was no "hostility," he went on to say that the laboring classes of Chinese immigrants posed a threat to American laborers and he supported restricting immigration. So although he may have claimed there was no hostility, Chinese immigrants were not welcome. It is also noteworthy that his above statement was not made on the floor of the House of Representatives; it was included in a prepared statement he submitted to be included in the Appendix.

In sum, even though anti-Chinese sentiment was present in all the Congresses included in the analysis, it was most prevalent in the earlier Congresses. The vast majority of the anti-Chinese remarks were made by Congressmen from the Pacific coast, specifically California. Even though the California Congressmen were overt and virulent in their dislike of the Chinese, this sentiment was not held by everyone. However, that the California Congressmen's remarks regarding the evilness and general undesirability of the Chinese were uncontested suggests that either their stance may have been a popular viewpoint or they were successful in obtaining the support of some of their fellow Congressmen on a quid pro quo basis[14].

---

[14] Although it is generally assumed that Congressmen engage in the practice of logrolling, agreeing to support a piece of legislation in exchange for support on another piece of legislation, such conversations did not occur on the floor of Congress and thus were not recorded in the Congressional Record during the Congresses included in this analysis. Members of Congress may have engaged in such bargaining outside of Congress, however, there is no record of these conversations and therefore no way of analyzing legislative discussions that occur in the hallways or private offices. It can only be assumed that favor currying may have occurred and could be a plausible explanation as to why the California Congressmen's remarks were uncontested.

Labor Competition

The anti-Chinese sentiment was also evident in the Congressional discussions regarding labor competition. Similar to the immigration discussions, within the labor discussions there were a few references to the Chinese as evil, although not as numerous nor as strident. Rather than making entire speeches regarding the evils of the Chinese, the references were single remarks within a speech or discussion used to reiterate a point rather than make one. Mr. Sargent of California used the allusion to evil as well as derogatory terminology in reference to the Chinese to make a point about white men not being able to compete with less expensive Chinese labor.

> **Mr. Sargent of California**: *Another evil of Chinese emigration is its injury to white labor. The merit is claimed for the Chinese that they are industrious and this is true of a considerable class of them, although as many are lazy, opium-stupefied drones. But their very industries are a source of injury to the community, in that they undersell other labor and work for prices on which no white man can support a family. Our growing young men and women find scant employment and in few avocations, because cheap Chinese labor is taken in preference by employers.* (Senate, May 1, 1876)

Mr. Clunie of California in discussing labor issues also referred to the Chinese as evil to reiterate his point of white workers needing protection from Chinese workers.

> **Mr. Clunie of California**: *The working men and women in the cities, and, in fact, all over the State, appeal to you to give them this legislation and any additional legislation necessary to rid the country of this evil. Their children are growing up*

> *and are anxious and willing to work, but they can not compete with these Mongolian invaders.* (House of Representatives, March 17, 1890).

Therefore, although the allusion to evil was not as overt, the fear of and hostility towards Chinese laborers was still present.

In addition to the infrequent references to the Chinese as evil there was also the occasional reference to criminal behavior. However, the references to violence in the labor discussions differed from those in the immigration discussions in that they alluded to the potential for violence against the Chinese rather than the criminality of the Chinese. Mr. Hager of California contended that if something was not done to control the immigration of Chinese laborers, white workers would be forced out of employment. The resulting desperation and hostility would erupt in violence.

> **Mr. Hager of California**: *It is impossible, because, as I say if they come down to twenty dollars a month the Chinese can make money at ten dollars a month; and one race must give way to the other; the result will be that either our white citizen labor will be entirely driven from every field of labor, or else, driven to desperation, with starvation before them, there will be an upheaval which will lead to scenes of violence and blood, however much we may deplore it, shocking to our humanity, and which may produce a thrill of horror throughout the civilized world.* (Senate, March 10, 1874).

Given the approximately dozen riots related to mining by 1850 and the work related riots of 1867 and 1871, Mr. Hager's assertions were not unmerited, what is remarkable is that the potential for violence was not discussed more frequently.

Given the proliferation and success of Chinese laborers and business owners, the public hostility against them and the anti-Chinese rhetoric and actions of the Workingmen's Party, it was assumed that the Congressional discussions would include references to the Chinese working for lower wages and thus making it difficult for white workers to compete with them. Beginning with the first Congress included in the analysis, the Congressmen from California vocalized their concern for white workers and their hostility towards Chinese laborers. Their arguments focused on the Chinese working for less money and thus making it difficult for whites to compete for jobs. In their speeches, Mr. Hager and Mr. Sargent of California argued, on more than one occasion, that the servile nature of Chinese laborers and their ability to live on extremely low incomes rendered competition unfair.

> **Mr. Sargent of California:** *They [*Chinese*] work at very moderate prices. They underbid and undersell all other kinds of labor. They necessarily thereby drive out other laborers, skilled and unskilled. They are exceedingly simple in their requirements for a living, living upon a few handfuls of rice per day.* (Senate, February 14, 1874)

> **Mr. Hager of California**: *...and they are entering into all the avenues where labor seeks employment. The result is they exclude our own citizens.....Our own citizen labor is unable to compete with this servile labor, because what will sustain a Chinaman will not sustain our citizen labor. If a citizen can afford to work for fifty dollars a month, a Chinese will do it for thirty...That is the condition there, so that there is no fair competition.* (Senate, March 20, 1874)

Whether Mr. Sargent's assertion of the extent that the Chinese undercut white labor was correct, was a moot point given that no Congressmen challenged his remarks indicating either it was common knowledge that the Chinese worked for less money than white workers or it was not an issue for them. Given the questions that the only two Senators to respond to Mr. Hager asked, it was probably more the latter than the former. Mr. Bayard of Delaware asked "Is it the cooly trade?"

and "Do they make their own contracts for labor?" while Mr. Merrimon of North Carolina asked "For what sort of labor are they used?" (Senate, March 20, 1874). Their questions suggest that they had relatively little knowledge of the issue.

The issues of labor competition and the affect of Chinese labor on white workers were raised in subsequent Congresses. These discussions were dominated by the Pacific coast Congressmen, especially those from California, until the 60th Congress in 1909 (see Table 4.4). By 1909 the concern over labor competition with the Chinese was an issue for Congressmen regardless of geographic area. In addition to being a concern for more Congressmen, the discussions regarding labor competition became more blatantly racial. The remarks made by Mr. Hayes of California, Mr. Clark of Missouri and Mr. Harrison of New York on February 25, 1909 pitted the white race against the Chinese. Mr. Hayes began the discussion of excluding Chinese laborers by stating the number of unemployed white men in comparison to the number of employed Japanese and Chinese. His assertion that the "rights" of the whites needed to be preserved was supported by Mr. Clark and Mr. Harrison.

> **Mr. Hayes of California**: *I say, Mr. Chairman, that at this moment there are 22,000 idle white men in the city of San Francisco alone, and every charitable institution there is maintaining, and has been for months, a system of supplying the necessities of these people who are out of work, and yet in my district there are probably 10,000 Japanese, I do not know how many Chinamen, nearly all of whom are employed. Now, Mr. Chairman, I say to you that the people of California, except the few who profit by their labor, which is generally given cheaper than white labor, are in favor of what they conceive to be the patriotic thing to do, and that is preserve the land of the Pacific coast for the Caucasian race [Applause.].....*

TABLE 4.4 Labor Competition in Congressional Discussions

Congressman & State	Location & Date	Quote
Mr. Sargent of California	Senate, February 13, 1874	"They [Chinese]* work at very moderate prices. They underbid and undersell all other kinds of labor. They necessarily thereby drive out other laborers, skilled and unskilled. They are exceedingly simple in their requirements for a living, living upon a few handfuls of rice per day. ....the other States will find themselves crowded, as our workingmen are crowded, by the presences of Chinese in great numbers...simply robs us of our material wealth to enrich China, and deprives our willing citizen laborers of the means of subsistence."
Mr. Hager of California	Senate, March 20, 1874	"...and they are entering into all the avenues where labor seeks employment. The result is they exclude our own citizens.....Our own citizen labor is unable to compete with this servile labor, because what will sustain a Chinaman will not sustain our citizen labor. If a citizen can afford to work for fifty dollars a month, a Chinese will do it for thirty...That is the condition there, so that there is no fair competition."
Mr. Hager of California	Senate, March 20, 1874	"It is impossible, because, as I say if they come down to twenty dollars a month the Chinese can make money at ten dollars a month; and one race must give way to the other; the result will be that either our white citizen labor will be entirely driven from every field of labor, or else, driven to desperation, with starvation before the, there will be an upheaval which will lead to scenes of violence and blood, however much we may deplore it, shocking to our humanity, and which may produce a thrill of horror throughout the civilized world."
Mr. Sargent of California	Senate, May 1, 1876	"Another evil of Chinese emigration is its injury to white labor. The merit is claimed for the Chinese that they are industrious and this is true of a considerable class of them, although as many are lazy, opium-stupefied drones. But their very industries are a source of injury to the community,

TABLE 4.4 Labor Competition in Congressional Discussions (continued)

Congressman & State	Location & Date	Quote
		in that they undersell other labor and work for prices on which no white man can support a family. Our growing young men and women find scant employment and in few avocations, because cheap Chinese labor is taken in preference by employers."
Mr. Mitchell of Oregon	Senate, May 16, 1876	"the effect of Chinese immigration upon the Pacific coast is to degrade the industry of the country, to subordinate the labor of the honest, hardworking, free American citizen to that of the dishonest, servile legions of a rice-eating and heathen race."
Mr. Page of California	House, April 22, 1880	"…my friends from New England will not listen to me when I appeal to them to stand by the laboring classes of the Pacific coast and tell them it is degrading to them to bring one hundred and fifty thousand Mongolian slaves and place them in the machine-shops, in the shoe-factories, in the watch-factories, in the cigar-factories, alongside the white laborers of the country. As before the war free labor refused to go South and enter into competition with the slave labor of South Carolina, Florida, and Louisiana, so Mr. Chairman, free white American labor shrinks from the contest when it has to enter into competition with the labor of one hundred and fifty thousand Mongolian slaves."
Mr. Morrow of California	House, March 17, 1890	"Mr. Speaker, the laws now upon the statute books provide for the exclusion of Chinese laborers from the United States. Commencing with the treaty of the 17th of November, 1880....Congress has been seeking to execute the will of the people of the United States, to exclude Chinese laborers from this country. For a time each act in turn had been deemed effective, but the immigration has continued in spite of legislation forbidding it."

TABLE 4.4 Labor Competition in Congressional Discussions (continued)

Congressman & State	Location & Date	Quote
Mr. Clunie of California	House, March 17, 1890	"...I desire to say my people are deeply interested in this subject. The farmers and fruit men who get the benefit of their cheap labor are willing to forego that advantage for the benefit of their own race. The working men and women in the cities, and, in fact, all over the State, appeal to you to give them this legislation and any additional legislation necessary to rid the country of this evil. Their children are growing up and are anxious and willing to work, but they can not compete with these Mongolian invaders."
Mr. Hayes of California	House, February 25, 1909	"I say, Mr. Chairman, that at this moment there are 22,000 idle white men in the city of San Francisco alone, and every charitable institution there is maintaining, and has been for months, a system of supplying the necessities of these people who are out of work, and yet in my district there are probably 10,000 Japanese, I do not know how many Chinamen, nearly all of whom are employed. Now, Mr. Chairman, I say to you that the people of California, except the few who profit by their labor, which is generally given cheaper than white labor, are in favor of what they conceive to be the patriotic thing to do, and that is preserve the land of the Pacific coast for the Caucasian race [Applause.]"
Mr. Hayes of California	House, February 25, 1909	"The labor market is greatly overcrowded there, and unless there can be some stop to the influx of the Oriental the time is not far distant when the common laborer of California and, doubtless, in time, the skilled labor, also, will be wholly monopolized by Orientals, because no white man and no white woman can compete with them."
Mr. Clark of Missouri	House, February 25, 1909	[in response to Mr. Hayes statements on the same day]* "...I congratulate him [Mr. Hayes] on believing in a white man's government....But it is not only organized labor that is against that immigration. It is every laborer in the United

TABLE 4.4 Labor Competition in Congressional Discussions (continued)

Congressman & State	Location & Date	Quote
		States who understands his rights and values his own interests [Applause]...The Caucasian race from the dawn of history has been the dominant race of the world; it is yet, and always will be as long as any of us are left. [Applause.]...We claim to be superior to everybody in everything. There is one mistake in that proposition. There is one thing that by reason of centuries of training and by disposition we are unable to do. We Can not compete with the Chinese in the matter of starvation. [Loud applause.] If you let them in here ad-libitum or even in large numbers, they will starve our laborers out. The gentleman from Iowa, Colonel HEPBURN, says that 500,000 Chinese laborers can be absorbed into the labor of the Untied States at this time. It is currently reported that there are millions of Americans out of employment in this country to-day. The gentleman from California {Mr. HAYES} says that 22,000 stand in bread lines in San Francisco alone. I would rather see 500,000 men and women of my own blood absorbed in the labor of this country. [Loud applause.]
Mr. Harrison of New York	House, February 25, 1909	"I think that he [Mr. Hayes]* will find that the people of the United States are a unit in demanding that this bar shall not be taken down and that our labor markets shall not be flooded with the hungry millions of the Orient....The question of the white civilization is at stake....Mr. Chairman, in its sum it is nothing more or less than our assertion of our rights to preserve the white civilization. [Applause.]"

* Explanation added

Mr. Clark of Missouri: *...I congratulate him* [Mr. Hayes] *on believing in a white man's government....But it is not only organized labor that is against that immigration. It is every laborer in the United States who understands his rights and values his own interests [Applause]...The Caucasian race from the dawn of history has been the dominant race of the world; it is yet, and always will be as long as any of us are left. [Applause.]...We claim to be superior to everybody in everything. There is one mistake in that proposition. There is one thing that by reason of centuries of training and by disposition we are unable to do. We can not compete with the Chinese in the matter of starvation. [Loud applause.] If you let them in here ad-libitum or even in large numbers, they will starve our laborers out. The gentleman from Iowa, Colonel HEPBURN, says that 500,000 Chinese laborers can be absorbed into the labor of the Untied States at this time. It is currently reported that there are millions of Americans out of employment in this country to-day. The gentleman from California {Mr. HAYES} says that 22,000 stand in bread lines in San Francisco alone. I would rather see 500,000 men and women of my own blood absorbed in the labor of this country. [Loud applause.]...*

Mr. Harrison of New York: *I think that he* [Mr. Hayes] *will find that the people of the United States are a unit in demanding that this bar shall not be taken down and that our labor markets shall not be flooded with the hungry millions of the Orient....The question of the white civilization is at stake....Mr. Chairman, in its sum it is nothing more or less than our assertion of our rights to preserve the white civilization. [Applause.]* (House, February 25, 1909)

In their remarks, all three Congressmen blatantly asserted that the Chinese laborers and their ability to work for lower wages were a threat to the Caucasian race. Although these three Congressmen were vocal in their beliefs, it can not be assumed that they alone thought the Caucasian race needed to be protected. Rather, given that after each of these statements and throughout Mr. Clark's comments, the transcriber of the Congressional Record noted the applause from the other Representatives and even denoted the difference in the volume with "loud applause" their beliefs were most likely shared by the majority of the House. Also of note, in all of the discussions included in the analysis of the opium laws these are the only comments for which applause was indicated.

In sum, concern for economic competition with the Chinese immigrants was present in all the Congresses included in the analysis. The majority of the statements and discussions regarding economic competition were made by or included Pacific coast, specifically California, Congressmen. By the 60th Congress economic competition was a concern for Congressmen regardless of geography. Although it may not have been an important issue for everyone, the applause in the House of Representatives from Mr. Hayes, Mr. Clark and Mr. Mitchell's discussion of preservation of the white race indicates their views may have been popular.

Political Competition

Although anti-Chinese sentiment and economic competition were more prevalent in the Congressional discussions, concerns regarding political competition were also voiced albeit rarely. On at least two occasions, once in both the Senate and House, Congressmen raised the issue of Chinese immigrants' political power or potential political power. On May 16, 1876 during discussions of Chinese immigration Mr. Merrimon of Delaware after listening to Mr. Mitchell of Oregon's lengthy speech extolling the "evilness" of Chinese immigration (see another excerpt from Mr. Mitchell's speech in Table 4.3) asked him how many of the Chinese were naturalized.

Mr. Mitchell of Oregon: *...you may not feel it here, but our shores, the golden shores of the Pacific are to-day being flooded with the serfs, the criminals, the mendicants, the opium-eating gamblers, the leprous prostitutes, the most debased, in every sense of the word, of the Chinese Empire. To permit this, when no possible good can come to the Chinese subjects, as I have already shown, and when, instead of adding to the intelligence, the wealth, the prosperity, the dignity of our country, it but brings poverty, disease, and pestilence, and crime, simply out of a desire on our part to adhere to a principle, is, to my mind, to subordinate the truest and best interests of this Government, the general welfare, and the domestic tranquility, to the vindication of a mere idea in political ethics. It is one, in my judgment, that cannot be sustained for one solitary moment by any element of true statesmanship; and, sir, if it is persisted in, I predict here and now that the people of the next centennial, if not of the next generation, will eat of its bitter fruits and drink of its poisoned waters.*

Mr. Merrimon of Delaware: *May I ask the Senator a question?*

Mr. Mitchell: *Certainly.*

Mr. Merrimon: *I ask whether any portion of the Chinese on our western shores are naturalized; and, if so, do they belong to the voting population of California and Oregon?*

Mr. Mitchell: *They are not naturalized; and not only that, but they do not desire to be naturalized; and that is the very point I have been trying to make, that the country from which they come is an exception to the nations of the world to which* *the doctrine of the right of expatriation ought to be extended by our country.*

Mr. Merrimon: *Suppose they are content to be naturalized and our people are content that they shall be and become voters among them?*

Mr. Mitchell: *That is simply supposing a case that never will occur, as I have been endeavoring to show. I have been endeavoring to show that all their inclinations and aspirations and dispositions are in the other direction. They do not desire either a change of government in their own country or a transfer of their allegiance to this.*

Mr. Sargent of California: *If my friend will allow me, I will say that the people of the Pacific coast do not wish them to be naturalized. Naturalization would only add to the mischiefs Put the ballot in the hands of the sixty thousand Chinese in California, and they would be marshaled in squads at the polls by their masters, the six companies, with ballots prepared beforehand and dictated to them, and the influence of white men in the government of California would soon cease to exist. California would be a mere Asiatic province.*

Mr. Mitchell: *This is unquestionably true, and the same thing applies in relation to the State of Oregon. The whole immigration is not a voluntary one; it is controlled, as stated by the Senator from California, by these six companies, by these masters, if you please, in whose control and under whose subjection is every Chinese, male and female, that comes from the empire to our shores; and, as stated, the ballot in their hands would but add to the horrors of the situation.* (Senate, May 16, 1876)

On the one hand, Mr. Sargent and Mr. Mitchell both state their belief that few Chinese immigrants would choose to become citizens of the United States, yet they fear that if the Chinese did naturalize and had the ability to vote then they would take over the state and white men would lose their political power. Realistically, given that the ratio of Chinese immigrants to California's total population was 1:11.5 in 1870 and 1:13 in 1880 (Seward, 1970) it was unlikely that the Chinese would outnumber California's voting population. In respect to Oregon, since Oregon had approximately 45,000 fewer Chinese immigrants than California in 1870 (Seward, 1970) it was even less likely that the Chinese immigrants would outnumber the eligible voters in Oregon. Thus, although Mr. Sargent and Mr. Mitchell perceived the Chinese immigrants political power as a threat to whites, it was a perceived rather than an actual threat.

The political power of the Chinese was also briefly mentioned in the House of Representatives in February 1909. While discussing Chinese immigration Mr. Hayes of California commented on Chinese labor and alluded to the Chinese's potential political power.

> **Mr. Hayes of California**: *I say to you that I believe it is an immediate, pressing necessity that something should be done to stop the influx of Orientals who have been coming to the Pacific coast and who, unless prevented, will absorb not only the entire labor there, but will buy up the land and come to possess and rule and control that fair country as they do or will soon do in Hawaii.* (House, February 25, 1909)

Although Mr. Hayes was not as specific as Mr. Sargent or Mr. Mitchell in stating his perception of the Chinese as a political threat, his comment that they would "control that country" implied a political as well as economic threat. Given that the Chinese Exclusion Act of 1882 and subsequent acts reduced the volume of Chinese immigration from a high of approximately 20,000 a year in the 1870's to a high of approximately 4,300 in the two and a half decades prior to 1909, the

Chinese population in the United States had significantly decreased (Li, 1916). Therefore, the likelihood of the Chinese outnumbering eligible California voters was even less than it was in 1876.

Regardless of perceived or actual threat, the discussion of naturalization and voting power of the Chinese immigrants was a mute point. When Congress passed the Naturalization Act of 1870, California successfully lobbied to include blacks but limit all other eligible groups to be "free white persons" (Kennedy, 1990: 38). Per Mr. Mitchell in the above referenced quote and mentioned frequently in immigration discussions, the majority of Chinese immigrants were not free; they came to America indebted by contract to six Chinese companies[15]. Also as indicated by Mr. Sargent's remarks referring to Chinese and whites as well as numerous other comments during the immigration and labor competition discussions (see quotes in Table 4.3 as well as quotes included in labor competition), the Chinese immigrants were considered a different race. Therefore, at the time of Mr. Mitchell, Mr. Merrimon and Mr. Sargent's discussion, per the

---

[15] The Chinese Six Companies were social organizations based on region of origin and blood (Tsai, 1986). Chinese immigrants arriving in the United States usually sought out people who spoke with their dialect (and thus came from the same or similar regions of China). In 1851 the Kong Chow Company was founded and accepted all Chinese except San Yi and Hakkas. The San Yi immigrants created the Sam Yup Company while the Zhongshan and Hakkas immigrants founded the Yeong Wo Company and Yan Wo Company, respectively. Around 1854 the Taishan created Ning Yeung Company and the Kaiping and Emping Chinese formed the Hop Wo Company. These six companies came together to form a federal association they called the Chinese Consolidated Benevolent Association but is known to Americans as the Chinese Six Companies. The Companies sent representatives to meet all arriving Chinese immigrants and provided them with the basic necessities and aided them in starting their new life in America. The Companies also provided Chinese immigrants with numerous services including but not limited to interpreters, lodging, employment, credit and loans, mediation, and arbitration (Tsai, 1986; Lyman, 1974). Essentially the Companies acted as a mutual aid society. However, those who opposed Chinese immigration accused the Companies of importing coolie labor and prostitutes under labor contracts that amounted to slave labor as well as operating gambling facilities and opium dens (Tsai, 1986).

Naturalization Act of 1870, the Chinese were legally prohibited from voting and thus had little political power. In addition, by the time of Mr. Hayes remarks in 1909, the 1882 Chinese Exclusion Act among others had also prohibited the naturalization of the Chinese[16] and thus their ability to vote, rendering the ability of the Chinese to govern the Pacific Coast legally improbable if not impossible despite Mr. Hayes concerns.

Localized Issue

Although anti Chinese sentiment and economic competition were present in all the Congresses included in the analysis, in the early Congresses they were a localized issue. Tables 4.3 and 4.4 illustrate that most of the anti Chinese comments were made by Pacific Coast Congressmen, specifically those from California. Given that Chinese immigration was most widespread in California (see Table 4.1); it is not surprising that the California Congressmen were concerned about Chinese immigration and labor.

The California Congressmen were aware of the localized nature of Chinese immigration and all its ramifications. On several occasions Mr. Sargent of California acknowledged that the majority of Congress and the United States may not have been aware of the issue but they needed to be.

> **Mr. Sargent of California**: *Senators must see the dangerous and disgusting nature of this encroaching element. The country must awake to the danger before it is too late. I have*

---

[16] In addition to Chinese immigrants not being allowed citizenship, since the male Chinese immigrants vastly outnumbered female Chinese immigrants and of the females who did immigrate many were employed as prostitutes, relatively few Chinese immigrants had children born in the United States. Thus it was unlikely that sufficient numbers of Chinese would be born in the United States to achieve the population necessary to become an actual political threat.

> *not waited to this hour to warn Congress and the country of these evils. On the 25th June, 1862, nearly fourteen years ago, I called to the attention of the House of Representatives...* (Senate, May 1, 1876)

By his own admission in 1876, Mr. Sargent had been advocating the need to restrict Chinese immigration, yet in fourteen years he had not been successful in persuading the rest of Congress of the urgency of the situation.

One of the tactics of Mr. Sargent, Mr. Hager and Mr. Page in pleading their case was on the one hand to admit that Chinese immigration was at the time largely an issue just for California and the Pacific Coast states, while also arguing that it would become a national problem either due to increasing immigration or migration across the United States. To make his point, Mr. Sargent referred to California as the gateway for Chinese immigration implying that it was just a matter of time before the Chinese migrated across the United States. Then the issue would be national rather than local.

> **Mr. Sargent of California**: *The matter is of very great local importance, and perhaps it is to be regretted that it is so local in its character that its importance cannot be fully estimated in other parts of the country ......I wish to call the attention of Senators to the fact that California and the Pacific States and Territories are simply the gateway which lets in the influx of Chinese population ...* (Senate, February 13, 1874)

While Mr. Sargent referred to California as a gateway, Mr. Hager focused on how the rapid increase in Chinese immigration (the greatest influx of Chinese immigration occurred in the 1870's) would render it a national problem.

> **Mr. Hager of California**: *It* [Chinese immigration] *is a subject of very considerable moment to us, I may say of the*

> *highest importance, and, although perhaps not well understood here, it is rapidly assuming such proportions as must necessary make it a national problem.* (Senate, March 20, 1874)

In the House of Representatives, Mr. Page referred to California's economic hardships occurring after the 1873 stock market crash and the volume of employed Chinese versus the unemployed whites for which the Chinese were blamed. He implied that California's economic hardships would spread across the nation if something was not done to end Chinese immigration.

> **Mr. Page of California**: *That its destructive influence on the industrial condition of California is the inevitable result which must follow its extension into every other State of the Union.* (House, February 10, 1875)

When pleas such as this seemed not to sway Congress, Mr. Sargent switched tactics, somewhat, and asked his fellow Senators to put themselves in California's "shoes" and ask how they would respond.

> **Mr. Sargent of California**: *Are the people of the East quite certain that, if the Chinese were to land in their midst in the proportion of one in every eight of the population of the several States, they would be as easy as to the future as now? They should try and put themselves in our place, and deal with this question as if they, too, had among them this strange and dangerously unassimilative people, increasing in numbers from year to year.....The question of the restriction of Chinese immigration to the United States concerns at present the people of the Pacific coast more than it does eastern communities.* (Senate, May 1, 1876)

Regardless as to whether Congressmen were swayed by the California Congressmen's statements, the question of Chinese immigration did evolve from a localized issue to a national one with the discussions and passage of the 1882 Chinese Exclusion Act and subsequent Chinese exclusionary acts[17]. Yet, despite the passage of the acts, some Congressmen may have still believed Chinese immigration was a local rather than national issue. Mr. Hepburn of Iowa indicated this in the House of Representatives in 1909 during a discussion about labor competition and Chinese immigration.

> **Mr. Hepburn of Iowa**: *If this matter could be submitted to the housekeepers of the United States, it would be decided against the foolish policy that we have adopted in obedience to the demands of Dennis Kearney and other sandlotters, agitators, and disturbers of the peace on the Pacific Coast.* (House, February 25, 1909)

Mr. Hepburn had argued that the Chinese were very good domestic servants and should be allowed to come to the United States to be employed in that occupation. He also implied that the exclusionary acts were not a good idea, yet they were passed because Congress gave into the demands of California and other Pacific Coast states due to the

---

[17] The Chinese Exclusion Act of 1882 prohibited the immigration of Chinese laborers, skilled and unskilled, as well as those Chinese employed in mining. Although concerns with Chinese immigration may have appeared to be localized, the Act was passed in the House by a vote of 201 for and 37 against with 51 Representatives not voting and in the Senate by a vote of 32 for and 15 against with 29 Senators absent (Li, 1916). The Geary Act of 1892 which extended the Chinese Exclusion Act for 10 years and required the Chinese to register and obtain certificates of residence or face deportation was passed in the House by a vote of 186 for and 27 against with 115 Representatives not voting and in the Senate with a vote of 30 for and 15 against with 43 Senators not voting. The passage of both anti-Chinese immigration acts by wide margins indicates that Chinese immigration had evolved from a local to national issue whether by actual concern or logrolling.

actions of Dennis Kearny and others who advocated against the Chinese and were instrumental in instigating the riots. Although the localized issue may not have been deemed worthy of national stature by all, Chinese immigration, labor competition and anti Chinese sentiment did evolve from localized to national, if not in actuality (as in the Chinese migrating in mass numbers across the United States) then in the form of federal laws.

While anti Chinese sentiment and fear of economic competition began as localized issues being the focus and concern primarily of California and other Pacific Coast Congressmen and eventually emerged as a concern for many regardless of geographic area culminating in the passage of several anti Chinese laws, fear of political competition remained localized. Political competition was mentioned or alluded to on just two occasions, both by Pacific coast Congressmen, during the discussions included in this analysis.

Opium Discussions

It was assumed that given the public association of the Chinese and smoking opium that the discussions regarding opium legislation would contain anti-Chinese rhetoric and be overtly biased against the Chinese. Although anti-Chinese rhetoric was utilized in the discussions regarding Chinese immigration and labor occurring during the same time frame and sometimes on the same day as the opium discussions, the opium legislation discussions did not contain as overtly biased rhetoric. In addition, in comparison to the discussions of Chinese immigration and labor, the opium discussions were to an extent a non event in that they were either very brief or non existent.

Even though the first opium law, the San Francisco city ordinance, was passed in 1876 and several states followed San Francisco's lead, there were no discussions of opium in the 43rd or 44th (1873-1876) Congresses. One of few references to opium was made by Mr. Hager of California when he was characterizing the Chinese during his statements about labor competition.

> **Mr. Hager of California:** *Another evil of Chinese emigration is its injury to white labor. The merit is claimed for the Chinese that they are industrious and this is true of a considerable class of them, although as many are lazy, opium-stupefied drones.* (Senate, May 1, 1876)

Other than this comment and Mr. Mitchell's reference to "opium-eating gamblers" on May 16, 1876, there was no mention of opium during these Congressional sessions. In the 46th and 51st Congresses, opium was referenced in the Index, but there were no discussions only statements in Congress that the legislation had been sent to committee and then when it was read in Congress and passed. Therefore, there were no discussions in Congress of either the 1880 treaty or the 1890 opium legislation. If there was any discussion it may have occurred in committee but there was no mention of a committee report.

In the 49th Congress, the 1887 opium legislation was discussed by Mr. Cox in the House in that he read the proposed 1887 bill as well as the 1880 treaty and stated that the current legislation was to enforce the 1880 treaty as requested by the President. Although he indicated no further discussion was necessary he reiterated his statements.

> **Mr. Cox of North Carolina**: *I do not suppose it is necessary to say anything more in regard to the bill. Mr. Speaker, the bill now presented for consideration is a means to carry out certain treaty stipulations between the Chinese Government and our own, which was ratified by the President in May, 1881. It related to what is known as the opium trade, to repress importation into the United States by Chinese subjects, and the importation by citizens of the United States of opium into any of the open ports of China, or transportation from one open port to another, or the buying and sale of opium in any such ports.....The manifest intent of this treaty is to prevent American citizens in China from engaging in this opium traffic, or in knowingly aiding others to do so. The*

> *treaty itself is not self-executing. Appropriated legislation is required to make it effective.* (House, February 8, 1887)

No other members of the House commented on the bill. It was read for a third time and passed with essentially no discussion.

Since there was essentially no discussion of these three laws and anti-Chinese concerns appear to have been localized to the Pacific Coast, how did the laws garner enough support for passage? Since the 1880 law was a treaty between the United States and China and the 1887 legislation enforced the treaty, that both were supported or requested, respectively, by the President may have been sufficient motivation for Congressmen to support their passage. The 1890 legislation which raised a tariff on the manufacturing of only smoking opium, however, was not related to the 1880 treaty nor was it specifically requested by the President, yet it still passed with no discussion indicating that perhaps the Pacific Coast Congressmen bargained with other Congressmen for their support of this legislation in exchange for support on other legislation. Since there were no discussions of the 1890 legislation on the floor of Congress, any conversations would have occurred outside of Congress in the halls or offices for which there is no record and can only be assumed. Thus logrolling may have occurred and been a factor in the passage of at least the 1890 law.

Although the 1880 treaty and the 1887 and 1890 opium legislation were passed with essentially no discussion in Congress, the 1909 law was discussed in both the House and the Senate albeit briefly. All of the opium discussions occurred in the Senate on January 26, 1909 (the bill was read and passed in the Senate on February 2nd with no discussion) and in the House on January 23rd and February 1st. These discussions focused on international necessity, taxes, and smoking opium.

Despite reports indicating that opium addiction was a growing problem in the United States (Morgan, 1974; Fernandez, 1998; Gray, 1998; Bonnie & Whitehead, 1999), the 1909 law seemed to be more about international politics than a concern for the health of Americans. The International Opium Commission consisting of the United States, "China, France, Germany, Great Britain, Japan, the Netherlands, Portugal, Russia, Austria-Hungary, Italy, Siam and Persia" (Wright, 1910; 3) met from February 1, 1909 through the 26th in Shanghai, China. The opium legislation was quickly pushed through Congress so the law would be in place by the beginning of the International Opium Commission. Per the Congressional discussions, it was believed that the United States needed to have a federal opium law in order to be in a good negotiating position at the International Opium Commission since the other nations in attendance had opium laws. In the House, Mr. Payne of New York spoke of the international importance on two occasions.

> **Mr. Payne of New York**: *Now I know that it is urged that the State Department desires that this bill pass, because there is to be a convention in Hongkong, about the 1st of February, of the powers, who are going to see if they can not stop the use of opium in the Chinese Empire, and this is to be a sort of inducement for the convention to get together, a sort of certificate of good faith on the part of the people in the United States that they do not propose to have opium coming in here prepared for smoking purposes.* (House, January 23, 1909)

> **Mr. Payne of New York**: *That convention meets at Hongkong to-day, and he [the Secretary of State] was particularly anxious that this bill should pass, because the United States had the initiative in calling that convention and it would strengthen the hands of the administration.* (House, February 1, 1909).

The international significance of the law was also discussed in the Senate where Mr. Lodge of Massachusetts opened the discussion of the legislation by stating its international importance.

> **Mr. Lodge of Massachusetts**: *the bill (S. 8021) to prohibit the importation and use of opium for other than medicinal purposes, which was reported this morning by the Committee on Finance. The international congress is now meeting at Shanghai, and it is very important that the bill should be promptly passed.* (Senate, January 26, 1909)

He reiterated the importance of the legislation in a later discussion with Mr. Bailey of Texas in which Mr. Bailey questioned the United States ability to pass a federal opium law whose intent was to protect health.

> **Mr. Lodge:** *...There is a meeting of an international commission in regard to this subject now in progress in Shanghai. We have American commissioners there. I think I am correct in saying that every important nation, except the United States, has adopted legislation of the character of this bill as a measure of hygiene and protection.*
>
> **Mr. Bailey of Texas:** *That is the point.*
>
> **Mr. Lodge:** *That, of course, is the real reason.*
>
> **Mr. Bailey:** *Then, Mr. President, if it is a matter of health, it is not within the jurisdiction of the Federal Government, and I must object to the consideration of the bill.*
>
> **Mr. Lodge:** *I was speaking of the views of other nations.*
>
> **Mr. Bailey:** *But I understood the Senator to say –*
>
> **Mr. Lodge:** *They think it is good to exclude the smoking of opium.*
>
> **Mr. Bailey:** *I think almost every State –*

> **Mr. Lodge:** *And I presume they have not supposed that would stand in they way.*
>
> **Mr. Bailey:** *I think probably every State in the Union has a law forbidding the smoking of opium. If they have not, I am sure they ought to have.* (Senate, January 26, 1909).

Mr. Lodge acknowledged that the purpose for the opium legislation was to place the United States on at least equal footing with the other nations on the Commission who already had such laws. Even though many states had opium legislation, it was believed a federal law was needed to achieve a position of power at the International Opium Commission.

Mr. Bailey's discussion with Mr. Lodge also illustrated the question of federal jurisdiction. In 1909 the federal government still held that the regulation of behavior was a state rather than federal power (Musto, 1999). Within the opium discussions some Congressmen questioned the federal government's power to pass laws regulating behavior. Since regulation of behavior was outside of the federal government's jurisdiction, the only power the federal government had or believed they had was regulation through taxation. The federal government began taxing opium imports in 1842 with a tariff of 75 cents per pound (Wright, 1910). In 1857, the tariff was increased to $1 per pound. By 1871, the federal government differentiated between opium and smoking opium, with the tariff for the former remaining $1 per pound and the latter $6. While the tariff for opium remained constant, the smoking opium tariff fluctuated. From 1885 to 1890 the smoking opium tariff was $10 per pound. The tariff was increased to $12 from 1890 to 1897, and then lowered to $6 until 1909. Given the federal governments history of taxing smoking opium, eliminating the tax and prohibiting behavior was a concern for a few Congressmen, specifically Mr. Bailey of Texas and Mr. Payne of New York.

Mr. Payne raised the issue of taxation and questioned whether it was wise to pass legislation that by prohibiting the importation of smoking opium would also eliminate the per pound tariff.

> **Mr. Payne of New York**: *If I thought, Mr. Speaker, that this bill would prevent the use of a pipe full of opium in the United States, I would still be disposed to give it consideration. But it will not prevent the use of it. Opium will still come in to be used for other purposes, and there is nothing in the bill, there can be nothing in any effective law passed by Congress, to prevent any person in the United States from preparing opium for smoking or using it as smoking material from the opium brought in for other purposes. It can not be done. We would have practically the same consumption of opium for smoking as we have now. Opium for smoking purposes produces a revenue of over $900,000 a year. That would cut us off from a million dollars of revenue, and we should gain nothing by the operation of the law....I am not willing to give up a revenue of $75,000 a month when it will do no good.* (House, January 23, 1909).

In this, Mr. Payne indicated that he did not think the legislation as written would decrease the practice of smoking opium and if the legislation would not prevent people from smoking opium then the government should not also lose the lucrative tariff. Thus, with the power Congress had, if the practice could not be stopped at least revenue could be raised. Instead of generating discussion, his comments were responded to by Mr. Mann of Illinois objecting to his long speech if he was going to object to the bill in the end.

> **Mr. Mann**: *I did not expect the gentleman to make a long speech on the bill and then in the end object to it.*

> **Mr. Payne:** *I object, Mr. Speaker. If the gentleman wants to make a statement, however, I will withhold my objection.*
>
> **Mr. Mann**: *O, Mr. Speaker, I do not believe in batting the air like the gentleman from New York {Mr. PAYNE}. I do not want to make a statement.*
>
> **The Speaker**: *Objection is heard.* (House, January 23, 1909).

Mr. Mann's comments imply that Mr. Payne is wasting time objecting to a bill that would be passed, perhaps due to pressure regarding the International Opium Commission.

While Mr. Payne focused on the lucrative revenue, in the Senate, Mr. Bailey was concerned with the federal government's power.

> **Mr. Bailey**: *Mr. President, the bill comes from a committee of which I have the honor to be a member, and while I thoroughly sympathize with the object of it, I have grave doubt that it is exactly the kind of legislation Congress is competent to enact. It is upon its face an effort to suppress the practice of smoking opium and this is clearly a police regulation.* (Senate, January 26, 1909).

Mr. Bailey's comment began a discussion of the power of Congress to protect the morals of United States citizens. A lottery law regulating morals had been deemed constitutional by the Supreme Court, thus it was argued that the opium legislation would also be constitutional. Throughout the discussion Mr. Bailey maintained his position; however Mr. Money of Mississippi ended the discussion by supporting Congresses power to pass the legislation.

> **Mr. Money:** *Now, as to this bill, I myself think that there is no police power in the General Government of any character whatever. There can not be, from the very nature of the case.*

> *It is one of the vast mass of residuary powers left by the Constitution inherent, inalienable in the States themselves, and it has been so held in every decision of the Supreme Court that I have ever read. That is still true; but we travel, in this bill, upon extremely narrow lines, which I hold, however, to be sufficient. We can declare what is not merchantable and what is merchantable; and, under the power to regulate commerce, we can say what can be imported and what can not be imported. We could absolutely forbid some sorts of commerce from entering this country at all; and in this case, in my opinion, we clearly have the right, although on a very narrow line, I must say, to take the action proposed by the bill. Whatever the ulterior object may be, the object on the surface is the one that we will consider, and that is, to forbid the importation into this country of an article which is not merchantable according to our way of thinking. I think that is quite sufficient, and I hope that this bill will pass without any further delay.* (Senate, January 26, 1909)

After Mr. Money's assertion that Congress had the power to pass the bill, the bill was read again and passed. Although the issue of federal power was to an extent resolved in the Senate, it was also questioned in the House by Mr. Gaines of West Virginia.

> **Mr. Gaines of West Virginia**: *They [the Philippine Islands] provided there that no person might use opium unless he registered himself as a confirmed opium smoker. We have no such power in this country. It takes plenary power to stamp out such a habit – if it can be suppressed at all – the full police power. Our Federal Government does not have it.* (House, February 1, 1909)

Therefore, Congress's power to pass and enforce the opium legislation, prohibiting behavior, was questioned in both the House and the Senate.

Despite these questions regarding the federal government's power to regulate behavior, the opium bill was passed.

In addition to the international necessity and the power of Congress, the discussions in both the House and Senate focused on one form of opium, smoking opium. Although studies had indicated that the United States had a problem with opium addiction not just smoking opium, both the law itself and the Congressional discussions regarding it focused on smoking opium. In the Senate, Mr. Bailey of Texas and Mr. Lodge of Massachusetts remarked on more than one occasion that the intention of the law was to prohibit the smoking of opium.

> **Mr. Lodge of Massachusetts**: *It is a tariff prohibition against the introduction of opium – opium prepared for smoking purposes. It admits all opium and its derivatives for medicinal purposes, but excludes smoking opium.* (Senate, January 26, 1909)

(For additional quotes, see also those previously included from Mr. Bailey). Within the Senate discussions, there was no mention of other forms of opium other than reiterating that opium could be imported for medicinal purposes.

The focus on smoking opium was also prevalent in the House discussions. However, the House discussions differed from the Senate discussions in that they made the connection between China and/or Chinese and smoking opium. Mr. Payne of New York voiced his concern that while smoking opium was primarily manufactured in China it could be manufactured in the United States from medicinal opium.

> **Mr. Payne of New York**: *The object of the bill is to prohibit the importation of opium prepared for smoking, or smoking opium....with a proviso that opium for medicinal purposes may be imported under rules and regulations prescribed by the Secretary of the Treasury and subject to the duties*

> *provided by law. ...smoking opium is manufactured abroad, exclusively in China. There is a process by which it can be manufactured in this country from medicinal opium, but Chinamen desire opium prepared for smoking in their own country; but rather than not have it at all they would take that prepared in this country undoubtedly.* (House, February 1, 1909).

He associated the smoking of opium with the Chinese and their desire of smoking opium to the extent that they would find ways to obtain smoking opium even if importation was prohibited. Mr. Gaines of West Virginia was of the same mind and also expressed concern that the Chinese if prohibited from importing smoking opium from China would begin manufacturing it here.

> **Mr. Gaines of West Virginia**: *Now unfortunately, because of the conservatism of the Chinese people, they so much prefer to have their opium prepared in China that the high rate of duty has not stimulated the manufacture of opium in this country; but it is a notorious fact, known of all men, that those who are addicted to the opium habit will secure the drug in some form, even though not the preferred form, if they are prevented from getting it in the form in which it is preferred. My belief and fear is that this proposition presented to the House of Representatives by the gentleman from Illinois would but stimulate the manufacture and preparation of opium for smoking in this country...*(House, February 1, 1909)

Mr. Payne's solution was to add a tariff to the manufacturing of smoking opium in the United States.

> **Mr. Payne of New York**: *This act might be greatly strengthened by putting a tax which would be prohibitive upon the manufacture of smoking opium in this country... That, in*

> *connection with this bill, as gentleman will readily see, will do very much to cut off the use of smoking opium in this country.* (House, February 1, 1909)

His suggestion of taxing the manufacturing of smoking opium follows Congress's tradition of regulating behavior through taxation.

Despite the available knowledge that the practice of smoking opium was not restricted to the Chinese (Morgan, 1974), the Congressmen only referred to the Chinese as smoking opium and did not acknowledge the practice of non Chinese smokers. In addition, the bill and the Congressmen's discussion focused on smoking opium and disregarded the problem with opium addiction specifically those addicted to laudanum or morphine. Therefore, although race was only briefly mentioned during the discussion period, by focusing on the use of smoking opium, a form of opium that well off whites, specifically white women who had the highest addiction rates, did not use but which was associated with the Chinese, the law did target Chinese immigrants although indirectly.

CONCLUSION

The analysis of the 1880, 1887, 1890 and 1909 opium laws and the Congressional discussions addressed the research questions discussed in Chapter Three. The second research question addressed the content of the laws and whether they were racially biased or race neutral in their wording. Three of the four opium laws were race neutral in their wording. The 1880 law may, with its restricting only Chinese immigrants from importing opium, on its face seem to be racially biased; however, since it was a treaty between the United States and China in which each nation prohibited only the citizens of the other nation from importing opium, it was race neutral in its wording. The 1887 law, however, since it created harsher penalties for Chinese was not race neutral. Both the 1890 and 1909 laws were race neutral in their wording, but focused on only the form of opium, smoking opium, that was generally associated with the Chinese. Therefore, the content of the wording of the opium laws changed slightly over time from race neutral to racially biased and then back to race neutral.

The fifth research question asked how minority groups were vilified during the period leading up to the enactment of the drug legislation. Anti-Chinese sentiment, although more prevalent in the earlier Congresses, was present in all the Congresses included in the analysis. The anti-Chinese rhetoric included terminology such as evil, curse, and plague as well as alluding to the depravity and criminality of the Chinese. The vast majority of the anti-Chinese remarks were made be Congressmen from the Pacific coast, specifically California. Even though the California Congressmen were overt and virulent in their dislike of the Chinese, this sentiment was not held by everyone. Still, the rhetoric regarding the evilness and general undesirability of the Chinese was, for the most, uncontested suggesting that this may have been the popular viewpoint. Thus, the Chinese were vilified during the period leading up to the enactment of the opium legislation.

Research questions three and four asked whether the discussions surrounding the opium legislation impacted their passage and whether competition for economic and political resources affected the drug laws. During this time the United States experienced an influx of Chinese immigration and an economic recession and the resulting competition for scarce jobs. Thus, it was not surprising that the anti-Chinese sentiment was most prevalent in immigration and labor discussions. Congressional discussions regarding Chinese immigration and the labor competition between Chinese immigrants who would work for lower wages and white laborers occurred before, during and after the enactment of the opium laws. Although immigration and labor issues were not specifically mentioned during the opium legislation discussions, since these issues completely surrounded the opium discussions they may have affected the opium legislation, especially since all the opium legislation focused in some way on the Chinese and excluded almost everyone else.

Although the anti Chinese sentiment and fear of economic competition were localized issues concerning primarily the California and other Pacific Coast Congressmen, they eventually became national concerns. The national concerns of the Congressmen were illustrated by the applause for Mr. Hayes, Mr. Clark and Mr. Mitchell's anti-Chinese and preservation of the white race discussion. Political competition was also present; however it remained a localized issue and was only referenced a few times. Additionally, given the number of Chinese in America at the time, it was a perceived rather than actual threat. Since political competition was barely mentioned and remained localized it is unlikely that it affected the opium legislation. However, given the focus on the Chinese working for lower wages when jobs were scarce and that the opium laws essentially restricted only the Chinese, economic competition most likely did affect the passage of the opium laws.

Finally, the first research question asked whether racism had been embedded in our drug laws. Although this question cannot be definitively answered since the actual intent of the Congressmen cannot be ascertained, a plausible case can be made that the 1887, 1890 and 1909 opium laws at least represent indirect institutional discrimination. The 1887 law created harsher penalties for the Chinese who imported opium into the United States than for the Americans who imported opium into China. Since there were essentially no discussions of this law in Congress, the intent of the Congressmen is unknown; however, the potential negative outcome due to the harsher penalties for the Chinese illustrates indirect institutional racism.

Although the 1890 and 1909 opium laws did not specifically reference the Chinese, they did focus on smoking opium which was generally associated with the Chinese. The 1890 law also prohibited the manufacturing of smoking opium for non citizens, thus all United States citizens could still manufacture smoking opium. Therefore, while they did not specifically reference the Chinese, by focusing on smoking opium the laws did indirectly target the Chinese immigrants. If the concern behind the laws was public health and lowering the addiction rates, the laws, given the available addiction studies, should have focused on opium, laudanum, and morphine rather than just smoking opium which did not have the highest addiction rates. Why focus on a form of opium that was not creating the most health problems? Given that the references in the Congressional discussions were all regarding the Chinese and their habit of smoking opium, it can be concluded that the focus on smoking opium was related to the general dislike of the Chinese immigrants.

Furthermore, the Congressional discussions indicated that the major concern with the laws was not public health. The 1880 and 1887 laws were the treaty and enforcement of the treaty with China while the 1909 law was primarily passed to establish a position of power for the United States at the International Opium Commission. Thus, these opium laws were passed not out of concern for public health but rather international diplomacy.

As previously indicated, the actual intention of the Congressmen is difficult, if not impossible, to ascertain. Nevertheless, their focus on the Chinese and smoking opium combined with the anti-Chinese immigration and labor competition discussions indicate that the laws, at the least, indirectly targeted the Chinese. It could be argued in terms of cultural relativity that perhaps at the time the anti-Chinese sentiment was not considered racist. However, Mr. Sargent of California, one of the more outspoken anti-Chinese Congressmen did acknowledge the prejudice against the Chinese during an immigration discussion.

> **Mr. Sargent of California**: *The prejudice of race cannot be considered when persons already among us appeal for protection....Is the desire of the Chinese to select our country as a place of residence so clear a natural right that, rather than gainsay it, we are willing to submit to the disorders which must grow out of the prejudice known to exist against them? As to this prejudice, is it not based upon some reason?* (Senate, May 1, 1876)

Mr. Sargent not only acknowledged the prejudice that existed against the Chinese, but also argued that it was justified. Given that there was no responding comment to his remark, it is probable that Mr. Sargent was not alone in his knowledge that the beliefs and actions against the Chinese were discriminatory. Therefore, given all of the above, racism was embedded in at least the 1887, 1890 and 1909 opium laws.

CHAPTER 5

The Marihuana Tax Act of 1937

Marijuana comes from the hemp plant *Cannabis sativa L* (Abadinsky, 2008; U.S. Department of Justice, 2008; Liska, 2004). *Cannabis sativa L* grows wild in most tropical and temperate regions, but grows best under the same conditions as corn (Abadinsky, 2008). For over 5,000 years it has been cultivated for a variety of purposes such as the manufacturing of clothing, paper, rope and paint (Abadinsky, 2008; Liska, 2004). The stem of the plant is used for its fiber, the seeds have been cultivated for feed mixtures and the oil has been used in paints. The leaves and resinous flowering tops (referred to as buds) contain the psychoactive drug delta9-tetrahydrocannabinol (THC) (Abadinsky, 2008; U.S. Department of Justice, 2008; Liska, 2004). Male plants are usually killed so the female will produce more resin to cover the buds when trapping pollen. Although marijuana can consist of the dried flowers, stems, seeds and leaves, currently growers concentrate on the flowering tops that contain the most THC (the leaves contain less THC while the stems, roots and seeds have almost no THC). Marijuana once cultivated can be smoked as a cigarette usually referred to as a joint, in a pipe called a bong, or as a blunt (a cigar with tobacco removed and replaced with marijuana and often a combination of drugs). It can also be added to foods or prepared as a tea.

GENERAL HISTORY OF MARIJUANA

Cannabis sativa L has existed for approximately 5,000 years during which it has been used by numerous societies around the world as a source of fiber for manufacturing, a food additive, a medicine and a psychoactive drug (Liska, 2004; Abadinsky, 2008; Sloman, 1979). According to Lusane (1991), during the 1600's African slaves brought the hemp plant with them to the American colonies where it also grew wild. Hemp was bountiful in the colonies and used to produce products such as clothes, paper, paint, ship sails, food oils, and rope. The entire plant was also used in numerous medicines and patent medicines for various ailments such as migraines and insomnia (Provine, 2007). In the mid 1800's, Parke-Davis and other pharmaceutical companies manufactured a tincture of cannabis.

From the 1600's until the 1800's, hemp was one of the most important crops in America (Lusane, 1991). Hemp was so important that the colony of Jamestown in Virginia passed a law in 1619 requiring farmers to grow it. By 1762, Virginia was imposing penalties on those who did not grow hemp (Sloman, 1979). Even though Virginia passed hemp laws there may not have been a dire need to impose the laws given the volume of people growing the crop including two United States presidents, Washington and Jefferson (Lusane, 1991; Sloman, 1979). The importance of hemp was also illustrated in that from "1631 until the 1800's" (Lusane: 29) it was legal tender. Although Kentucky and Missouri were the major areas for hemp cultivation, it was grown all over the South and had towns and counties named for it (i.e. "Hempstead, Long Island; Hempstead County, Arkansas; and Hempstead County, Texas" (Lusane: 29)).

At the beginning of the twentieth century, marijuana began to appear in Texas border towns and New Orleans (Inciardi, 1992; Bonnie & Whitehead, 1999). Although Americans knew of the various uses of marijuana, smoking was not designated as a problem until the late 1910's and early 1920's when it was reported that Mexican immigrants were bringing it across the border. It was then assumed that the smoking of marijuana had been introduced in America by the Mexican immigrants who brought the habit with them (Musto, 2002). However, at the turn of the century the American Black Cavalry stationed near the Mexican border smoked marijuana as did sailors who brought the drug back from South and Central America (Sloman, 1979). Therefore, although Mexican immigrants may have brought the practice with them in the 1920's, Americans had already been smoking marijuana. Regardless of actual origin, public perception linked smoking marijuana to Mexicans (Sloman, 1979; Provine, 2007; Musto, 2002).

As in the case of opium and the Chinese, popular belief negatively associated marijuana with Mexicans. Stories told of Mexicans smoking marijuana going crazy and killing people (Bonnie & Whitehead, 1999). Mexicans under the influence of marijuana were bloodthirsty and three times as adventurous (Bonnie & Whitehead, 1999), and had "superhuman strength" (Provine, 2007: 83). It may have been acknowledged that anyone, whites included, was prone to violence and crime when high on marijuana, but popular belief held that Mexican laborers were responsible for a disproportionate amount of violent crimes (Bonnie & Whitehead, 1999). There were also reports of Mexicans enticing schoolchildren to try the drug (Provine, 2007). At times, marijuana was even referred to as the Mexican opium (Inciardi, 1992). These images of violent Mexicans high on marijuana were repeatedly cited in multiple public forums (i.e. newspapers, magazines, radio, and public speeches), eliciting fear among whites (Provine, 2007). Hearst newspapers were one of the major sources of the proliferation of racial stories associating Mexicans with marijuana use and violence (Lusane, 1991). Lusane (1991) contends that Hearst's interest was due in part to Pancho Villa's army seizing 800,000 acres of Hearst's land. Regardless of why, Hearst newspapers helped spread anti-Mexican and anti-marijuana sentiment. Despite the association with Mexicans and the growing concern about the drug, marijuana was predominately considered a local problem until approximately 1933 (Sloman, 1979).

Although Louisiana was the first state to enact an anti-marijuana law in 1922 (Liska, 2004), Texas and New Mexico also quickly passed anti-marijuana legislation with little discussion other than references to its Mexican origins, criminal conduct of Mexicans and the "killer weed" (Bonnie & Whitehead, 1999). By 1933, 33 states had passed anti-marijuana legislation. Four years later, all 48 states and the District of Columbia had anti-marijuana laws (Liska, 2004). Societal fear of marijuana was so great that three states' (Illinois, Missouri, and Utah) laws maximum penalty for the possession of a marijuana cigarette was a life sentence. At the same time there were also demands for bans on Mexican immigration to decrease job competition (Bonnie & Whitehead, 1999) which will be discussed in more depth under Mexican immigration.

State pressure and anti-marijuana sentiment lead the Secretary of Treasury, under the Food and Drug Act, to prohibit the importation of cannabis for other than medical purposes and required it to be listed in a product's ingredients in 1915 (Bonnie & Whitehead, 1999). In January 1937 a few marijuana bills were introduced in Congress: the Treasury introduced H.R. 6385, the Hatch bill originally introduced in 1935 and the Fish bill (Sloman, 1979). Since H.R. 6385 addressed the issues covered in all the bills, the others did not progress. After approximately seven months and some revisions H.R. 6385 became the Marihuana Tax Act of 1937. The Act classified marijuana as a narcotic, subjected it to prohibitions similar to that of opium and cocaine in the Harrison Narcotics Act, and made the illegitimate use and sale of it a felony (Inciardi, 1992; Lusane, 1991). Although, the Marihuana Tax Act of 1937 was race neutral in its wording, research (Provine, 2007; Bonnie & Whitehead, 1999; Lusane, 1991; Liska, 2004; Abadinsky; 2008; Musto, 2002) has frequently implied that racism was involved and the law was influenced by the association between Mexicans and marijuana use and the stories of Mexicans high on marijuana committing violent crimes.

The rapidity of the passage of the state and especially federal marijuana laws is often credited to Harry Anslinger, the Commissioner of the Federal Bureau of Narcotics, and his campaign against marijuana (Liska, 2004). Anslinger originally campaigned for state legislation but around 1934 he began promoting the need for a federal marijuana law (Bonnie & White, 1999; Provine, 2007). During his support and in lobbying and testifying for the marijuana legislation, Harry Anslinger made references to the dangers of Mexican and black use of marijuana (Lusane, 1991). The media actively covered Anslinger's campaign publicizing the stories of violence committed by those high on marijuana which some refer to as his "gore file" (Provine, 2007; Sloman, 1979). In addition to the print media publicizing his campaign, Commissioner Anslinger also spoke on numerous radio programs, spoke in a variety of public forums, wrote magazine articles, and gave hundreds of lectures on the increasing prevalence of marijuana and crimes associated with it as well as naming it a cause of insanity and linking it to children.

MEXICAN IMMIGRATION

After the completion of the Mexican railroad and the Revolution of 1910 which resulted in an economic recession, Mexicans migrated north to the United States (Handman, 1930). Mexicans immigrated to America because it was a neighboring nation, the standard of living was higher, World War I created a labor shortage in America, immigration policies permitted low wage laborers, and in California and Texas land prices had increased necessitating cheap labor (Handman, 1930; Taylor, 1930; Molina, 2006). For Mexican workers cheap labor by American standards was still higher than their standard of living. According to Handman (1930), with the influx of Mexican immigrants by 1930 in Texas and California the American tenant farmer had been replaced by the Mexicans, railroad track foreman preferred Mexican laborers, and Mexican laborers did more work than white laborers for half the pay. Although not supported by documentation other than a footnoted story, Handman also alleged that due to the migratory nature of their labor, Mexicans used and sold narcotics during the winter when they were not working; thus alluding to the alleged association between Mexicans and marijuana.

Although the exact number of Mexican immigrants is unknown due to people entering the country illegally, approximations of the total Mexican population were created by comparing census reports and immigration records (Bloch, 1929). The census reports from 1870 to 1920 illustrate the increasing Mexican born population (see Table 5.1). From 1881-1890 1,913 Mexicans legally immigrated to the United States. In the following decade another 971 Mexicans legally entered the United States. Despite the relatively small number of Mexicans legally immigrating to America, per the 1900 census 103,393 Mexicans (people born in Mexico rather than of Mexican descent) resided in the United States (Bloch, 1930; Batten, 1930). By the 1910 census the Mexican population had risen to 221,915 but between the two censuses only 41,490 Mexicans legally enter the country (Bloch, 1930). From this Bloch concluded that approximately 100,000 Mexicans illegally entered the country during that ten year period. Per their calculations, between 1910 and 1920 152,541 Mexicans legally immigrated to the United States but the 1920 census reported the Mexican population as 486,418 indicating, according to Bloch, that approximately 200,000 Mexicans entered the country illegally. Regardless of legal or illegal entry, from 1900 to 1920 the Mexican immigrant population increased more than four fold.

Table 5.1
Number of Population Born in Mexico and Residing in United States*

1870	42,435
1880	68,399
1890	77,853
1900	103,393
1910	221,915
1920	486,418

* From Bloch (1929)

In the 1920's Mexican immigration continued to increase (Bloch, 1929). From 1920 to 1927 339,988 Mexicans legally immigrated to the America. Even accounting for those who returned to Mexico or had died, by 1927 the Mexican population totaled more than 801,000 without including approximations for those who illegally entered the country. Thus, Bloch estimated that the Mexican population was over one million with the vast majority living in the Southwest (see Table 5.2). Bonnie and Whitehead (1999) also found that the majority of Mexican immigrants resided in the southwest. Between 1915 and 1930, 590,765 Mexicans immigrated to America, two-thirds of whom settled in Texas. By 1930, the Mexican born population was approximately one and a half million with just under 90% residing in Arizona, California, Colorado, New Mexico and Texas (Alvarez, 1966).

Table 5.2
Mexican Population by State in 1920*

Texas	251,827
California	88,7771
Arizona	61,580
New Mexico	20,272
Kansas	13,770
Colorado	11,037
Oklahoma	6,884
Illinois	4,032
Missouri	3,411
New York	2,999
Iowa	2,650
Nebraska	2,611
All other states	16,574

* From Bloch (1929). Only includes information for legal Mexican immigrants.

As Table 5.2 illustrates, although Mexican immigrants may have settled primarily in the Southwest they did migrate to other parts of the country. Mexican laborers migrated to the industrial region in the Midwest and other major commercial centers (Bonnie & Whitehead, 1999). Both the railroads and the steel industry who employed large numbers of Mexicans, transported Mexican laborers from the Southwest to the Midwest and other locations, thus aiding in the volume of Mexican migration, because of the ability to pay them lower wages (Taylor, 1930) and specifically for the steel industry to break the 1919 strike (Levenstein, 1968). By 1930, the Mexican population in Chicago had reached 30,000, more than seven times Illinois' Mexican population in 1920.

With the advent of the Great Depression, the demand for immigrant labor rapidly decreased until it was almost nonexistent (Alvarez, 1966). The decrease in labor demand coincided with a significant decrease in Mexican immigration beginning in 1930. From July, 1929 to March, 1930 only 10,500 Mexicans legally entered the United States (Batten, 1930). In addition to the depression and increased competition for labor, Batten attributed part of the decrease in immigration to a law passed on March 4, 1929 making it a felony to illegally enter the country. Prior to this law, a Mexican caught illegally entering the country was just deported.

Even though industries such as the railroads, agriculture and steel sought out Mexican laborers who would work for lower wages (Levenstein, 1968), anti-Mexican sentiment never reached the level of anti-Chinese sentiment in that it did not result in the volume of riots and deaths. Despite this, labor organizations sought to restrict Mexican immigration to decrease the competition between white and Mexican laborers (Molina, 2006). The American Federation of Labor (AFL) lobbied throughout the 1920's to have Mexican immigration restricted (Levenstein, 1968). However, during Congressional hearings in 1920 Mexican agricultural workers were depicted as ideal laborers because of their physical ability to do the work (Molina, 2006). The AFL attempted but failed to have Mexico included in the National Origins Act of 1924 which established immigration quotas of 2% for the countries included in the Act (Levenstein, 1968; Bloch, 1930). Though they continued to lobby for Mexican immigration restrictions, they met with opposition from businesses and industries as well as the

Secretaries of State, Agriculture and the Interior. At the close of the 1920's the AFL's efforts remained unsuccessful[18].

According to Molina (2006) after Mexico was not included in the 1924 National Origins Act, those opposing Mexican immigration began depicting Mexicans as "racially inferior and diseased" (29). Articles relating to Mexican inferiority were published with "titles such as 'The Menace of Mexican Immigration,' 'The Influx of Mexican Amerinds,' and 'Mexicans or Ruin'" (Molina: 32). Although laws restricting Mexican immigration were not passed, during the Depression federal, state and local governments engaged in the unconstitutional deportation of Mexicans, known as repatriation (Balderrama, 2005; Johnson, 2005). In some areas, such as Los Angeles, police would go to public places where Mexicans gathered, put them on buses and immediately drive to the border (Johnson, 2005). Repatriation was partly justified as a way to decrease welfare costs as well as lower job competition during the mass unemployment of the Depression (Balderrama, 2005; Katz, Stern & Fader; 2007; Johnson, 2005). The exact number of Mexicans, American and Mexican born, repatriated to Mexico is unknown. According to Katz, Stern & Fader (2007) more than 400,000 people of Mexican ancestry were deported, while Johnson (2005) estimated the number to be closer to one million. Therefore, although the federal

---

[18] During the 1920's when the AFL unsuccessfully lobbied for Mexican immigration restrictions to decrease labor competition, both Congress and the Presidency were Republican (Senate.gov, 2008; House.gov, 2008). From the 66th Congress beginning in 1919 through the 72nd Congress ending in 1933 both the Senate and the House of Representatives were controlled by Republicans. Likewise the Presidency was held by Republicans Harding (1921-1925), Coolidge (1925-1929) and Hoover (1929-1933). It was not until after Democrats took control of Congress and the Presidency in 1933 that legislation protecting employees rather than employers garnered any measure of success. Most notable was the passage of the 1935 Wagner Act which protected workers' right to unionize. Thus the AFL's unsuccessful attempts to restrict Mexican immigration may have been due more to the government's support of employer rights rather than support for Mexican immigration.

government did not pass laws restricting Mexican immigration during this time, the United States did substantially decrease the Mexican population through repatriation.

THE MARIHUANA TAX ACT

The Marihuana Tax Act was enacted on August 2, 1937 and was effective as of October 1, 1937. The Act levied a tax on marijuana for importers, manufacturers, producers, and medical practitioners. Section Two of the Act required all people who handled marijuana transactions to register and pay a yearly tax. The tax varied from one dollar, three dollars and $24. Producers, medical practitioners and anyone importing or manufacturing marijuana for research purposes were taxed one dollar. Those who dealt with marijuana but were not medical practitioners paid the higher tax of $3, while importers or manufacturers of marijuana for non research purposes were taxed $24 a year. In addition to being taxed, Section 6 of the Act required those who prescribed or dealt marijuana to others to keep a record of how much marijuana was transferred and to whom. For these records, dealers had to purchase the forms (referred to as bills) from the federal government for two cents each. The bills required the name and address of the purchaser as well as the amount of marihuana. By the Act, the dealer had to provide the purchaser with a bill as well as keep his own copy.

Although Section Two of the Act required registration and payment of a yearly registration (occupational) tax, Section 7 of the Act levied another tax on the transfer of marijuana by the ounce. For those who were properly registered the tax per ounce of marijuana was one dollar, but for those not registered the tax was $100 per ounce. Payment of the tax was denoted by a stamp created by the Treasury and affixed to the bill. The transferee paid the dollar tax while the transferor was liable for the $100 tax if not properly registered. Thus, Section 7 created a $100 per ounce "penalty" tax on marijuana if not properly registered. Section 12 of the Act also addressed penalties.

Anyone violating any provision of the Act could be penalized by up to a $2,000 fine, five years in prison or both subject to the courts discretion. Thus, the Act created more than one tax as well as bills and stamps that had to be purchased in advance and penalties.

Per the text of law, no racial or ethnic distinction is made regarding people who import, manufacture, produce, sell, dispense or deal with marijuana. References to people were usually referred to as "any person" that was defined at the beginning of the Act as:

> *(a) The term "person" means an individual, a partnership, trust, association, company, or corporation and includes an officer or employee of a trust, association, company, or corporation, or a member or employee of a partnership, who, as such officer, employee, or member, is under a duty to perform any act in respect of which any violation of this Act occurs.* (The Marihuana Tax Act of 1937)

Although the Act does distinguish between importers, manufacturers, medical practitioners, and non medical dealers, it is based on occupational purpose rather than race. In addition, there is no reference to Mexico or Mexicans any where in text of the Act. Therefore, the Marihuana Tax Act is race neutral in its wording.

CONGRESSIONAL DISCUSSIONS

As, if not more important, than the wording of the laws is the social context from which they emerged. Analysis of the latent content of the discussions occurring on or around the discussions of the Marihuana Tax Act did not yield the expected themes of anti-Mexican sentiment, vilification of Mexicans and labor competition. Instead the discussions illustrated themes regarding the commercial aspects of hemp manufacturing, taxing, the vilification of marijuana, lack of knowledge of marijuana, and the use of newspaper accounts as factual support.

References to Mexicans and Mexico

Given the increase in Mexican immigration and the migration of Mexican immigrants to the Midwest it was assumed that the influx of Mexican immigrants would foster anti-Mexican sentiments within the Congressional discussions of the Marihuana Tax Act. It was also assumed, given that the Marihuana Tax Act was created, discussed and passed during the Great Depression, that the Congressional discussions would include references to job competition, specifically discussions of Mexican immigrants taking jobs away from white workers because they were willing to work for less money. Of the Congressional discussions included in this analysis, there were no discussions of labor competition or Mexican immigration and essentially no anti-Mexican sentiment. Mexican immigration was mentioned a few times but only to state that a bill had been referred to a committee.

It was also assumed that the Congressional discussions regarding marijuana would include references to Mexican savagery or brutality while using marijuana. Contrary to what was expected, the majority of Congressional discussions did not focus on Mexicans or their use of the drug. Although public opinion may have associated marijuana use and the crime and violence associated with marijuana use with Mexicans, there were few references to Mexicans included in the discussions. During the discussion on the House floor on June 14, 1937 when the bill was debated, read and passed there was no reference to Mexicans or Mexico. However, there were a few derogatory references made against Mexicans during the House's Ways and Means committee hearings on marijuana. Of note is that both of the references were provided by Harry Anslinger, Commissioner of the Federal Bureau of Narcotics.

Although Anslinger did not read the letter verbatim he did highlight the crime and provide copies of the letter for the committee to read. The letter was from Floyd K. Baskette, the City Editor of the Alamosa Daily Courier.

> *Two weeks ago a sex-mad degenerate, named Lee Fernandez, brutally attacked a young Alamosa girl. He was convicted of assault with intent to rape and sentenced to 10 to 14 years in the state penitentiary. Police officers here know definitely that Fernandez was under the influence of marihuana.*
>
> *But this case is one in hundreds of murders, rapes, petty crimes, insanity that has occurred in southern Colorado in recent years....*
>
> *The people and officials here want to know why something can't be done about marihuana. The sheriff, district attorney, and city police are making every effort to destroy this menace. Our paper is carrying on an educational campaign to describe the weed and tell of its horrible effects....*
>
> *I wish I could show you what a small marihuana cigarette can do to one of our degenerate Spanish-speaking residents. That's why our problem is so great; the greatest percentage of our population is composed of Spanish-speaking persons, most of who are low mentally, because of social and racial conditions* (Taxation of Marihuana, April 27, 1937a: 32).

Although, per Baskette, southern Colorado had numerous crimes related to marijuana, the only crime he specifically referenced was that of a man with a Hispanic surname alluding that he is Mexican. Later in the letter he referred to Mexican immigrants as "our degenerate Spanish-speaking residents" (Taxation of Marihuana, 1937a: 32). From the contents of the letter one might, regardless of correctness, assume that it was just the Mexican residents who used marijuana and committed crimes under its influence.

In addition to the Baskette letter, Anslinger also provided the Ways and Means committee with a copy of Dr. Frank Gomila, Commissioner of Public Safety, and Madeline Gomila's article "Marihuana – A More

Alarming Menace to Society than All other Habit Forming Drugs" which discussed information from various newspapers regarding the dangers of marijuana, its prevalence and various crimes committed under the influence of marijuana. In the article Gomila and Gomila state "that Colorado reports that the Mexican population there cultivates on an average of 2 to 3 tons of the weed annually. This the Mexicans make into cigarettes, which they sell at two for 25 cents, mostly to white high school students" (Taxation of Marihuana, 1937a: 33). Thus, Gomila and Gomila associated Colorado's marijuana problems with Mexicans.

Within the committee hearings the only other references to Mexico or Mexicans referred to either the terminology or the origins of marijuana. Matt Rens of Rens Hemp Co. when proposing changes to the wording of H.R. 6906 during the Senate Subcommittee of the Committee on Finance hearings opposed the use of the term marihuana because it "is purely a localized term of Mexican (Indian) origin, and has no more general significance and is no more universally recognized than 'bhang', 'hashish', and similar local terms" (Taxation of Marihuana, 1937b: 23-24). Dr. William Woodward, legislative counsel for the American Medical Association, also had issue with the use of the term marihuana, "the term 'marijuana' is a mongrel word that has crept into this country over the Mexican border and has no general meaning, except as it relates to the use of Cannabis preparations for smoking" (Taxation of Marihuana, 1937a: 90). References to marijuana's Mexican origin similar to that made by Rens were the norm rather than Dr. Woodward's comments. Therefore, despite Dr. Woodward's comment most references to the terminology or origins of marijuana tended to be race neutral.

Although some of the statements are derogatory towards Mexicans, overall there were few references to Mexicans or Mexico in all the discussions on the Congressional floor or in the committee hearings. Rather than vilifying Mexicans, the drug itself was vilified by focusing on the crimes committed by those under its influence, its link to insanity, and its prevalence among children, specifically high school students.

Vilification of Marijuana

Within the Congressional discussions marijuana was vilified through rhetoric and by associating the drug with crime, insanity, and children. In terms of rhetoric, marijuana was referred to as evil and a menace. In the first and relatively few references to marijuana in the Congressional Record for the 75th Congress, Mr. Hamilton Fish included a transcript of his radio speech in the Appendix in which he referred to marijuana as evil and a menace.

> **Mr. Fish**: *Marihuana is used largely in the form of cigarettes, which cause delusions and produce insanity and often lead to atrocities that only a drug-soaked mind could conceive. Marihuana is a sinister drug that has only recently become available and popular among the younger element. It is much cheaper than cocaine, heroin, or morphine, and to that extent more dangerous, and is fast becoming a menace.*
>
> *There should be drastic laws not only against the importation of the ingredients but even more so against the manufacture and sale of marihuana in cigarettes or in any other form. This is a matter for the State legislatures and the Congress to take up and adopt effective legislation without further delay to curb and, if possible, wipe out this growing evil and menace to the youth of America.* (Appendix for House of Representatives, February 24, 1937).

Despite his remarks appearing in the Appendix rather than being stated on the floor of the House it is likely that his fellow Congressmen heard them given they were from a public radio address. Similar rhetoric was more prevalent in the committee hearings. The Chairman of the Ways and Means committee in discussing the necessity of the proposed legislation referred to marijuana as "the evil that exists" (Taxation of Marihuana, 1937a:115). Mr. Vinson and Commissioner Anslinger also referred to marijuana as a menace, but Anslinger added another dimension by discussing how rapidly the drug had spread.

> **Mr. Vinson**: *When was this brought to your attention as being menace among our own people?*
>
> **Mr. Anslinger**: *About 10 years ago---*
>
> **Mr. Vinson**: *Why did you wait until 1937 to bring a recommendation of this kind?*
>
> **Mr. Anslinger**: *Ten years ago we only heard about it throughout the Southwest. It is only in the last few years that it has become a national menace. It has grown like wildfire, but it has only become a national menace in the last 3 years. It is only in the last 2 years that we have had to send reports about it to the League of Nations.* (Taxation of Marihuana, 1937a: 20)

Mr. Reed reiterated Mr. Anslinger's assertion that marijuana was a national concern in the House of Representatives.

> **Mr. Reed of New York**: *This demoralizing dope is sold by a class of degenerate peddlers in dens, dives, and on the streets of cities throughout the country.*" (House of Representatives, June 14, 1937)

Thus, through the use of terminology such as menace and evil, Commissioner Anslinger and the Congressmen were able to vilify marijuana and instill some level of urgency by discussing how rapidly it had become a national concern.

As alluded to by Mr. Fish's radio address, support for the

marijuana legislation was also garnered by associating the drug with crime, insanity and children. In part of his opening comments to the Ways and Means hearing, Mr. Hester illustrated how the three were usually linked to the drug.

> **Mr. Hester**: *...Inhibitions are released. As a result of these effects, many violent crimes have been and are being committed by persons under the influence of this drug. Not only is marihuana used by hardened criminals to steel them to commit violent crimes, but it is also being placed in the hands of high-school children in the form of marihuana cigarettes by unscrupulous peddlers. Its continued use results many times in impotency and insanity.* (Taxation of Marihuana, 1937a: 6)

Mr. Hester's statement was indicative of how associations with crime, insanity and children were used to vilify marijuana. Rarely was one discussed without linking the drug to another. However, of the three, associating the drug with and crime and children were the most prevalent.

<u>Crime & Insanity</u>:
In Congress and the committee hearings the vilification of marijuana was illustrated by references to heinous crimes committed by those under its influence. The crimes discussed seemed to be the more extreme and salacious crimes. Although the cases discussed were relatively few in number, the level of violence seemed to capture the Congressmen's attention. The most sensational cases involved decapitation and an ax murder both purportedly committed under the influence of marijuana. Mr. Reed of New York referenced these cases when discussing the necessity of the marijuana legislation before the House of Representatives voted.

> **Mr. Reed of New York**: *The testimony given by experts shows that the use of the drug leads to insanity and crime... a*

> *case was presented to us from California where 'a man under the influence of marihuana actually decapitated his best friend and then, coming out of the effects of the drug, was as horrified as anyone over what he had done'. Another case is recorded where 'A young boy who had become addicted to smoking marijuana cigarettes, in a fit of frenzy because, as he stated while still under the marihuana influence, a number of people were trying to cut off his arms and legs, seized an ax and killed his father, mother, two brothers, and a sister, wiping out the entire family except himself.* (House of Representatives, June 14, 1937)

Although he only presented two cases, the two cases were the most sensational. Of note, the case of the young man killing his family with an ax was also mentioned in the 1936 film Reefer Madness.

Even though Mr. Reed mentioned crimes in the House, the majority of the crimes were presented in the committee hearings by Commissioner Anslinger. Anslinger began his account of the crimes by stating how people on marijuana behave.

> **Mr. Anslinger**: *Some people will fly into a delirious rage, and they are temporarily irresponsible and may commit violent crimes. Other people will laugh uncontrollably. It is impossible to say what the effect will be on any individual.* (Taxation of Marihuana, 1937a: 21)

With this statement he established the link between marijuana use and crime and then went on to support the assertion with examples of crimes. Table 5.3 contains most of the crimes that Anslinger referred to in the House Ways and Means hearings and the Senate Finance Subcommittee hearing. Between the two committees Anslinger referenced approximately eight specific cases (some cases were referenced in both committees) and stated that there were many other violent cases for which he provided no documentation. In the Senate

Finance Subcommittee, Anslinger not only spoke of the cases, but he also circulated a photograph of a victim whose head had been "smashed." Given that no one questioned the association of marijuana and criminal behavior and that both committees recommended the legislation, apparently, eight extreme cases was enough evidence to support the link between marijuana and crime or it was already a widely held belief.

In addition to fortifying the association between marijuana use and crime, Anslinger also linked marijuana to insanity. Before the Senate Finance Subcommittee he stated that although marijuana affects people differently continued use leads to insanity.

> **Mr. Anslinger:** *I believe in some cases one cigarette might develop a homicidal mania, probably to kill his brother. It depends on the physical characteristics of the individual. Every individual reacts differently to the drug. It stimulates some and others it depresses. It is impossible to say just what the action of the drug will be on a given individual, or the amount. Probably some people could smoke five before it would take effect, but all the experts agree that the continued use leads to insanity. There are many cases of insanity.* (Taxation of Marihuana, 1937b: 14)

In addition to this statement, within his discussion of some of the criminal cases he also alluded to marijuana causing insanity by saying one of the defendants was found "mentally deranged" (Taxation of Marihuana, 1937b: 12). Anslinger alleged that "all the experts agree" (Taxation of Marihuana, 1937b: 14), yet he did not present scientific studies as support just letters and Dr. Gomila's article that relied

Table 5.3 Mr. Anslinger's Crime Account

"Here is a gang of seven young men, all seven of them, young men under 21 years of age. They terrorized central Ohio for more than 2 months, and they were responsible for stick-ups. They all boast they did those crimes while under the influence of marihuana." (Taxation of Marihuana, 1937a: 22)
"There was one town in Ohio where a young man went into a hotel and held up the clerk and killed him, and his defense was that he had been affected by the use of marihuana." (Taxation of Marihuana, 1937a: 22)
"In Florida a 21-year-old boy under the influence of this drug killed his parents and his brothers and sister. The evidence showed that he had smoked marihuana. In Chicago, recently two boys murdered a policeman while under the influence of marihuana. Not long ago we found a 15-year-old boy going insane because, the doctor told the enforcement officers, he thought the boy was smoking marihuana cigarettes. They traced the sale to some man who had been growing marihuana and selling it to these boys all under 15 years of age, on a playground there." (Taxation of Marihuana, 1937a: 23)
"Here in Colorado- and Colorado seems to have had a lot of cases of violence recently- in Alamosa County, and in Huerfano County the sheriff was killed as the result of the action of a man under the influence of marihuana. Recently, in Baltimore a young man was sent to the electric chair for having raped a girl while under the influence of marihuana." (Taxation of Marihuana, 1937a: 23)
"...last January I tried a murder case for several days, of a particularly brutal character in which one colored young man killed another, literally smashing his face and head to a pulp, as the enclosed photograph demonstrates. One of the defenses was that the defendant's intellect was so prostrated from his smoking marihuana cigarettes that he did not know what he was doing. The defendant was found guilty and sentenced to a long term of years." [letter read by Anslinger who also distributed the photograph] (Taxation of Marihuana, 1937b: 11)
"I have a few cases here that I would just like to tell the committee about. In Alamosa, Colo., they seem to be having a lot of difficulty. The citizens petitioned Congress for help, in addition to the help that is given them under the State law. In Kansas and New Mexico also we have had a great deal of trouble. Here is a typical illustration: A 15-year-old boy, found mentally deranged from smoking marihuana cigarettes, furnished enough information to the police officers to lead to the seizure of 15 pounds of marihuana. That was seized in a garage in an Ohio town. These boys had been getting marihuana at a playground, and the supervisors there had been peddling it to children, but they got rather alarmed when they saw the boys developing the habit and

Table 5.3 Mr. Anslinger's Crime Accounts (continued)

particularly when this boy began to go insane. In Florida some years ago we had the case of a 20-year-old boy who killed his brothers, a sister, and his parents while under the influence of marihuana. Recently, in Ohio, there was a gang of very young men, all under 20 years of age, every one of whom confessed that they had committed some 38 holdups while under the influence of the drug. In another place in Ohio a young man shot the hotel clerk while trying to hold him up. His defense was that he was under the influence of marihuana." (Taxation of Marihuana, 1937b: 12)

heavily on newspaper accounts. Despite the lack of scientific support, given that no one questioned the link to insanity and Mr. Hester and Mr. Reed among others also made the connection, the belief that marijuana use led to insanity may have been widely held among the Congressmen.

Children:

In addition to the association of crime and insanity with marijuana, the drug was vilified by associating its use with children. During his testimony before the House of Representatives Ways and Means committee Anslinger discussed how marijuana users were different from heroin or morphine users in that they were much younger.

> **Mr. Anslinger:** *this drug is not being used by those who have been using heroin and morphine. It is being used by a different class, by a much younger group of people. The age of the morphine and heroin addict is increasing all the time, whereas the marihuana smoker is quite young.* (Taxation of Marihuana, 1937a: 24)

To support his assertion that marijuana users were much younger, Anslinger read a statement from Dr. Bromberger who was a psychiatrist at Bellevue Hospital in New York.

> **Mr. Anslinger**:...*Dr. Walter Bromberger, a distinguished psychiatrist in New York, has made this statement: Young men between the ages of 16 and 25 are frequent smokers of marihuana; even boys of 10 to 14 are initiated (frequently in school groups); to them as to others, marihuana holds out the thrill. Since the economic depression the number of marihuana smokers was increased by vagrant youths coming into intimate contact with older psychopaths.* (Taxation of Marihuana, 1937a: 24)

Although this was the only support Anslinger provided for the age of marijuana users, he also alluded to age in his description of the crimes (see Table 5.3). Whenever age was mentioned in reference to crimes, it was a fifteen year old or someone under the age of 20 or 21.

Even without substantial documentation of the age, Congressmen associated marijuana use with children. In the House of Representatives both Mr. Buck and Mr. Reed argued that one of the worst aspects of the marijuana trade was it being supplied to high school students.

> **Mr. Buck of California**: *The worst thing about this trade is not that hardened criminals use the drug to steel themselves for their operations but it is being peddled by itinerant dealers and peddlers throughout the country and sold to our high-school students, starting the young out as drug addicts.* (House of Representatives, June 14, 1937)

> **Mr. Reed of New York**: *The most alarming aspect of this illicit traffic is the sale of marihuana cigarettes to the boys and girls, especially those of high-school age.* (House of Representatives, June 14, 1937: 5689)

Although in a submission to the Appendix rather than on the floor of the House, Mr. Fish also associated marijuana use with children. He, however, not only associated marijuana use with children, but also stated that it was almost always used by young people.

> **Mr. Fish of New York**: ... *a narcotic that is being extensively used by the younger generation of America.* (Appendix for the House, February 23, 1937)

Given that his statement was submitted for inclusion to the Appendix, other Representatives may not have read it. However, since it was the transcript of his radio address his perception of young people being the primary users of marijuana may have supported or influenced public as well as the Congressmen's opinion.

Regardless of personal or public opinion or evidence of the age of marijuana users, in both the committee hearings and on the floor of Congress the association between high school students (or young people) and marijuana use was rarely, if ever, questioned. Rather than questioning the age of users, Congressmen focused on how young people obtained the drug.

> **Mr. Lewis**: *Where do the victims get it?*
>
> **Mr. Reed**: *I think what the chairman wants to know is how high-school children are able to get it. Is it not true that there are illicit peddlers who hang around the high-school buildings, and as soon as they find out that there is some boy to whom they think they can sell it, they make his acquaintance?*
>
> **Mr. Hester**: *Yes. I read in the newspapers not long ago that a place on Twelfth Street was raided, where a lady was selling marihuana.* (Taxation of Marihuana, 1937a: 17)

Mr. Lewis did not question that high school students' used marijuana, instead he was concerned with how they obtained the drug. In asking his question he referred to the high school students as victims. Whether they were the victims of the drug or drug dealers was not specified, but referring to users as victims, to an extent, vilifies marijuana as a perpetrator.

In sum, rather than the expected vilification of Mexicans, the Congressional and committee hearing discussions illustrated that marijuana, itself, was vilified. Commissioner Anslinger and Congressmen expressed their anti-marijuana sentiment and referred to marijuana as evil and a menace. The drug was also vilified by associating users with heinous crimes while under the drug's influence, implying that continued use would lead to insanity, and focusing on teenage use.

Effect on Hemp Manufacturing

Although marijuana was vilified, references to marijuana's association with crime, insanity and children did not dominate the discussions. More prevalent than the vilification of marijuana were the discussions of the potential effects of the legislation on hemp industries. In the 1930's hemp was still deemed one of the most important, if not the number one, crop in America by the USDA (Lusane, 1991). The hemp industry had a significant role in the manufacturing of products such as clothing, paper, rope, paint, varnish and birdseed. The concern of the hemp manufacturers was indicated in both their presence and their testimony. Three of the twelve people who testified before the Ways and Means committee represented hemp or hemp product manufacturers, while four of the seven people testifying before the Senate Finance Subcommittee represented five hemp manufacturers. In total, between the two committees eight hemp or hemp product manufacturers were represented by the seven men's testimony.

The hemp manufacturers were concerned that the marijuana legislation would adversely affect their industry. They sought confirmation from the committees that if the legislation were passed their industries could still legitimately produce and manufacture hemp and hemp products. Mr. Scarlett representing Wm. G. Scarlett & Co. expressed concern for his industry since the proposed legislation included seeds in the definition of marihuana.

> **Mr. Scarlett**: *We handle a considerable quantity of hempseed annually for use in pigeon feeds. That is a necessary ingredient in pigeon feed because it contains an oil substance that is a valuable ingredient of pigeon feed, and we have not been able to find any seed that will take is place.* (Taxation of Marihuana, 1937a: 73-74)

Mr. Scarlett's testimony before the Ways and Means committee mirrored the concerns and testimony of the other hemp manufacturers. Given that different and more hemp manufacturers testified before the Senate Finance Subcommittee that met approximately two months after the Ways and Means committee, whatever assurances the manufacturers received from the committee did not alleviate their concerns. In the Senate Finance subcommittee hearing the hemp manufacturers first stressed the necessity of the hemp plant to their industry with statements similar to Mr. Scarlett's and then questioned the wording of the legislation.

At the beginning of the Senate Finance Subcommittee hearing, Mr. Hester was aware of the hemp manufacturer's concerns. He began his testimony by stating the plants industrial uses.

> **Mr. Hester**: *The plant also has many industrial uses. From the mature stalks fiber is produced which in turn is manufactured into twine, and other fiber products. From the seeds, oil is extracted which is used in the manufacture of such products as paint, varnish, linoleum, and soap. From hempseed cake, the residue of the seed, after the oil has been extracted, cattle feed and fertilizer are manufactured. In addition the seed is used as special feed for pigeons.* (Taxation of Marihuana, 1937b: 5-6).

Later in his statement he attempted to reassure the hemp manufacturers that their industries would not be adversely affected by the legislation.

> **Mr. Hester**: *The production and sale of hemp and its products for industrial purposes will not be adversely affected by this bill. In general, the term "marihuana" is defined in the bill so as to include only the flowering tops, leaves, and seeds of the hemp plant and to exclude the mature stalk, oil, and meal obtained from the seeds of the plant, and sterilized seed, incapable of germination.* (Taxation of Marihuana, 1937b: 7)

Despite Mr. Hester's assurances some of the Congressmen were also concerned that the legislation would be detrimental to the hemp industries. Senator Brown questioned Commissioner Anslinger about the protection of legitimate practices.

> **Mr. Brown**: *Now, Commissioner Anslinger, I do not know whether you are the best man to answer this question, or Mr. Hester. What dangers, if any, does this bill have for the persons engaged in the legitimate use of the hemp plant?*

> **Mr. Anslinger**: *I would say they are not only amply protected under this act, but they can go ahead and raise hemp just as they have always done.* (Taxation of Marihuana, 1937b: 17)

Although Commissioner Anslinger assured Mr. Brown that the legislation protected legitimate producers and manufacturers, the hemp manufacturers still harbored concerns.

Once they had been assured that they would be protected under the legislation, the representatives of hemp manufacturing focused on the wording of the legislation.

> **Mr. Johnson**: *We have no dispute whatever with Mr. Hester and Mr. Anslinger, or the Government. We have gone over the testimony carefully, and we find that the testimony of Mr. Hester and others shows rather definitely that there is no deleterious matter or property in the stalk or the fiber. As I showed the chairman the other day, the leaves and the seeds are the parts of the plant that contain marihuana.*
>
> *The fiber, stalk, or hurd has nothing in it, and the fiber in which we are interested is an important part of the industry. It is used in the making of fine papers, condenser tissues, carbon paper, Bible paper, and all other types of fine papers, including cigarette papers.*
>
> *As there is no marihuana and no resin in the stalk, we think the phraseology should be changed in the bill to some degree, not to change the merits of the bill, but the phraseology, so that it can be made clear that there is no deleterious property in the stalk or in the fiber. Very great industries can be worked in this country. I can readily visualize without much difficulty 25,000 or 30,000 or 40,000 acres of hemp, with 200,000 acres of flax being used in the paper industry and in the plastic industry, concerning the gentleman just testified.* (Taxation of Marihuana, 1937b: 29)

Mr. Johnson's concern of the wording was reiterated by the other hemp manufacturer representatives. Several of the manufacturers submitted suggested changes which the committee eventually approved and changed the definition of marijuana in the final version of the Act to:

> *(b) The term "marihuana" means all parts of the plant Cannabis sativa L., whether growing or not; the seeds thereof; the resin extracted from any part of such plant; and every compound, manufacture, salt, derivative, mixture, or preparation of such plant, its seeds, or resin- but shall not include the mature stalks of such plant, fiber produced from*

> *such stalks, oil or cake made from the seeds of such plant, any other compound, manufacture, salt, derivative, mixture, or preparation of such mature stalks (except the resin extracted there from), fiber, oil, or cake, or the sterilized seed of such plant which is incapable of germination. (The Marihuana Tax Act of 1937,* Public No. 238, 75th Congress)

The final version of the Act differentiated between what parts of *cannabis sativa L* were and were not considered marijuana. With the change in the wording of the legislation the hemp manufacturers received some assurance as to the future of their industry.

Despite the changes, there were still some concerns regarding the affect of the legislation on the hemp industry when it was discussed in the House of Representatives. Even though the hemp manufacturers seemed to have their concerns assuaged by the end of the Senate Finance Subcommittee hearing, some Congressmen still expressed concern that their state's legitimate hemp industry would be adversely affected.

> **Mr. Robison of Kentucky**: *Mr. Speaker, reserving the right to object, of course, I am opposed to the use of the drug taken from hemp, but is this bill so drawn that it will not interfere with or injure the production of hemp for commercial purposes in a legitimate way?*

> **Mr. Buck**: *This bill defines marijuana so that every legitimate use of hemp is protected.*

> **Mr. Robison of Kentucky**. *The gentleman from [Mr. Fred M. Vinson] is present. Kentucky is a hemp-producing State. I would like to have a statement from the gentleman from Kentucky [Mr. Vinson].*

> **Mr. Fred M. Vinson**: *The industry was represented in the person of Mr. Lozier and it was agreed that the language in the bill took care of the industrial end of it.* (House, June 14, 1937: 5690)

Thus, regardless of the assurances made during the committee hearings, some people remained concerned about the potential adverse effect of the legislation on the legitimate commercial enterprises of the hemp industry up to the legislative vote.

Taxation

Equally, if not more prevalent than the concerns regarding the protection of legitimate uses of *cannabis sativa L*, within the Congressional and committee discussions was the focus on taxation. As previously discussed the Marihuana Tax Act required those whose occupation dealt with marijuana to register and pay a yearly fee and levied a per ounce tax on the transfer of marijuana. The lengthy tax discussions addressed primarily two issues: whether Congress had the power to levy the tax and concerns over the amount of the tax.

When Congress passed the first opium laws it held that the regulation of behavior was a state rather than federal power (Musto, 1999). The marijuana legislation discussions illustrated that Congress still questioned the extent of federal jurisdiction. In both the Ways and Means and the Finance Subcommittee hearings the Congressmen and speakers discussed in depth the purpose of the tax and why the proposed legislation was modeled after the Harrison Narcotics Act and the National Firearms Act. In his opening statement to the Ways and Means committee Mr. Hester acknowledged the purpose of the marijuana legislation.

> **Mr. Hester:** *The purpose of H.R. 6385 is to employ the Federal taxing power not only to raise revenue from the marihuana traffic, but also to discourage the current and*

> *widespread undesirable use of marihuana by smokers and drug addicts and thus drive the traffic into channels where the plant will be put to a valuable industrial, medical, and scientific uses.* (Taxation of Marihuana, 1937a: 7)

Per Mr. Hester, the purpose of the proposed legislation was to raise revenue and to regulate the illegitimate use of marijuana (the smoking of marijuana). While he asserts that the legislation has dual purposes, the discussions regarding regulation of behavior and statements such as Mr. Reed's on the House floor indicated that the primary purpose of the bill was regulating the use of marijuana.

> **Mr. Reed of New York:** *Mr. Speaker, the Congress from time to time has passed legislation to suppress the traffic in narcotics. This has been done with some measure of success by invoking the taxing power of the Federal Government. The bill, H.R. 6906, now before the House for consideration, has for its chief purpose the suppression and, if possible, the destruction of traffic in a deadly drug sold in the form of a cigarette. This new smoke is known by several names, but the name applied to it in this country is marihuana.* (House of Representatives, June 14, 1937:5689)

Since neither Mr. Hester nor Mr. Reed's statements were questioned, the dual nature of the legislation with its primary purpose being the regulation of behavior may have been widely accepted.

Given that the purpose was to in some way regulate behavior, the committees discussed at length how Congress could pass legislation that was beyond its powers. Mr. Hester's statement before the Ways and Means committee provided a thorough summary of the arguments presented and discussed.

> **Mr. Hester**: *The imposition of an occupational tax enables the Government constitutionally to make it illegal to engage in*

the occupation without payment of the tax. Thus, unless the Congress in this bill imposes the occupation tax upon the producers of hemp, Congress cannot make the production of hemp for illicit purposes illegal. Hence, if the occupational tax is not imposed upon producers, marihuana may be legally produced for illicit purposes. Furthermore, the imposition of an occupational tax enables the Government to require the taxpayer to furnish the information in connection with the business taxed. This would permit the Government to ascertain where the legitimate production of hemp is being carried on, and, having this information it can stamp out the illicit production more effectively. Obviously, therefore, the legitimate producers of hemp cannot be further exempted from the provisions of the bill. Otherwise the bill cannot be enforced....

The primary purpose of this legislation must be to raise revenue, because we are resorting to the taxing clause of the Constitution and the rule is that if on the face of the bill it appears to be a revenue bill, the courts will not inquire into any other motives that the Congress may have had in enacting the legislation.

This bill is modeled on the Harrison Narcotics Act and the National Firearms Act. The Harrison Narcotics Act has been sustained by the Supreme Court, the first time by a 5-to-4 decision, and a second time by a 6-to-3 decision. The Supreme Court in March of the year sustained the constitutionality of the National Firearms Act, insofar as it related to the occupational tax.

...The Supreme Court has held that where on the face of act it appears to be a taxing measure, the fact that it happens to be prohibitive in character will not affect the constitutionality of it. But we have tried throughout this measure not to interfere materially with the production of marihuana, but to permit it, and to do it in a manner which

> *will enable the Government to stamp out this illicit traffic in the sale of it.* (Taxation of Marihuana, 1937b: 8-9)

Since Congress deemed the regulation of behavior outside of the federal government's power, the only power they believed they had was regulation through taxation. By levying an occupational tax they could monitor the legitimate production of hemp and penalize illegitimate production by imposing the higher tax ($100) per ounce of marijuana transferred on those who did not properly register and pay the occupational tax as well as the $2,000 fine and/or five years of imprisonment for violating the Act. Thus, they could indirectly regulate behavior by levying and enforcing the occupational tax.

Mr. Hester's statement also illustrated that for the proposed legislation to be constitutional it had to appear to be a revenue bill rather than regulatory. Although it was not within Congress's power to pass regulatory legislation, the passage and success of the Harrison Narcotics Act[19] and the National Firearms Act[20] indicated to Congress that it was possible to pass legislation with the purpose of regulating behavior as long as it purpose appeared to be taxation. Mr. Hester used the Harrison Narcotics Act and the National Firearms Act to illustrate that Congress had previously passed regulatory legislation in the form of revenue bills that the Supreme Court had deemed constitutional. Per Mr. Hester's assertions, so long as the marijuana legislation appeared, on its face, to be a taxing measure then that it also acted in a prohibitive way would not affect its constitutionality. In other words, as long as

---

[19] The Harrison Narcotics Act required all persons importing, manufacturing, selling and dispensing cocaine and opiates to register with the Treasury Department (Inciardi, 1992). They were required to keep to records of all transactions and pay special taxes. Through this Act the federal government regulated narcotics through taxation rather than prohibiting them outright which was deemed the regulation of behavior and outside the scope of the federal government's power.

[20] The National Firearms Act required all importers, manufacturers and dealers of firearms to register and pay a yearly occupational tax (www.atf.gov, 2008).

the text of the legislation focused on levying an occupational and transfer tax and enforcing those taxes and did not mention the regulation of behavior, it was within the power of Congress and, thus, constitutional. That it also succeeded in prohibiting marijuana trafficking was not an aspect the Supreme Court would address.

Although the contention that Congress could constitutionally regulate behavior through its power of taxation was almost unanimously accepted by the end of the committee hearings and was not raised during the Congressional discussions, there was one individual that remained unconvinced. Dr. Woodward, the legislative council for the American Medical Association, repeatedly questioned Congresses power to pass the legislation. He argued that Congress did not have the power to regulate medical practices which the occupational tax would. In his arguments before the Ways and Means committee he voiced the medical professions' objection to the legislation by referring to previous legislation that attempted to require physicians to obtain a permit to prescribe narcotics.

> **Dr. Woodward**: *...To go back, if you will, to about 1929 or 1930, when a bill was before Congress proposing to require every physician in the United States who desired to prescribe or dispense narcotic drugs to obtain a Federal permit before he did so, the medical profession objected to any such Federal control, even if it had been possible. It was not only impracticable, because of the size of the country and the number of physicians, but clearly, I think, most of us will admit, a law of that kind is clearly beyond the power of Congress*. (Taxation of Marihuana, 1937a: 93)

Not only did he not receive any support for his position, he was subjected to approximately 22 pages of questions from the committee members and participants as to his expertise, association with the American Medical Association and knowledge of marijuana. He was questioned more than any other person who spoke in either committee and at times the Congressmen seemed antagonistic. At one point, after Dr. Woodward stated that little if any scientific research had been presented to support the idea that marijuana use led to crime and insanity and was most prevalent among children, Mr. Cooper criticized, and to an extent, mocked him.

> **Mr. Cooper**: *With all due deference and respect to you, you have not touched, top, side, or bottom, the question that I asked you. I asked you: Do you recognize that a difficulty is involved and regulation necessary in connection with marihuana?*

Later during the barrage of questions from the Congressmen, the Chairman chastised Dr. Woodward for not coming prepared with 'constructive proposals' (Taxation of Marihuana, 1937a: 116).

> **Mr. Chairman**: *If you want to advise us on legislation, you ought to come here with some constructive proposals, rather than criticism, rather than trying to throw obstacles in the way of something that the Federal Government is trying to do. It has not only an unselfish motive in this, but they have a serious responsibility.* (Taxation of Marihuana, 1937a: 116)

Despite the reaction of the Committee to his objection to the legislation, Dr. Woodward maintained that the medical professions primary concern was the requirement of registration and occupational taxes in addition to those required by the Harrison Narcotics Act. According to him, if the marijuana legislation was included in the Harrison Narcotics Act the medical profession would have no objection because they would only have to register and pay one occupational tax rather than two.

As Dr. Woodward objected to medical professionals having multiple occupational taxes, the hemp industry representatives objected to the amount of tax some producers would incur. Per the proposed legislation doctors, dentists, veterinarians and other medical practitioners would be taxed one dollar (Taxation of Marihuana, 1937b). Marihuana producers would be taxed $5 per year, while importers, manufacturers and compounders would pay $24. Mr. Moksnes, representing the Amhempco Corporation, raised issue with the proposed legislation levying the occupational tax of $5 on marijuana producers given that some producers grew such small quantities that the tax would be prohibitive.

> **Mr. Moksnes**: *We have to contract our seed from the growers in Kentucky, that was covered by Mr. Rens, and their acreage runs anywhere from a quarter of an acre up, and we have no objection to the bill. In fact, any attempt to prevent the passage of a bill to protect the narcotic traffic would be unethical and un-American. That is not the point, but we do believe that a tax of $5 is going to be prohibitive for the small dealer as well as the man that grows the hemp; not only the seed dealer, but the man that grows the crop, because he will average- I do not know what the average will be, but they raise as little as 2 acres.*
>
> **Senator Brown**: *As I understand it, Mr. Hester can take care of the dealer.*
>
> **Mr. Hester**: *The dealer; yes.*
>
> **Senator Brown**: *That will be generally agreed, that he will be exempted from that tax.*
>
> **Mr. Hester**: *From the transfer tax. He will be exempted from the transfer tax.*
> **Mr. Moksnes**: *That is the deal. That is the transfer tax, but how about the grower of the seed?*

> **Senator Herring:** *The man who only grows one-eighth of an acre with a $20 or $25 crop cannot be harmed much. He does not have much at stake.*
>
> **Mr. Hester**: *He would just have to add the occupational tax on to the price that he sells to the dealer in the city.*
>
> **Senator Herring**: *Of course, that would make it pretty difficult for him to compete with the producer who had 10 or 15 acres.*
>
> **Mr. Moksnes**: *You see we are dependent on the small growers down in the Kentucky River bottoms to furnish our seed. They are small growers who probably do not have over 10 or 15 acres of land, distributed among several crops. If he has to pay $5 an acre-*
>
> **Mr. Hester**. *Not $5 an acre- $5 a year.*
>
> **Mr. Moksnes**: *I mean $5 a year, and he only has a quarter or half an acre, that tax is going to be prohibitive, we are going to lose the small growers, and it is the combination of growers that we have to depend on.* (Taxation of Marihuana, 1937b: 27)

Per Mr. Moksnes since some producers grew small quantities of the plant they might not have been able to offset the $5 occupational tax. Mr. Moksnes' concerns for the small farmers were reiterated by Mr. Johnson who represented Chempsco, Inc. and Hemp Chemical Corporation.

> **Mr. Johnson**: *Now, on this question of the tax, and the constitutionality of the law, I am firmly convinced that the farmers' can be reduced to $1 and the law still be*

> *sustained...In my judgment a $1 tax on the farmer is sufficient. To my mind this industry is going to be more affected by the regulations, but I have no doubt Mr. Anslinger and the gentlemen associated with him, with their wide experience and with their desire to do justice, will work out regulations far more important than the law which will be fair to industry and the farmer.* (Taxation of Marihuana, 1937b: 31)

Both Mr. Moksnes and Mr. Johnson wanted the proposed legislation to be changed from requiring a $5 a year occupational tax for producers of marijuana to $1. Both argued that their industries relied on small growers who might decide not to grow marijuana if the $5 occupational task made it difficult for them to compete with larger growers. If this occurred their industries would be adversely affected by having fewer suppliers. By the end of the committee hearings the hemp manufacturers successfully persuaded the Congressmen to change the wording of the legislation and lower the occupational tax for all producers to one dollar.

In sum, one of the most prevalent themes in the marijuana legislation discussions was taxation. It was determined that although not a formal power of Congress, marijuana use could be regulated through the Congressional power of taxation. Though the Marihuana Tax Act, on its face appeared to be a revenue bill, most Congressmen and committee participants acknowledged by word or lack of disagreement that its primary purpose was the regulation of marijuana use and trafficking. The major disagreements were not over whether Congress should pass the legislation but how it could create constitutional legislation and how much individuals should be taxed.

References to Newspaper Stories

Although not necessarily a topic of discussion, during the marijuana legislation, of note was the volume of references to newspaper stories. Several committee participants quoted newspapers to either make or support a point. Mr. Hester in his opening statement to the Ways and Means committee referenced editorials and a cartoon in the Washington Times, Washington Post and thé Washington Herald.

> **Mr. Hester**: [quoting a Washington Post editorial] *With a Federal law on the books a more ambitious attack can be launched. It is time to wipe out the evil before its potentialities for national degeneracy become more apparent. The legislation just introduced in Congress by Representative Doughton would further this end. Its speedy passage is desirable.* (Taxation of Marihuana, 1937a: 6)

Mr. Hester used these references as support for the necessity of the proposed legislation. Perhaps not at the time but in review, Mr. Hester's use the editorials in some way makes it seem that he was taking cues from the media. In other words, the media was dictating policy rather than the legislature. Furthermore, Mr. Doughton, the Chairman of the Ways and Means committee, at the end of the hearings quoted the same Washington Times editorial that Mr. Hester read in the opening statements of the hearings.

> **The Chairman**: *I would like to read a quotation from a recent editorial in the Washington Times: 'The marihuana cigarette is one of the most insidious of all forms of dope, largely because of the failure of the public to understand its fatal qualities. The Nation is almost defenseless against it, having no Federal laws to cope with it and virtually no organized campaign for combating it. The result is tragic. School children are the prey of peddlers who infest school neighborhoods. High-school boys and girls buy the destructive weed without knowledge of its capacity of harm, and conscienceless dealers sell it with impunity. This is a national problem, and it must have national attention. The*

> *fatal marihuana cigarette must be recognized as a deadly drug, and American children must be protected against it.'*
>
> *That is a pretty severe indictment. They say it is a national question and that it requires effective legislation. Of course, in a general way, you have responded to all these statements; but that indicates very clearly that it is an evil of such magnitude that it is recognized by the press of the country as such.* (Taxation of Marihuana, 1937a:120).

Given that both men quoted this editorial and used it as support for the legislation, they were influenced by it as others may have been.

Since several people referred to and read newspaper articles and editorials during the committee hearings and few, if any, questioned their inclusion, it appears to have been a common or at least acceptable practice. People may be influenced by what is written in newspapers, but the extent of the influence on the Congressmen was surprising. Depending on the quality of the publication, a newspaper can be a source of information, but is it acceptable for newspapers to be essentially the only source of information? Mr. Dingle's remarks in the Ways and Means hearings indicated that at least for him and potentially others, newspapers were his primary source of information on marijuana.

> **Mr. Dingle**: *We know that it is a habit that is spreading, particularly among youngsters. We learn that from the pages of the newspapers.* (Taxation of Marihuana, 1937a: 117)

It was assumed that if an argument was presented as to why legislation was necessary, it would be accompanied by statistical data and/or scientific research. However in the case of the marijuana legislation there was essentially no scientific documentation presented. Dr. Woodward, the only person who seemed to truly object to the legislation rather than its language, noted the lack of evidence.

> **Dr. Woodward**: *That there is a certain amount of narcotic addiction of an objectionable character no one will deny. The newspapers have called attention to it so prominently that there must be some grounds for their statements. It has surprised me, however, that the facts on which these statements have been based have not been brought before this committee by competent primary evidence. We are referred to newspaper publications concerning the prevalence of marijuana addiction. We are told that the use of marihuana causes crime.*
>
> *But yet no one has been produced from the Bureau of Prisons to show the number of prisoners who have been found addicted to the marihuana habit. An informal inquiry shows that the Bureau of Prisons has no evidence to that point.*
>
> *You have been told that school children are great users of marihuana cigarettes. No one has been summoned for the Children's Bureau to show the nature and extent of the habit among children.* (Taxation of Marihuana, 1937a: 92).

In his statement, Dr. Woodward highlighted the major issue with referencing newspapers articles as support, that there was no scientific evidence presented to support the information in the newspapers. Without scientific evidence linking marijuana use with crime and insanity or indicating that young people are the primary users, how did the Congressmen differentiate between fact and fiction, especially when the majority of the newspaper references were editorials that are more often opinion and not necessarily fact?

Lack of Knowledge & Discussion

Although the over reliance on newspaper articles as support was disturbing, perhaps a more disconcerting aspect of the Marihuana Tax Act Congressional discussions was the lack of knowledge and the lack of discussion in Congress. The lack of the knowledge of the proposed legislation and marijuana was evident in both the committee hearings and Congress. Despite articles, editorials and cartoons about marijuana in the press, the 1936 depiction of marijuana in Reefer Madness, and Commissioner Anslinger's public campaign (in the form of articles and public speeches) against it, some of the committee participants did not understand what marijuana was. Even the representatives of the hemp manufacturers acknowledged that people within the industry did not know that hemp and marijuana were from the same plant. According to Mr. Johnson, representing Chempsco, Inc. and Hemp Corporation, the Minnesota hemp producers did not know that the hemp plant contained marijuana.

> **Mr. Johnson**: *...As a matter of fact these people in Minnesota did not know until 2 months ago that the hemp which they grew there contained marihuana. Until this agitation came up they did not dream of it, and they were as much surprised as anyone else.* (Taxation of Marihuana, 1937b: 31)

In his statement, Mr. Johnson also indicated that the hemp growers were not the only ones who did not realize that marijuana and hemp came from the same plant. This assertion was supported when Mr. Scarlett who represented Wm. G. Scarlett & Co. acknowledged his own failure to associate marijuana with hemp.

> **Mr. Scarlett**: *Until Monday of this week we did not know there was any connection between the two. When this bill came out and we saw that it was called a bill to impose an occupational excise tax upon dealers in marihuana we paid no attention to it. Nobody in the seed trade refers to hempseed as marihuana.*
>
> *Hempseed is a harmless ingredient used for many years in the seed trade. They say that hemp and marihuana are one and the same thing, but it was not until Monday that we knew they were.* (Taxation of Marihuana, 1937a: 76)

Since the hemp manufacturers, prior to a few days before the Ways and Means committee hearing, were not aware that marijuana came from the same plant as hemp products, their presence at the hearings and concern for the future of their industry was not surprising.

The hemp manufacturers were not the only people who did not know what marijuana was, the committee members also had questions.

> **Mr. Reed**: *Several people have talked to me about marihuana and they have impressed me with the fact, that they are different plants. I think that ought to be cleared up in the public mind, so that we may know we are dealing with hemp. It appears that it is grown in back yards, but I suppose a good many people have the idea that it is some sort of a new species of plant in this country.*
>
> **Mr. Disney**: *Down in our part of the country I understand marihuana grows everywhere, just as an ordinary weed. I would like to get a clear understanding on that.*
>
> **Mr. Reed**: *In other words, it is hemp growing wild, is it not?*
>
> **Mr. Disney**: *I do not know.*
>
> **Mr. Reed**: *There seems to be quite a good deal of confusion about it, and the newspapers are publishing stories about it, and we might as well clear up that situation and say that we are not dealing with the ordinary hemp plant, wild or cultivated, if that is right.* (Taxation of Marihuana, 1937a: 76)

Even after three days of testimony in the Ways and Means committee, Mr. Reed and Mr. Disney still needed clarification of what marijuana was and how it was related to hemp. Their confusion may have stemmed from the lack of scientific evidence presented in the hearings.

However, given the volume of anti-marijuana publicity in the 1930's, it was assumed that the Congressmen would have had some basic knowledge of marijuana other than its supposed linked with children, crime and insanity.

In addition to their lack of knowledge regarding marijuana, the committee participants also questioned why there was suddenly such a necessity to pass marijuana legislation. Since states had been passing anti-marijuana laws since 1914 and there were numerous newspaper articles discussing marijuana (Bonnie & Whitehead, 1974), it would not have been presumptuous to assume the Congressmen would have had some knowledge of marijuana and the proposed legislation despite the fact that it had only been introduced in Congress in January. Mr. Brown in discussion with Mr. Anslinger questioned why the use of marijuana had become so prevalent given that they had only heard about the drug in the last year.

> **Mr. Brown**: *What has caused the new dissemination of it? We did not hear anything of it until the last year or so.*
>
> **Mr. Anslinger**: *...I do not know just way the abuse of marihuana has spread like wildfire in the last 4 or 5 years.* (Taxation of Marihuana, 1937b: 15)

Mr. Brown's remark indicated that, at least, he had only heard about marijuana in the last year, yet per Commissioner Anslinger the drug had been a problem for the last 4 to 5 years. The disconnect between when the drug became a problem and when the Congressmen learned about the drug, let alone the need for legislation was also raised by Mr. Vinson.

> **Mr. Vinson**: *When was this brought to your attention as being menace among our own people?*
>
> **Mr. Anslinger**: *About 10 years ago-*

> **Mr. Vinson**: *Why did you wait until 1937 to bring in a recommendation of this kind?*
>
> **Mr. Anslinger**: *Then years ago we only heard about it throughout the Southwest. It is only in the last few years that it has become a national menace. It has grown like wildfire, bit it has only become a national menace in the last 3 years. It is only in the last 2 years that we have had to send reports about it to the League of Nations.* (Taxation of Marihuana, 1937a: 20)

In his remarks, Mr. Vinson voiced a common concern among the committee members regarding the apparent suddenness of the legislation. If marijuana had been a national issue for three years and Commissioner Anslinger had known about it for ten, why had it not been presented to Congress?

Dr. Woodward, the chief objector to the legislation, implied that the legislation had be prepared in secret and the professions that would be most affected were not informed and perhaps intentionally not informed.

> **Dr. Woodward**: *We cannot understand yet, Mr. Chairman, why this bill should have been prepared in secret for 2 years without any intimation, even, to the profession, that it was being prepared.* (Taxation of Marihuana, 1937a: 116)

Regardless of the accuracy of Dr. Woodward's insinuation, for many in the committee the proposed legislation and the need for it seemed to come out of nowhere.

The relative suddenness of the legislation was also illustrated by the Congressional Record. Within the Congressional Record the volume of discussion on the marijuana legislation was significantly less than that of the early opium laws. There was no discussion of marijuana during the 74th and 75th Congresses other than in the House on June 14, 1937. During those two Congresses marijuana was mentioned in Congress but only to say that a bill had been referred to a committee – a few sentences buried within thousands of pages of the Congressional Record. Even on the day the Marihuana Tax Act was discussed in the House of Representatives the discussion comprised only approximately a page and a half of the Congressional Record whereas the verbatim reading of the bill itself constituted approximately 2 and a half pages of the Record. Additionally, the bill was read three times (but only printed once).

Although no specific reason was stated in the Congressional Record as to why there seems to be little if any discussion of the Marihuana Tax Act prior to it being passed, it can be inferred from the discussions that did take place that the Congressmen lacked knowledge of the bill. The Marihuana Tax Act was brought to the House floor on June 10, 1937; however, despite the four days of Ways and Means hearings and their report, the Representatives had little knowledge of the bill.

> **Mr. Snell**: *What is this bill?*
>
> **Mr. Rayburn**: *It has something to do with something that he called marihuana. I believe it is a narcotic of some kind.*
>
> **Mr. Fred Vinson**: *Marihuana is the same as hashish.* (House of Representatives, June 10, 1937)

The discussion of the bill was then delayed until Monday June 14th. Mr. Buck commented on the delay in his remarks submitted for inclusion in the Appendix.

> **Mr. Buck of California**: *Late yesterday afternoon, the chairman of the Ways and Means Committee [Mr. Doughton] endeavored to secure unanimous consent for the immediate*

> *consideration of the bill, to the enactment of which I am sure there can be no serious or well-founded opposition. In view of the lateness of the hour and in view of the fact that some of the Members then present on the floor were apparently not informed as to the necessity for the legislation, Chairman DOUGHTON did not press his request. The bill, however, will be called up, if not on Monday next, at the earliest practicable opportunity. In the hope of saving time in its consideration and in order that Members of the House may be familiarized with just what the bill proposes to do...*(Appendix for House of Representatives, June 11, 1937: 1440).

According to Mr. Buck the legislation was delayed due to lack of time for a discussion on Friday and because some of the Representatives were not aware of the necessity of the legislation, which given Mr. Snell's question might be interpreted as some Representatives had no knowledge of the bill.

Even with four days to familiarize themselves with the bill, the Representatives comments on June 14th indicated that they still had little knowledge of it or even of what constituted marijuana.

> **Mr. Meeks**: *Is the substance that is called marihuana used in the manufacture of commercial articles for sale besides drugs and cigarettes?* (House of Representatives, June 14, 1937: 5690)

Had Mr. Meeks read the information from the Ways and Means committee he would have known that many commercial products were manufactured from the same plant as marijuana. While the Representatives may not have known about the bill on June 10th, they had the opportunity to familiarize themselves with the Ways and Means' report. That some of the Representatives, given Mr. Meeks question, did not read that information does not speak highly of them making informed decisions and to an extent caring about making informed decisions.

CONCLUSION

The analysis of the Marihuana Tax Act of 1937 and the Congressional discussions addressed the research questions discussed in Chapter Three. The second research question addressed the content of the laws and whether they were racially biased or race neutral in their wording. The Marihuana Tax Act made no mention of Mexicans or any other racial or ethnic group and in general referred to people using either the neutral phrase "any person" or by referring to occupations dealing with marijuana such as importer and producer. Therefore, the content of the wording of the Marihuana Tax Act was race neutral.

The fifth research question asked how minority groups were vilified during the period leading up to the enactment of the drug legislation. Although anti-Mexican sentiment may have been voiced by labor unions, the press and private citizens, within the Congressional discussions regarding and surrounding the Marihuana Tax Act Mexicans were only negatively associated with marijuana a few times. The half a page or less of those comments as compared to approximately 150 pages of committee hearing testimony and Congressional discussion that had no mention of Mexicans or Mexico does not support a contention that Mexicans were vilified prior to the passage of the Act.

Rather than a minority group being vilified, marijuana itself was vilified by referring to it as an evil and a menace. Marijuana was also vilified by associating its use with causing people to commit crime and go insane. The evilness of marijuana was further solidified by claiming children, specifically high school students, used it most frequently and then referring to them as victims. Thus, contrary to expectations the drug rather than a minority group was vilified during the legislative process.

Although marijuana was vilified in the Congressional discussions, the evilness of it did not dominate the discussions. Instead, one of, if not, the most prevalent theme in the marijuana legislation discussions was taxation. Per their discussions the Congressmen seemed more concerned with whether they had the power to pass the legislation than with the consequences of marijuana use. They determined that although not a formal power of Congress, marijuana use could be regulated through the Congressional power of taxation. Though the Marihuana Tax Act, on its face appeared to be a revenue bill, most Congressmen and committee participants acknowledged by word or lack of disagreement that its primary purpose was the regulation of marijuana use and trafficking. Thus the major discussions were not about the consequences of marijuana or whether Congress should pass the legislation, but how it could create constitutional legislation and how much individuals should be taxed.

Research questions three and four asked whether the discussions surrounding the marijuana legislation impacted its passage and whether competition for economic and political resources affected the drug law. Although, the United States had experienced an influx in Mexican immigration until approximately 1930 and during the 1930's federal, state and local governments were repatriating hundreds of thousands of Mexicans, there were no references to labor or political competition surrounding the marijuana discussions. Perhaps, this was the case because by 1937 the Mexican population in the United States had already been substantially diminished by repatriation. Regardless, since there were no references, the surrounding discussions did not impact the marijuana legislation.

Finally, the first research question asked whether racism had been embedded in our drug laws. Without knowing the actual intent of the Congressmen this question cannot be definitively answered. However, sometimes a Congressmen's beliefs, if not intent, can be ascertained through analyzing the content of their Congressional discussions. Due to the lack of discussion on the floor of Congress and because only the Congressmen who were members of the Ways and Means and Senate

Finance subcommittee were present at the hearings and even then did not dominate the discussions (the invited speakers all of whom were not members of Congress dominated the testimony), determining the beliefs, let alone the intent of the Congressmen is problematic. The lack of discussion combined with the lack knowledge and an over reliance on newspapers for information raises a few questions. If they did not know what the bill was and they were unclear as to what constituted marijuana, why was the legislation passed, let alone put to a vote without more discussion? Since no scientific or statistical documentation was presented, on what did they base their decisions? If it was newspapers as it appeared to be given some of the Congressmen's comments, they did contain anti-Mexican sentiment and may have influenced them. However, given that the newspapers read during the hearings made few references to Mexicans and it is unknown what articles the Congressmen read on their own, determining how they may have influenced the Congressmen is beyond the scope of this research.

Given that within the more than one hundred and fifty pages of committee hearing testimony and Congressional discussions only a few derogatory references were made towards Mexicans and that the majority of the discussions related to Congresses power to pass the legislation, the protection of the legitimate commercial uses of *cannabis sativa L*, and how much people should be taxed, the analysis does not support racism being embedded in the Marihuana Tax Act.

CHAPTER 6

Anti-drug Abuse Act of 1986: Cocaine and Crack Cocaine

Cocaine comes from the shrub *Erythroxylon coca* (Liska, 2004). The coca shrub is primarily grown in South American countries. Peru, Bolivia, and Columbia are currently the worlds first, second and third, respectively, leading producers of the coca leaves, coca paste[21] and cocaine base. Columbia, however, leads the world in processing cocaine. The coca shrub is not grown in the United States and, thus, cocaine is imported.

When chemists isolate cocaine from the leaves of the coca plant it is called cocaine base (Liska, 2004). The cocaine base is processed into cocaine hydrochloride (powder form). Each time cocaine changes hands while it is trafficked it may be cut with more chemicals (lidocaine, procaine, inositol, etc.) decreasing its purity. As of 2007, the average purity of cocaine in the United States was 53-59% (U.S.

[21] The coca leaves are "mashed and treated with alkali to free the alkaloid. Kerosene or gasoline is used to extract the cocaine, followed by addition of sulfuric acid to precipitate a crude, semisolid product called *cocaine sulfato* (coca paste) " (Liska, 2004: 183). The coca paste is mixed with tobacco or marijuana and smoked (Liska, 2004; Abadinsky, 2008). Coca paste is also called bazuco and for a time in the United States, "bubble gum."

Drug Enforcement Administration, 2010). Cocaine is a water-soluble hydrochloride salt that can be snorted or injected (often referred to as mainlining) (Liska, 2004).

Crack is a derivative of cocaine, a freebase form that emerged in the mid 1980's in large cities (Liska, 2004). Crack is prepared by cooking cocaine in a mixture of baking soda (sodium bicarbonate) and water (Liska, 2004; Abadinsky, 2008). The baking soda turns the water-soluble cocaine into water-insoluble free base which floats to the surface, is skimmed out and then dried. When dry it has a rock like appearance and is broken into pieces called crack or rock. When it is heated it makes a crackling sound hence the name crack. Even though crack is a mixture of cocaine, baking soda, salt and a few other substances its purity level averages 80%. Crack is smoked by heating it in a pipe to a vapor and then inhaling the vapor. Smoking freebase cocaine sends the drug to the brain more quickly than snorting or smoking cocaine hydrochloride (seconds rather than minutes). Doses of 25-100 milligrams of cocaine when snorted take 15 to 30 minutes to take effect.

GENERNAL HISTORY OF COCAINE AND CRACK

Although cocaine did not receive much public or governmental attention until the late 1800's and early 1900's, according to some its existence dates back 4,000 years to when native Andean populations used (and continue to use) the coca leaf in rituals and as gifts (Abadinsky, 2008). Andean porters and guides also chewed[22] the leaves because it gave them energy and reduced hunger (Liska, 2004). In the 1200's the Incas used it as "an agent for communicating with the

[22] The leaves of the coca shrub can be chewed in a manner similar to that of chewing tobacco by packing the leaves between the teeth and cheek where saliva will act as a natural extract (Liska, 2004). Chewing the coca leaves does not result in drug dependency even if used daily because less than .025-.045 grams of cocaine is absorbed into the user's bloodstream.

gods" (Liska, 2004: 38) and deemed its leaves sacred. The mestizo people from Argentina to Columbia still consider the shrub sacred and use it in social, religious and healing rituals.

In 1855, German chemists isolated alkaloidal (pure) cocaine from the coca leaf of the coca plant (Liska, 2004; Abadinsky, 2008). Three decades later, Sigmund Freud began using, prescribing and advocating for cocaine fostering its popularity in Europe. Around the same time in the late 1880's in the United States the use of cocaine was widely supported by doctors and pharmacists (Musto, 1999, Inciardi, 1992). Cocaine was an ingredient in many patent medicines and achieved popularity as a tonic, a hay fever remedy, a cure for opium and alcohol addictions and in beverages such as Coca-cola (which was originally marketed as a remedy for depression), wine, and cordials (Musto, 1999, Inciardi, 1992; Liska, 2004). By 1908 there were more than forty brands of drinks containing cocaine (Abadinsky, 2008).

Around the turn of the century, while Californians feared the Chinese and opium smoking, the South feared blacks and cocaine (Musto, 1999, Inciardi, 1992; Abadinsky, 2008). Newspaper articles alleged widespread use of cocaine among blacks and alluded to an association of use and violence (Abadinsky, 2008). The popular belief was that the stimulating properties of cocaine would make blacks disregard the boundaries of Jim Crow laws and attack whites and more specifically rape white women (Musto, 1999, Inciardi, 1992). Stories also abounded that blacks on cocaine had superhuman strength, cunning, and efficiency, improved gun marksmanship, and became impervious to .32 caliber bullets (Musto, 1999; Lusane, 1991). In 1910, testimony before a House committee addressed these stories and included "the colored people seem to have a weakness for it [cocaine]. ....They would just as leave rape a woman as anything else and a great many of the southern rape cases have been traced to cocaine" (Inciardi, 1992: 82). During Prohibition these fears were heightened due to allegations that with the scarcity of alcohol, blacks were using cola drinks laced with cocaine or cocaine itself. Despite popular belief, there was no evidence of the prevalence of cocaine use among blacks or support for cocaine causing a crime wave (Inciardi, 1992; Abadinsky, 2008); rather it was the perception, the anticipation, of black rebellion.

The fear of cocainized blacks began around the same time as the fear of Chinese and opium in the 1870's. The rise in fear of drug using blacks coincided with the end of slavery, the vote being extended to blacks, and blacks being elected to Congress among other public offices. Thus, the fear of cocaine using blacks was growing in popularity as blacks political power was increasing. Since the association of cocaine and blacks spanned several decades, it also coincided with a peak in lynching (Musto, 2002), legal segregation, and restrictive voting laws enacted to remove blacks from the political arena. Given the economic (end of slavery and entry into work force) and political advancements and subsequent loss of political power of blacks at the time, the negative association to cocaine may have been linked to a perceived political threat.

Unlike opium, the fear of cocaine and blacks did not result in race and drug specific federal legislation. Cocaine remained federally unregulated until the 1906 Food and Drug Act and the Harrison Act of 1914 which designated it as a narcotic and required dealers to register and pay a tax (Liska, 2004; Abadinsky, 2008). After World War I medical use of cocaine declined almost to obscurity and in 1922 the federal government prohibited the importation of coca leaves and cocaine except for limited medical purposes.

Cocaine use decreased from the 1930's to 1960 and was associated with those at the fringes of society and thus considered deviant (Abadinsky, 2008). With the changes in societal attitudes towards recreational drug use in the late 1960's and 1970's cocaine was no longer associated with society's fringes but with the upper class and societal elite (Abadninsky, 2008; Reinarman & Levine, 1997). In the mid 1980's a new form of cocaine, a derivative called crack became popular in a number of large cities, New York, Miami and Los Angeles in particular. Popular belief held that crack users and dealers were much younger than those involved with cocaine or heroin and more violent. Numerous news articles and televisions segments focused on cocaine and particularly crack propagating the association between crack and violence. While crack may have seemed to explode onto the drug markets, its popularity began to diminish by 1989.

Despite the hype surrounding crack, studies indicate that crack was not as addictive or as popular as it was portrayed in the media (Abadinsky, 2008; Reinarman & Levine, 1997; Fagan & Chin, 1991; Johnson, Golub, & Fagan, 1995; Ray & Ksir, 1993). Some studies indicate that crack is more addictive than alcohol but less than nicotine (Abadinsky, 2008), while others have found no addictive difference between cocaine and crack (Abadinsky, 2008; Fagan & Chin, 1991). According to Johnson, Golub, and Fagan (1995), crack was not instantly addictive as it was portrayed nor did its use spread across the United States. Even in its peak years, crack abuse was only widespread within the urban underclass. Per the National Household Survey on Drug Abuse in 1991 of respondents 12-17 years of age only 0.4% reported using cocaine in the last 30 days, those 18-34 2%, and of those over 35 only 0.5% used cocaine (Ray & Ksir, 1993). In 1991 only 3% of high school seniors reported ever having used crack. Furthermore, the survey indicated that from 1974 to 1990 the percentage of 18-25 year olds who had used cocaine in the last 30 days never exceeded 10%.

REVERSE DISCRIMINATIONAND "WELFARE QUEENS"

During the Reagan era and his "war on drugs" the 1986 Anti-Drug Abuse Act established mandatory minimum sentences for offenses, including drugs (Fernandez, 1998). The guidelines differentiated between drugs, amounts of drugs, and prior criminal records among other things. The most controversial aspect of the guidelines was the differentiation between crack cocaine and cocaine sentences. Possession of 5 grams of crack cocaine carried a 5 year sentence whereas 500 grams of cocaine were required for the same sentence. The rationale was that crack was more addictive than cocaine and was devastating the inner cities. While the guidelines purportedly took race out of the equation because the focus was on the offense rather than the offender, they have resulted in disproportionate outcomes negatively affecting minorities, specifically African Americans and Hispanics, which government bureaucrats and criminologists often refer to as a disparity in sentencing rather than discrimination.

While the sentencing guidelines may have claimed to be race neutral, the context from which they emerged was not. Beginning in the late 1970's the Republican Party began propagating the idea that racism was no longer a serious factor in American life (Lusane, 1991). Contrary to the idea that the Civil Rights era alleviated racism, a 1990 National Opinion Research Center poll found that a majority of whites believe that blacks are more likely to be lazy, are less intelligent than whites, and would rather live on welfare. Apostle, Glock, Piazza, and Suelzle (1983) also found that whites believe that blacks are less intelligent than whites, are less fortunate than whites "because God made it so" (p. 50), are born without the abilities of whites and should not receive preferential treatment due to government intervention (e.g. Affirmative Action). Although the Republican Party might have said racism was no longer a factor that is not necessarily the message that Reagan set forth in his Presidential campaign or his time in office (Lusane, 1991; Edsall & Edsall, 1992).

Following the California v. Bakke (1978) decision, that stated while race should not determine admission it could be a factor, there was a backlash of whites claiming reverse discrimination (Pholmann, 1999). Reverse discrimination claims involved allegations of unqualified blacks taking jobs away from white workers and taking the place of more qualified whites in colleges (Pholmann, 1999; Glazer, 1975). Coupled with the end of a recession and high unemployment, reverse discrimination gave the perception of economic threat pitting black against white for limited resources. In response, the Reagan administration not only ceased enforcing all affirmative action regulations, but also argued against them in court.

In discussing social service policies, Reagan referred to "welfare queens" (Feagin & Vera, 1995). References to welfare queens when speaking of black women gave rise to the myth of lazy women who live well off welfare instead of getting a job and have child after child to supplement the benefits. Similar to reverse discrimination, "welfare queens" were deemed less deserving and consequently an economic threat to tax payers who fund social services. One of Reagan's major initiatives was cutting the social services budget (Lusane, 1996).

Prior to 1986, African Americans political power was increasing. Since the passage of the 1965 Voting Rights Act, black voter registration and turnout increased. When unified, blacks had the political power to be a deciding factor in Presidential elections (Edsall & Edsall, 1992; Lusane, 1996). Jesse Jackson campaigned for the Democratic Presidential nomination in 1984 and 1988. Although he did not win the nomination he garnered 16% of the primary vote in 1984 (Pohlmann, 1999). African Americans were also elected to Congress, chaired committees, and the Congressional Black Caucus (CBC) was active. Thus, the increase in black political power could be perceived as a political threat. Of note, Reagan met once briefly with the CBC and then refused to meet with them for the remainder of his two terms. Also, it was during Reagan's administration that the CBC's funding was challenged resulting in the loss of their offices on Capitol Hill and some of their power (being on Capitol Hill was essential to lobbying efforts)

THE ANTI-DRUG ABUSE ACT OF 1986

The Anti-Drug Abuse Act was enacted on October 27, 1986. The 86 page comprehensive law addressed numerous acts and issues including but not limited to: Narcotics Penalties and Enforcements Act, Drug Possession Penalty Act, Juvenile Drug Trafficking Act, Assets Forfeiture Amendments Act, Money Laundering Control Act, Armed Career Criminals, Narcotics Traffickers Deportation Act, Interdiction, Treatment and Rehabilitation, Drug-Free Communities and School Act,

Ballistic Knife Prohibition, Homeless Eligibility Clarification Act and Commercial Motor Vehicle Safety Act. Through the multiple acts it was comprised of, the Anti-Drug Abuse Act discussed numerous issues such as drug treatment, drug education, various types of drugs, and interdiction strategies, established sentencing guidelines for the drugs, and established various committee's and associations to study drugs.

Due to the extensiveness of this law, this research focused on the section of the law, the Narcotics Penalties and Enforcements Act, which became the most controversial aspect of the Anti-Drug Abuse Act of 1986 due to the penalties for cocaine and crack cocaine. The Act established a two tier system of mandatory minimum and maximum sentences for heroin, cocaine, freebase (crack) cocaine, PCP, LSD, and marijuana as well as enhancements for prior drug and other felony convictions. Section 401 (b)(1) subsection (1)(A) created a minimum sentence of 10 years and a maximum of life for anyone possessing 1 kilogram of heroin, 5 kilograms of cocaine, 50 grams of freebase (crack) cocaine, 100 grams of PCP, 10 grams of LSD or 1000 kilograms of marijuana. If death or serious bodily injury resulted from the drug the minimum sentence would be increased to 20 years and/or a maximum fine of four million dollars for individuals or ten million for non individuals. In addition, enhancements were created for individuals who had prior drug or felony convictions. One or more priors increased the sentence to a minimum of 20 years and if death or serious injury resulted the minimum sentence increased to life and/or a maximum fine of eight million dollars for individuals and twenty million for non individuals.

Section 401(b)(1) subsection (B) created the second tier of penalties for those possessing smaller quantities of a drug. It created a minimum sentence of 5 years and a maximum of 40 years for possessing 100 grams of heroin, 500 grams of cocaine, 5 grams of freebase (crack) cocaine, 10 grams of PCP, 1 gram of LSD or 100 kilograms of marijuana. If death or serious injury occurred due to the drug the penalty increased to a minimum of 20 years and a maximum of life and/or a fine of two million dollars for individuals and five million for non individuals. In the event of prior drug or felony convictions the minimum increased to ten years and the maximum to life. In the case of death or serious injury, the penalty increased to a minimum of life and/or a maximum fine of four million dollars for individuals and ten million for non individuals.

The creation of the mandatory minimum sentences in subsections (1)(A) and (B) established a legal difference between cocaine and freebase (crack) cocaine. Five grams of crack cocaine required a minimum five year sentence, but to receive the same sentence for cocaine one had to possess 500 grams. Similarly, 50 grams of crack cocaine required a minimum ten year sentence, but for the same sentence someone had to possess 5 kilograms (or 5,000 grams) of cocaine. Thus to incur the same sentence, the quantities of cocaine had to be 100 times that of crack. After the Act was passed, this difference between cocaine and its derivative, crack cocaine, sparked debate and raised questions as to why the difference in quantities of the two drugs was so great. Were the harsher penalties for crack cocaine due to it being a more severe drug or because of the belief that cocaine was used primarily by the upper classes and whites and crack cocaine by the lower classes and minorities?

In addition to establishing mandatory minimum and maximum sentences and fines, both subsections also stated that any one possessing the indicated amount of one of the specified drugs was not eligible for probation, a suspended sentence, or parole. Thus all persons violating this Act were required to serve the mandatory minimum prison sentence even if they were first time offenders. Even after the mandatory prison sentence was served, the Act required supervised release. Possession of the larger quantities of drugs specified in subsection (1)(A) required first time offenders to complete 5 years of supervised release and those with priors to do 10 years. Those convicted under subsection (B) of possessing smaller quantities of drugs had to complete four years of supervised release if they had no priors and eight years if they did. With the creation of the mandatory minimum sentences, supervised release, and the elimination of probation, suspended sentences and parole, the Anti-Drug Abuse Act established the harshest penalties to date for cocaine and crack as well as the other drugs specified.

Section 401 (b)(1) subsections (1)(A) and (B) are included below. Per the text of the law, no racial or ethnic distinction was made regarding people who violated the Act or who were addressed in any way within the Act. References to people were usually referred to as "such person."

> *SEC. 1001. SHORT TITLE.*
>
> *This subtitle may be cited as the "Narcotics Penalties and Enforcement Act of 1986".*
>
> *SEC. 1002. CONTROLLED SUBSTANCES ACT PENALTIES. Section 401(b)(1) of the Controlled Substances Act (21 U.S.C. 841(b)(1)) is amended –*
>
> *(1) by redesignating subparagraph (C) as subparagraph (D); and*
> *(2) by striking out subparagraphs (A) and (B) and inserting the following in lieu thereof:*
> *"(1)(A) In the case of a violation of subsection (a) of this section involving –*
> *"(i) 1 kilogram or more of a mixture or substance containing a detectable amount of heroin;*
> *"(ii) 5 kilograms or more of a mixture or substance containing a detectable amount of –*
> *"(I) coca leaves, except coca leaves and extracts of coca leaves from which cocaine, ecgonine, and derivatives of ecgonine or their salts have been removed;*
> *"(II) cocaine, its salts, optical and geometric isomers, and salts of isomers;*

"(III) ecgonine, its derivatives, their salts, isomers, and salts of isomers; or

"(IV) any compound, mixture, or preparation which contains any quantity of any of the substance referred to in subclauses (I) through (III);";

"(iii) 50 grams or more of a mixture or substance described in clause (ii) which contains cocaine base;

"(iv) 100 grams or more of phencyclidine (PCP) or 1 kilogram or more of a mixture or substance containing a detectable amount of phencyclidine (PCP);

"(v) 10 grams or more of a mixture or substance containing a detectable amount of lysergic acid diethylamide (LSD);

"(vi) 400 grams or more of a mixture or substance containing a detectable amount of N-phenyl-N-[1-(2-phenylethyl)-4-piperidinyl] propanamide or 100 grams or more of a mixture or substance containing a detectable amount of any analogue of N-phenyl-N-[1-(2-phenylethyl)-4-piperidinyl] propanamide; or

"(vii) 1000 kilograms or more of a mixture or substance containing a detectable amount of marihuana; such person shall be sentenced to a term of imprisonment which may not be less than 10 years or more than life and if death or serious bodily injury results from the use of such substance shall be not less than 20 years or more than life, a fine not to exceed the greater of that authorized in accordance with the provisions of title 18, United States Code, or $4,000,000 if the defendant is an individual or $10,000,000 if the defendant is other than an individual, or both. If any person commits such a violation after one or more prior convictions for an offense punishable under this paragraph, or for a felony under any other provision of this title or title III or other law of a State, the United States, or a foreign country relating to narcotic drugs, marihuana, or depressant or stimulant substances, have become final, such person shall be sentenced to a term of

imprisonment which may not be less than 20 years and not more than life imprisonment and if death or serious bodily injury results from the use of such substance shall be sentenced to life imprisonment, a fine not to exceed the greater of twice that authorized in accordance with the provisions of title 18, United States Code, or $8,000,000 if the defendant is an individual or $20,000,000 if the defendant is other than an individual, or both. Any sentence under this subparagraph shall, in the absence of such a prior conviction, impose a term of supervised release of at least 5 years in addition to such term of imprisonment and shall, if there was such a prior conviction, impose a term of supervised release of at least 10 years in addition to such term of imprisonment. Notwithstanding any other provision of law, the court shall not place on probation or suspend the sentence of any person sentenced under this subparagraph. No person sentenced under this subparagraph shall be eligible for parole during the term of imprisonment imposed therein.

"(B) In the case of a violation of subsection (a) of this section involving –
"(i) 100 grams or more of a mixture or substance containing a detectable amount of heroin;
"(ii) 500 grams or more of a mixture or substance containing a detectable amount of –
"(I) coca leaves, except coca leaves and extracts of coca leaves from which cocaine, ecgonine, and derivatives of ecgonine or their salts have been removed;
"(II) cocaine, its salts, optical and geometric isomers, and salts of isomers;
"(III) ecgonine, its derivatives, their salts, isomers, and salts of isomers; or

"(IV) any compound, mixture, or preparation which contains any quantity of any of the substance referred to in subclauses (I) through (III);";

"(iii) 5 grams or more of a mixture or substance described in clause (ii) which contains cocaine base;

"(iv) 10 grams or more of phencyclidine (PCP) or 100 grams or more of a mixture or substance containing a detectable amount of phencyclidine (PCP);

"(v) 1 gram or more of a mixture or substance containing a detectable amount of lysergic acid diethylamide (LSD);

"(vi) 40 grams or more of a mixture or substance containing a detectable amount of N-phenyl-N-[1-(2-phenylethyl)-4-piperidinyl] propanamide or 10 grams or more of a mixture or substance containing a detectable amount of any analogue of N-phenyl-N-[1-(2-phenylethyl)-4-piperidinyl] propanamide; or

"(vii) 100 kilograms or more of a mixture or substance containing a detectable amount of marihuana; such person shall be sentenced to a term of imprisonment which may not be less than 5 years and not more than 40 years and if death or serious bodily injury results from the use of such substance shall be not less than 20 years or more than life, a fine not to exceed the greater of that authorized in accordance with the provisions of title 18, United States Code, or $2,000,000 if the defendant is an individual or $5,000,000 if the defendant is other than an individual, or both. If any person commits such a violation after one or more prior convictions for an offense punishable under this paragraph, or for a felony under any other provision of this title or title III or other law of a State, the United States, or a foreign country relating to narcotic drugs, marihuana, or depressant or stimulant substances, have become final, such person shall be sentenced to a term of imprisonment which may not be less than 10 years and not more than life imprisonment and if death or serious bodily

> *injury results from the use of such substance shall be sentenced to life imprisonment, a fine not to exceed the greater of twice that authorized in accordance with the provisions of title 18, United States Code, or $4,000,000 if the defendant is an individual or $10,000,000 if the defendant is other than an individual, or both. Any sentence imposed under this subparagraph shall, in the absence of such a prior conviction, include a term of supervised release of at least 4 years in addition to such term of imprisonment and shall, if there was such a prior conviction, include a term of supervised release of at least 8 years in addition to such term of imprisonment. Notwithstanding any other provision of law, the court shall not place on probation or suspend the sentence of any person sentenced under this subparagraph. No person sentenced under this subparagraph shall be eligible for parole during the term of imprisonment imposed therein.* (Public Law 99-570)

Although the Act did mention Latin America and other foreign nations it was to designate where funds or military equipment such as aircraft would be located. Thus the references were based on locations rather than race. Therefore, the Anti-Drug Abuse Act is race neutral in its wording.

CONGRESSIONAL DISCUSSIONS

As, if not more important, than the wording of the laws is the social context from which they emerged. Analysis of the latent content of the discussions occurring on or around the discussions of the Anti-Drug Abuse Act did not yield the expected themes of vilification of Latinos/Hispanics and African Americans, job competition and welfare queens. Instead the discussions illustrated themes regarding the vilification of cocaine and crack, the association of the drugs with children, addiction and crime, and more subtle implications of race and class than expected.

Given that popular belief held that crack cocaine use was associated with the lower classes and minorities while cocaine use was associated with the upper classes and whites, it was assumed that this would foster anti-minority sentiment within the Congressional discussions of the Anti-Drug Abuse Act in that the discussions of the drugs and their penalties would include derogatory comments about African Americans and Latinos/Hispanics and would focus on their use of the drug rather than other segments of the U.S. population. It was also assumed that since the Act was created, discussed and passed in the mid-eighties when the United States had recently emerged from the 1981 recession and the California v. Bakke decision, that the Congressional discussions would include references to job competition, specifically discussions involving reverse discrimination and minorities, in particular African Americans, taking jobs away from more qualified white workers because of Affirmative Action. It was also assumed that since there had been an ongoing debate over the welfare system and the term welfare queen had been used in reference to black women the Congressional discussions would include references to welfare queens.

Of the Congressional discussions included in this analysis, there were only a few discussions regarding job competition, however, contrary to expectations they focused on foreign job competition and the comparable worth of men's and women's wages rather than competition between whites and minorities due to reverse discrimination. Similarly, although there were discussions utilizing the term "welfare queen," it was not in reference to Black women but defense contractors. Furthermore, although the term "reverse discrimination" was used approximately 30 times in the discussions included in the analysis most of them were used in reference to Rehnqiust's Chief Justice of the Supreme Court nomination and in regard to Edwin Meese's alleged bad choices and criminal activity. Of the few "discussions" that directly mentioned reverse discrimination as it related to affirmative action, most were insertions into the Record of the same Washington Post article "Goals aren't quotas: but they do help achieve more balanced employment:"

> [excerpt from article] *In recent weeks, we have heard much talk of the debate within the Reagan administration over the efforts of Attorney General Edwin Meese to jettison the use of goals and timetables under affirmative action programs. Meese asserts that goals often turn into quotas and hence discriminate unfairly against better qualified whites. His opponents counter that goals are not quotas, only voluntary targets that help employers focus their efforts on improving their record in hiring women and minorities.*
>
> *Thus far, Meese's opponents have the better argument. While the Justice Department has offered little evidence that goals are actually quotas in disguise, civil rights advocates have pointed to studies showing that employers who fail to meet their goals have not been penalized by the government...Nevertheless, this is not the reverse discrimination that the attorney general deplores.* (132 Cong Rec E 797).

Although the article mentioned reverse discrimination, it states that since goals are not the same as quotas they are not considered reverse discrimination. Since multiple Congressmen submitted the article for inclusion in the Record without contradicting its content, they must have supported the argument that contrary to Meese's claims goals and quotas are two different things. Also of note, the article was not read in Congress; in fact, the majority of the references aside from those involving Justice Rehnquist were submitted for insertion rather than stated in Congress, indicating perhaps that reverse discrimination was not an issue of great importance at that time.

Overall there were few references to job competition, welfare queens, and reverse discrimination. Also contrary to expectations, rather than overtly vilifying African Americans and Hispanics/Latinos with references to their violence while using crack cocaine the association of the drug to minorities was much more subtle. Instead the more overt vilification was of cocaine and crack through rhetoric and associating them with harm to children, rising crime and instant addiction.

Vilification of Cocaine and Crack

Throughout the Congressional discussions included in this analysis cocaine and crack cocaine were vilified through rhetoric and by associating the drug with children, addiction and crime. In terms of rhetoric, cocaine and crack cocaine (and occasionally drugs in general) were referred to as an "epidemic." The term epidemic was used in two ways: in reference to the rapid increase of the drugs in society and in reference to a sickness from which the United States needed to be protected. Due to the emergence of crack in the mid 1980's and its supposed rapid escalation many of the discussions alluded to the proportional aspect of an "epidemic."

Although Congress had been discussing America's drug problem throughout the 99th Congress, the first mention of crack was not until March 21, 1986 when Mr. Rangel of New York submitted a statement and newspaper article for submission into the House's Record.

> **Mr. Rangel of New York**: *I wish to bring to the attention of our colleagues an article by Peter Kerr that appeared in the March 20, 1986, New York Times, entitled "Extra-potent cocaine: use rising sharply among teenagers." This dramatic piece confirms what many of us in the Congress who have the responsibility for reviewing federal drug abuse policy have known for some time; that the availability of "crack" – cocaine in its purest state – at low street prices will only expand the abuse of cocaine nationwide.*

> *...[reading from the article] As recently as last fall government officials who monitor drug abuse warned of the growing popularity of crack among cocaine users generally. But the speed with which crack use spread to teen-agers, including youths who had little or no previous involvement with drugs, has alarmed experts.* (132 Cong Rec E 944)

Even after Mr. Rangel's submission, crack was not mentioned again until April 22, 1986 when Mr. Chiles of Florida on the behalf of himself, Mr. Evans, Mr. Boren, Mr. Moynihan, Mr. Nunn, Mr. Gorton, Mr. Hollings and Mr. DeConcini submitted a statement and newspaper articles to the Senate's Record. If there was grave concern over crack and its proliferation, it was not initially being voiced on the floor of Congress or for submission into the Record. And despite Mr. Rangel's assertion that those reviewing federal drug abuse policy had known about crack for sometime, Mr. Chiles indicated that his knowledge dated from approximately January of 1986.

> **Inserted by Mr. Chiles of Florida:** *...Six months ago, I did not know about rock or crack cocaine or what it was.* (132 Cong Rec S 6968: June 1986)

Once crack did become a topic of discussion in Congress, it joined cocaine in being referred to as an epidemic due in part to its rapid proliferation. Mr. Rangel, in the first mention of crack, quoted the New York Times use of the term.

> **Inserted by Mr. Rangel of New York***: [quoting New York Times article} ...What is most frightening about crack is that it has made cocaine widely available and affordable for abuse among our youth. ...Mr. Speaker, I am afraid that the crack epidemic will only get worse, before it gets better.* (132 Cong Rec E 944)

Mrs. Hawkins of Florida also referred to crack as an epidemic, however she made it specific to her home state.

> **Mrs. Hawkins of Florida**: *...Florida is under a crack epidemic right now.* (132 Cong Rec S 9742)

In addition, to using the term "epidemic" to refer to the increasing volume of drugs, Congressmen also made remarks about being "under siege" (Mr. Chiles, 132 Cong Rec S 16338), it "snowing cocaine" (Mrs. Hawkins, 131 Cong Rec S 2350), and it being a "deluge" (132 Cong Rec S 12222). Thus, through the use of terminology such as epidemic, siege and deluge, the Congressmen were able to vilify cocaine and crack and instill some level of urgency by discussing how it was rapidly increasing in prevalence.

The term "epidemic" was also used in reference to a sickness from which the United States needed to be protected. According to Mr. Garcia of New York, drugs, especially cocaine and crack represented a threat to Americans.

> **Mr. Garcia**: *We are currently experiencing a drug epidemic, particularly a cocaine epidemic in this country. The influx of cocaine has increased 500 percent in the last year, exploding the drug crisis and threatening our society. It is the use of "smokeable cocaine," known as crack, that has intensified the epidemic and forced everyone to take notice. Crack probably poses the greatest drug threat to uses and society to date,* because *it is extremely addictive, with addiction taking hold even after a single use.* (132 Cong Rec H 6224)

Besides the use of the term epidemic, cocaine and crack were also referred to as a plague and a scourge, reinforcing the allusion to sickness and adding an association with death. Mr. Byrd of West Virginia, on more than one occasion, referred to crack as a "scourge" and then commented on the number of deaths due to crack use.

> **Mr. Byrd of West Virginia**: *...The newest scourge on the streets is a frightening low-cost substance called crack, which is drawing more and more attention due to its super potency. This form of cocaine which users freebase, has been proved lethal time and again, and it's responsible for an alarming number of episodes of death and injury in recent weeks.* (132 Cong Rec S 9652)

> **Mr. Byrd of West Virginia**: *Crack, a form of cocaine, is the newest scourge on the streets. It is a frightening, low-cost substance which is drawing more and more attention because of its super potency. Its use often results in death. It is extremely addictive – dependence can be established in as few as two or three episodes.* (132 Cong Rec S 10781)

Mr. Biaggi of New York used similar tactics in the House of Representatives when he referred to the crack as having caused "a very serious tear in the fabric of our society" and stated that it was "killing our kids" (132 Cong Rec H 4311). In associating crack, and ultimately cocaine, with death, the Congressmen buttressed their standpoint of the evilness of the drugs.

In addition to being associated with sickness and death, the Congressmen also alluded to the destruction caused by crack and cocaine. In their rhetoric, crack and cocaine became the cause of the destruction of health, resources, family and society in general. In his speech on the floor of the House, Mr. Strang of Colorado used a newspaper article from the Pubelo Chieftain to bolster his assertion that cocaine and crack reap destruction.

> **Mr. Strang of Colorado**: [reading from "Drug war should be everyone's concern" in Pueblo Chieftain by Dr. Otis Bowen, Secretary of Health and Human Services] *...Our nation faces a crisis that literally is a personal disaster for many of us. Cocaine use and the use of crack is growing in our schools, in*

> *the workplace, and in our homes. Commentators have called it a plague, a snowstorm, an avalanche and a flood. But whatever metaphor you choose the picture is always the same – millions of users, billions in wasted resources, and innumerable stories of pain and despair.* (132 Cong Rec H 8794)

Mrs. Hawkins of Florida used a similar tactic in the Senate by quoting an anti-cocaine group's report stating that "cocaine destroys physical health, cocaine divides families. Cocaine reduces productivity. Cocaine results in death. Cocaine is anti-American; antifamily; and antireligion." (131 Cong Rec S 6016). In associating cocaine with the deterioration of family, health and productivity, the members of Congress reiterated the "evilness" of the drug.

Table 6.1 contains all of the above referenced quotes as well as some additional quotes that illustrate the cocaine and crack rhetoric used in the Congressional discussions. The table also illustrates two other aspects of discussions. First, although the cocaine and crack rhetoric utilizing terminology such as "epidemic" and "scourge" was voiced at some time by the majority of the members of Congress, the Congressmen and women from Florida and New York were the most active, with Mrs. Hawkins spearheading the anti drug legislation. Their vigorous support of the legislation may have been due in part to the general consensus that New York and Florida were the two states affected the most by drugs and in the case of Mr. Rangel, he was the chairmen of the Select Committee on Narcotics Abuse and Control. Even though the Florida and New York Congressmen were more outspoken, almost every member of Congress commented on the bill at

TABLE 6.1 Cocaine and Crack Rhetoric in Congressional Discussions

Congressmen & State	Quote
Mr. Pepper of Florida	"Mr. Speaker, we know that one of the great menaces to the security if our country and the health or our people is the drug menaces. This committee, in every way it can, is mobilizing the might of this Nation to resist that dangerous menace and invasion of our country brining death and devastation to so many, and imposing such heavy costs upon so many public bodies of this country in trying to meet that onslaught and invasion." (131 Cong Rec H 1126)
Mrs. Hawkins of Florida	"Mr. President, it is snowing cocaine in Florida. And we are all in for some tough sledding." (131 Cong Rec S 2350).
Mrs. Hawkins of Florida	"Cocaine can cause addiction, paranoia, permanent brain damage, and death. Cocaine ruins minds, marriages, finances and lives. …As Citizens Against Cocaine states in its strategy report: ...For cocaine is America's public enemy No. 1 because cocaine destroys human potential. It enslaves the user; and changes his personality. Cocaine destroys physical health, cocaine divides families. Cocaine reduces productivity. Cocaine results in death. Cocaine is anti-American; antifamily, and antireligion." (131 Cong Rec S 6016).
Inserted by Mr. Rangel of New York	"…I wish to bring to the attention of our colleagues an article by Peter Kerr that appeared in the March 20, 198(New York Times, entitled "Extra-Potent cocaine: Use Risin Sharply Among Teen Agers." …Increasing, Mr. Speake members are inquiring of the select committee; What is crack How is it different from cocaine? Where is it all comin from? Mr. Kerr answers these questions very succinctly. Crack is purified cocaine in pellet form that sells in vials for as little as $5. Users smoke it, creating a powerful stimulating effect on the nervous system. Unlike regular cocaine, crack takes effect in seconds and induces a greater high, experts say. Compared with users of regular cocaine, crack users experience a stronger yearning for the drug and

TABLE 6.1 Cocaine and Crack Rhetoric in Congressional Discussions (continued)

Congressmen & State	Quote
	become addicted more quickly. What is most frightening about crack is that it has made cocaine widely available and affordable for abuse among our youth. …Mr. Speaker, I am afraid that the crack epidemic will only get worse, before it gets better." (132 Cong Rec E 944)
Mr. Garcia of New York	"We are currently experiencing a drug epidemic, particularly a cocaine epidemic in this country. The influx of cocaine has increased 500 percent in the last year, exploding the drug crisis and threatening our society. It is the use of "smokeable cocaine," known as crack, that has intensified the epidemic and forced everyone to take notice. Crack probably poses the greatest drug threat to uses and society to date, because it is extremely addictive, with addiction taking hold even after a single use." (132 Cong Rec H 6224)
Inserted by Mr. Chiles of Florida	"…Six months ago, I did not know about rock or crack cocaine or what it was." (132 Cong Rec S 6968: June 1986)
Mr. Biaggi of New York	"Mr. Speaker, there is a very serious tear in the fabric of our society, and it's called crack – smokable freebase cocaine. It's killing our kids, and sending violent crime statistics sky high. Having just come onto the scene in the last year, crack is one of the most addictive drugs known to man." (132 Cong Rec H 4311)
Mr. Waldon of New York	"Mr. Speaker, the madness which is crack has no respect for social, professional or economic status. Crack usage is the evidence that our society may in fact be losing control of itself." (132 Cong Rec H 5939)
Mr. Chiles of Florida	"Newsweek calls it a plague, according to Time, the rate of addiction to rock cocaine may prove worse than the wave of heroin addiction in the late 1960's. The Washington

TABLE 6.1 Cocaine and Crack Rhetoric in Congressional Discussions (continued)

Congressmen & State	Quote
	Post says that rock has swept affluent and poor neighborhoods alike." (132 Cong Rec S 7637)
Mr. Bumpers of Arkansas	"...The use of cocaine, which is the most addictive and powerful of all narcotic drugs, has become an epidemic in our society." (132 Cong Rec S 8695)
Mr. Strang of Colorado	[reading from "Drug war should be everyone's concern" by Dr. Otis Bowen in Pueblo Chieftain] "...Our nation faces a crisis that literally is a personal disaster for many of us. Cocaine use and the use of crack is growing in our schools, in the workplace, and in our homes. Commentators have called it a plague, a snowstorm, an avalanche and a flood. But whatever metaphor you choose the picture is always the same – millions of users, billions in wasted resources, and innumerable stories of pain and despair." (132 Cong Rec H 8794)
Mr. Byrd of West Virginia	"...The newest scourge on the streets is a frightening low-cost substance called crack, which is drawing more and more attention due to its super potency. This form of cocaine which users freebase, has been proved lethal time and again, and it's responsible for an alarming number of episodes of death and injury in recent weeks." (132 Cong Rec S 9652)
Mrs. Hawkins of Florida	"...Florida is under a crack epidemic right now." (132 Cong Rec S 9742)
Mr. Byrd of West Virginia	"Crack, a form of cocaine, is the newest scourge on the streets. It is a frightening, low-cost substance which is drawing more and more attention because of its super potency. Its use often results in death. It is extremely addictive – dependence can be established in as few as two or three episodes." (132 Cong Rec S 10781)
Mr. Chiles of Florida	"Much of that problem has been magnified and come to our attention because of the deluge we have seen of crack-

TABLE 6.1 Cocaine and Crack Rhetoric in Congressional Discussions (continued)

Congressmen & State	Quote
	cocaine in this country. It has hit us like a tidal wave." (132 Cong Rec S 12222)
Mr. Chiles of Florida	"…We have to ask ourselves why has that happened. It has happened because we are a nation under siege. We are under siege with the onslaught of drugs that have come into our country." (132 Cong Rec S 16338)

least once. Second, the quotes contained in Table 6.1 allude to how support for the legislation was garnered by associating the drugs with children, addiction and crime. These associations were used to vilify cocaine and crack. Rarely was one discussed without linking the drug to another. However, of the three, associating the drug with children was the most prevalent.

Children:

In Congress the vilification of cocaine and crack was also illustrated by associating its use with children. The association with children included those as young as eight, high school students and college students. In the Senate Mr. Sasser of Tennessee discussed how children were linked to the drugs.

> **Mr. Sasser of Tennessee**: …*In just a short period, the use of crack has reached epidemic proportions. It threatens to scar an entire generation of young people. Statistics show that one of every six of teenagers will have experimented with cocaine before they graduate from high school. That is a truly frightening statistic. And the picture is getting worse. Surveys show that 61 percent of all high school seniors have tried an illegal drug at least once. The simple fact is that students are used to the presence of drugs in their life experience. …So*

> *that puts it well within reach, at $10, of most high school students. ...Crack is so easy to manufacture that drug dealers can set up shop near a school and entice students to purchase drugs. Incredible as it may seem, while it is a crime to sell drugs to minors, it is not a separate crime to employ minors in drug dealing. By the same token, while it is a crime to sell drugs near a school, it is not a separate crime to manufacture them near a school. By creating these new offenses we are offering law enforcement a new tool to prosecute these vicious dealers who would destroy our youth for profit.* (132 Cong Rec S 10655)

Mr. Sasser's statement was indicative of how associations with children were used to vilify cocaine and crack. He highlighted several concerns about children. First, that the escalating use of crack would affect the future of an entire generation alluding to crack destroying their lives. He supported this concern by referencing statistics indicating that one in six high school students will try cocaine. Furthermore, with crack being inexpensive ($10) compared to other drugs it was affordable for high school students. In addition, not only were drug dealers selling near schools in order to entice students to use the drug, but they were also employing the students. In one statement Mr. Sasser addressed several concerns that were reiterated by his fellow Congressmen (see Table 6.2 for additional quotes).

Although Mr. Sasser highlighted almost all of the Congressmen's concerns regarding children, Mrs. Hawkins and Mr. Leahy addressed an additional concern.

> **Mr. Leahy of Vermont**: ... *From 1983 to 1984, cocaine related deaths increased 77 percent nationwide, while requests for treatment for cocaine use have risen 600 percent in the past 3 years. Thousands of individuals were arrested for selling drugs in the close vicinity of elementary*

TABLE 6.2 Concerns About Children in Congressional Discussions

Congressman & State	Quote
Mr. DioGiardi of New York	"...In one jurisdiction in my congressional district, the dropout rate in high schools is three times the average of the district and it is basically tied into drug abuse." (131 Cong Rec H 1126)
Mrs. Hawkins of Florida	"Mr. President, a very disturbing report was featured recently in the Washington Post's Health Magazine. The title says it all: "Drug Use Tops 60's Level." In this article, the results of a recent Washington Post-ABC News nationwide survey, half the individuals between the ages of 18 and 30 said they have tried marijuana and 1 in 5 said the have used cocaine." (132 Cong Rec H 4565).
Mr. Bumpers of Arkansas	"...As Senator Chiles has pointed out, young children are often indispensable to rock dealers and are used as deliveries, customer hustlers, and police lookouts. They are paid for their work with a dose of rock or crack and soon become hard addicts themselves. Thus our children are being victimized by these ruthless cocaine dealers, and it is time we put a stop to this deplorable situation before these children's lives are completely destroyed." (132 Cong Rec S 8695)
Inserted by Mr. Hamilton of Indiana	"The senseless cocaine-related deaths of promising young athletes and the emergence of "crack," a cheap and extremely addictive form of cocaine, have raised public concern and prompted a new round in the war against drugs. Both the President and Congress are developing plans to strike at drug suppliers and the demand for drugs. Americans spend over $100 billion each year on illicit drugs, making us the western world's largest consumer of illicit drugs. Many view drug use as our biggest social problem. Cocaine is particularly popular. Once too expensive for most Americans, cocaine can sell for about $50 a gram, making it cheaper than an ounce of marijuana. At least 5 million Americans regularly use cocaine. A 1985 survey showed almost two-thirds of high school seniors had used illicit drugs." (132 Cong Rec E 3142)
Mr. Waldon of New York	"...I firmly believe and have consistently stated that drugs are the scourge of today's society. Let us use all of our power to save the children of this generation.

TABLE 6.2 Concerns About Children in Congressional Discussions (continued)

Congressman & State	Quote
	...I am alarmed by the presence of all types of drugs in and near our schools. In New York alone more than 3,750 individuals were arrested for selling drugs in the vicinity of public schools. More than one-half of those arrested were near elementary schools. Seventy-nine percent of the people arrested were over 20 years of age. Children as young as 8 and 9 years old have been introduced to crack. What this means is that adult drug dealers for their own personal economic gain are seducing children into a life of drug dependency. We must educate our children to the dangers of drug abuse in general, but especially we must inform and educate them as to the deadly substance "crack." ...My colleagues, this is a sad period in the history of America when we hear of young people who are in the prime of their lives as were Len Bias and Don Rogers having their lives snuffed out by this human destroyer which is crack." (132 Cong Rec H 5939)
Mr. Leahy of Vermont	"...Drug abuse among young people has spread to all parts of the country and entered every segment of society. More and more children from families of all income levels, from rural as well as urban communities, are smoking marijuana, using cocaine, and experimenting with other dangerous drugs. ... From 1983 to 1984, cocaine related deaths increased 77 percent nationwide, while requests for treatment for cocaine use have risen 600 percent in the past 3 years. Thousands of individuals were arrested for selling drugs in the close vicinity of elementary schools. Drug merchants are now pushing anew craze that is sweeping the Nation. It's called crack. Crack is available to the young, and it will be in the schools this fall. I have heard horror story after horror story involving children as young as 9 who are already crack users. The sellers also use these young children as lookouts and as workers in houses that manufacture crack. One hit costs just $10. Users say addiction can begin after only the second use of crack." (132 Cong Rec S 12231)

TABLE 6.2 Concerns About Children in Congressional Discussions (continued)

Congressman & State	Quote
Mrs. Hawkins of Florida	"Mr. President, the impact of drug abuse is eating away at our society. Everything these deadly substances touch turns to death and despair. It is especially heartbreaking to see the devastating affect of illegal drugs on our children. To think of a single child falling under the seductive spell of illegal drugs is almost too much to take. To realize that a child who should be enjoying his or her innocence and the carefree years for youth has already become a slave to a chemical master is a tragedy. It is more a tragedy to realize that many of the kids hooked on drugs are disadvantaged having been raised in poverty." (132 Cong Rec S 13738)

schools. Drug merchants are now pushing a new craze that is sweeping the Nation. It's called crack. Crack is available to the young, and it will be in the schools this fall. I have heard horror story after horror story involving children as young as 9 who are already crack users. The sellers also use these young children as lookouts and as workers in houses that manufacture crack. One hit costs just $10. Users say addiction can begin after only the second use of crack. (132 Cong Rec S 12231)

Mrs. Hawkins of Florida: *Think of the threat this poses to our children and our neighborhoods. We all know that kids are curious. ...But crack does not give a kid a chance. There is no such thing as "experimenting" when it comes to crack. Crack steals your future and robs your soul on its first shot. There are no second chances. Crack is not just dangerous. It is deadly, and it is frightening. But instant addiction does not tell the whole story for crack – there is more. And it gets worse. Crack is cheap. And by cheap I do not mean $50 a shot, or*

> *even $30 dollars. I mean $5-15 dollars. For the price of a couple of movie tickets, our kids can be hooked for life.* (132 Cong Rec S 4706)

In addition to highlighting the concerns of young children using, the availability of drugs near schools, drug dealers employing children and the inexpensiveness of crack, Mr. Leahy and Mrs. Hawkins also mentioned addiction. Per Mrs. Hawkins crack was instantly addictive, while Mr. Leahy claimed it was addictive after the second use. Regardless of when addiction occurred, per both, crack was highly addictive and therefore even more dangerous for children who would be attracted to it due in part to the low cost. Implying that the combination of the low price, availability near schools and instantaneous addiction would lead to a generation of young people addicted to crack who have no futures.

When voicing their concerns regarding the volume of young people experimenting with cocaine or crack many of the Congressmen referred to studies to support their stance. In his previously mentioned statement, Mr. Sasser claimed that surveys indicated that one in six teenagers would experiment with cocaine before graduating from high school and 61% of seniors had tried illegal drugs. Mr. Hamilton of Indiana provided similar data in a prepared statement for insertion into the Record that stated "a 1985 survey showed almost two-thirds of high school seniors had used illicit drugs" (132 Cong Rec E 3142). In his statement he had been discussing cocaine and then referenced the 1985 survey implying that two-thirds of high school students had used cocaine. However, the survey referred to illicit drugs which cocaine may or may not have been included. Both Mr. Sasser and Mr. Hamilton's use of the studies to imply that cocaine was widely used was misleading in that the studies were about illegal drugs in general rather than cocaine and crack, specifically. Additionally, given that the National Household Survey of Drug Abuse indicated that from 1974 to 1990 the percentage of 18-25 year olds who had used cocaine in the last 30 days never exceeded 10% and that Monitoring the Future's surveys indicated that in 1986 only 12.7% of high school seniors had used cocaine in the last year and only slightly more than 4% had used crack cocaine, Mr. Sasser and Mr. Hamilton's use of illegal drug use surveys indicating that 61% or more of seniors had used drugs was extremely misleading and made it seem that cocaine and crack use among children was more prevalent than it was.

Mr. Dole also presented statistics, first noting the increase in cocaine users in general and then focusing on teenagers.

> **Mr. Dole of Kansas:** *...cocaine use in the United States is up. The number of coke users climbed to 5,800,000 last year, compared with 4,200,000 in 1982. This is frightening. It is a one-fourth increase in the number of cocaine consumers over a 4-year period. ...cocaine normally is a powder and is snorted by its users. But it can be processed into freebase and crack, which is smoked. Younger people, it seems, are attracted to the smokeable forms. The survey discloses that 44 percent of American youth between the ages of 12 and 17 have used cocaine and have freebased cocaine. At the same time, the survey showed that the dangers of cocaine use are widely recognized; 92 percent of the people questioned said they regarded cocaine as a great risk.* (132 Cong Rec S 16013)

No one questioned 44% of 12 to 17 year olds having used cocaine and freebase cocaine as being too high a percentage. While Mr. Hamilton, Mr. Sasser and Mr. Dole in their statements focused on high school students as did most Congressmen, Mrs. Hawkins also voiced and supported her concerns for college students.

> **Mrs. Hawkins of Florida**: *These findings come from a new survey of young Americans conducted for the National Institute on Drug Abuse by the University of Michigan. The core of the survey consisted of interviews with 1,100 students, 19 to 22 years old, enrolled in 2- and 4-year colleges across*

> *the country. ...Among students, 30 percent conceded that they had tried cocaine by the time they finished their senior year of college. Unlike other drug use, cocaine experimentation continued to grow each year after high school.* (132 Cong Rec S 9049)

Regardless of type of statistics presented, they were not questioned. None of the Congressmen asked who did the study if the information was not provided, how the statistics were generated, or questioned the numbers presented. Given the variety of statistics and percentages indicated, it was assumed that someone would question whether it was 30%, 44% or two-thirds of young people. Essentially, if a Congressman presented statistics or numbers of any sort to support his/her argument, their authenticity was assumed. As previously mentioned, the data provided by the Congressmen indicated use percentages much higher than those indicated by the National Household Survey on Drug Abuse or Monitoring the Future. Therefore, while support was provided, its accuracy was neither questioned nor confirmed.

Addiction:

In addition to associating children with the use and selling of cocaine and crack, the drug crack was vilified by discussing its addictiveness. Although the addictiveness of cocaine was occasionally mentioned, most of the references to addiction focused on crack. The Congressmen did not devote discussions to crack's addictiveness; instead their remarks were included in their statements about children and the drug in general. Within these discussions, crack's addictiveness was addressed in two ways: how highly addictive it was and how many people were addicted. Of the two, the former was more prevalent.

When commenting on how addictive crack was, the Congressmen either referred to it as highly addictive or the "most addictive drug known to man" (Mrs. Hawkins, 132 Cong Rect S 4706). To bolster their assertions of its addictiveness, the Congressmen often stated that people became addicted to crack after one use.

> **Mr. Sasser of Tennessee:** *...crack is a particularly dangerous drug. It is highly addictive. Some say that one use of crack and you are hooked. Crack is also cheap. A vial of crack costs as little as $10. ...Crack is as dangerous as any drug on the street – and more addictive than almost any of them.* (132 Cong Rec S 10655)

Mr. Sasser's statement was indicative of the general consensus among the Congressmen of crack's addictiveness; it was addictive in one use and more addictive than most drugs. While Mr. Sasser did not mention specific drugs other than crack, Mrs. Hawkins compared crack's addictiveness to cocaine's.

> **Mrs. Hawkins of Florida as read by Mr. Thurmond:** *...It is hard to exaggerate the threat posed by crack. According to Arnold Washton, a psychopharmacologist at Fair Oaks Hospital in Summit, New Jersey, "Crack is the most addictive drug known to man right now... it is almost instantaneous addiction, whereas if you snort coke it can take two to five years before addiction sets in. There is no such thing as the 'recreational use' of crack."* (132 Cong Rec S 4706)

In stating that crack was instantaneously addictive whereas it may take two to five years to become addicted to cocaine, Mrs. Hawkins bolstered her stance on the dangerousness of crack due to it being not only highly addictive but more addictive than other known drugs. (See Table 6.3 for additional quotes regarding crack's "one puff" addictiveness)

TABLE 6.3 Additional Addiction Comments in Congressional Discussions

Congressmen & State	Quote
Mrs. Hawkins of Florida	" ...Some psychopharmacologists have said that crack can be addicting after just one use. This hyper-addicting power combined with its bargain basement prices on the street -- sometimes going for as little as $5 to $10 per dose – gives crack the potential for infiltrating into every corner of our society and enslaving its uses to a deadly master, chemical addiction." (132 Cong Rec S 9428)
Mrs. Hawkins of Florida	"...crack being the cheap form, the deadly form of cocaine that becomes addictive with one puff." (132 Cong Rec S 9742)
Mrs. Hawkins of Florida	""free basing" – he relates – creates a false feeling of grandeur, illusions of wisdom, sexual prowess and infinite power. These sensations can be followed by anxiety, paranoia and hallucinations. Once the drug has been consumed, the user is left in a depressed state, crawling on the floor in a desperate search for one last crumb of cocaine for a final hit. Just one more hit. One hit is too many and a thousand are not enough." (132 Cong Rec S 14825)
Mr. Waldon of New York	"...I firmly believe and have consistently stated that drugs are the scourge of today's society. Let us use all of our power to save the children of this generation. Crack is so extremely addictive that it only takes one time to get hooked. Let us, Mr. Speaker, pledge to crack down on crack." (132 Cong Rec H 5939)

As indicated by Mrs. Hawkins statement, although infrequently, some Congressmen supported their addiction assertions by referring to health care professionals and/or data. Mr. Strang of Colorado supported his views on cocaine and crack by reading an article from the Pueblo Chieftan by Dr. Otis Bowen, the Secretary of Health and Human Services.

> **Mr. Strang of Colorado**: [reading from "Drug war should be everyone's concern" by Dr. Otis Bowen in Pueblo Chieftain] *...But the truth is more brutal than that.*
>
> *Any use is misuse. Clinical studies demonstrate that cocaine is addictive and dangerous. When snorted it can cause nasal congestion and nosebleeds, sexual dysfunction, cardiac arrhythmia, convulsions, coma, respiratory collapse, agitated or paranoid behavior, and death.* (132 Cong Rec H 8794)

Within the article Dr. Bowen stated that clinical studies indicated that cocaine was addictive. Although he did not specify why or how addictive cocaine was, just mentioning clinical studies may have provided enough support for some and apparently did for Mr. Strang since he presented the article. Given that the statement came from the Secretary of Health and Human Services may have also been influential for not only the Congressmen, but also for whoever read the article.

Mrs. Hawkins was one of the few Congressmen to present data in support of how many people were addicted to the drugs.

> **Mrs. Hawkins of Florida**: *The grip of these poisons on our society is staggering. Between 2 and 3 million Americans are seriously addicted to cocaine. Six million persons use it at least once a month. More than 25 million American have tried cocaine and 5,000 Americans sample it for the first time every day.* (132 Cong Rec S 12599)

Both Mr. Strang and Mrs. Hawkins statements refer to cocaine yet both had been discussing cocaine and crack. In discussing both drugs and then presenting support for the addictiveness of cocaine they implied by association that crack was also addictive. However, Mr. Strang's clinical studies and Mrs. Hawkins data only referred to cocaine; they did not provide support for crack. The only support for crack's addictiveness was provided by Mrs. Hawkins when she referred to psychopharmacologists saying crack was addictive after one use. Neither the accuracy of the information regarding cocaine nor the lack of scientific support for crack was questioned.

The lack of data on crack cocaine was noted by one Congressman, Mr. Rockefeller of West Virginia.

> **Mr. Rockefeller of West Virginia**: *...My distinguished colleagues have just talked about "crack," freebase cocaine. National data still needs to be developed on the scope of the use of this drug, but we don't need studies to know that "crack" has made its way to small communities as well as large cities and that it has come to our schools.* (132 Cong Rec S 10425) August 5, 1986

Mr. Rockefeller, on the one hand, acknowledged the need for data to ascertain the prevalence of crack, but then claimed that studies were not needed to know that the use of crack had spread and that crack was being used in schools. If the scarcity of data on crack necessitated studies, how did Mr. Rockefeller know crack use had spread? Where did he obtain his information? Given the volume of newspaper and magazine articles whether read or referred to in Congress and submitted to the Record, it is highly likely that for many of the Congressmen the media was their source of information. Mrs. Hawkins alluded to this in the Senate.

> **Mrs. Hawkins of Florida:** *The media, local and national, from one end of the country to the other have been doing their job. They have been educating the public to the scope and nature of the threat. Two of the major networks, CBS and NBC, have aired documentaries on cocaine. The news magazines – Time, Newsweek, and U.S. News & World Report – have run cover stories on cocaine, and its chemical cousin, crack.* (132 Cong Rec S 12599)

Per Mrs. Hawkins the media had been educational for the public which includes her and her fellow Congressmen. Although the media outlets may have presented accurate information, hard data on cocaine and crack should also have been obtained and utilized in decision making. Also of note, Mr. Rockefeller made the above statement on August 5, 1986, approximately two months before the Anti-Drug Abuse Act was passed indicating that the Congressmen may have passed the Act without having concrete information on crack and for some also knowing they lacked said information. Which raises the question, why would they pass the legislation when they lacked information? Given the volume of newspaper and magazine articles addressed in Congress, perhaps the media's campaign influenced their willingness to pass legislation without accurate information.

Crime:

In addition to associating cocaine and crack with children and addiction, the drugs were vilified by associating them with crime. Given the current and long time association between drugs and crime, it was assumed that the Congressional discussions would include references to crime. Of the Congressional discussions included in this analysis, crime was included but more infrequently than expected. When crime was discussed, it was suggested that use of cocaine or crack led to criminal behavior. Although Mrs. Hawkins succinctly stated her view of the relationship between drugs and crime by stating "drug addiction turns people into walking crime machines," (132 Cong Rec S 13741), most Congressmen, including herself, tended to be more verbose in their statements. In their comments in the Senate, the Florida Senators, Mrs. Hawkins and Mr. Chiles, illustrated how crime was usually linked to drugs.

> **Mrs. Hawkins of Florida:** *we need to focus more attention on cocaine, regarded by many experts as the most addictive and most destructive drug to date. People on cocaine resort to all kinds of tricks to acquire the drug. They are not beyond*

> *lying, cheating, or stealing to get the money to buy drugs. They are devious and scheming, with little regard for those who may be hurt in the process. Cocaine destroys the moral fiber of the user.* (132 Cong Rec S 14825)
>
> **Mr. Chiles of Florida:** *...but now the new wave of crack cocaine that you cannot experiment with; if you try it once, chances are that you will be hooked. If you use it up to three times, we know that you will become hooked, and it is the strongest addiction that we have found. We find again once people are hooked, all they can think about is staying high, that euphoria which they get, but there is a corresponding down that is just as deep in its trough as the high is at the crest of the wave. And so we find that people, when they are addicted, will go out and steal, rob, lie, cheat, take money from any savings, take refrigerators out of their houses, anything they can get their hands on to maintain that habit. That, of course, has caused crime to go up at a tremendously increased rate in our cities and in our States – the crime of burglary, robbery, assault, purse snatching, mugging, those crimes where people are trying to feed that habit.* (132 Cong Rec S 16338)

Their statements were indicative of how crime was associated with and used to vilify cocaine and crack. While using the drugs, people will do anything regardless of harm to themselves or others to obtain money to buy more drugs. In their quest for drugs people will deplete personal and perhaps family financial resources as well as resort to committing crimes for financial gain such as robbery and burglary.

Although neither Senator offered data in support of their statements, support was provided on a few occasions. Instead of documenting the rise in crime with statistics from the Federal Bureau of Investigations Uniform Crime Report, the Congressmen relied on defendant and inmate studies. Mr. Rangel of New York, discussing drugs in general, contended that drugs would cost the United States billions of dollars because of rising crime rates and prison populations associated with drug use.

> **Mr. Rangel of New York**: *At home we have a problem that is estimated to cost our Nation some $100 billion to $125 billion. The street crime certainly is increasing as a result of drug abuse. Of course, our jails, our prisons, where even in the city of New York, the inmate population, 60 percent of it is attributed to drug abuse.* (131 Cong Rec H 1126)

His assertion that drugs account for the majority of the prison population, was later supported by Mrs. Hawkins.

> **Mrs. Hawkins of Florida:** *...There is an unmistakable relationship between drug use and the crime rate. ...James K. Stewart, Director of the National Institute of Justice, the Justice Department's principal research agency, described the researchers working on the study as amazed at the findings. ..The study was based on urinalysis tests administered to 14,000 defendants charged with misdemeanor and felony crimes. Cocaine turned out to be the drug of choice in New York...Over all, the study found that 56 percent of the men tested in New York and 69 percent of the women tested had used drugs. In Washington, the figure was 56 percent for both sexes.* (132 Cong Rec S 7135)

As in the cases of children and addiction, no one questioned the defendant or inmate data. For the defendant data, whether the defendants were using during the commission of the crime or at the time of arrest was not asked. Given that no one questioned the crime statistics linking crime and cocaine nor the association itself, the belief that drugs led to criminal behavior may have been widely held among the Congressmen.

In addition to linking cocaine and crack to increasing financial crimes and the inmate population, some of the Congressmen associated them with murder. In the Senate, Mrs. Hawkins stated that cocaine emergency room visits and deaths had increased significantly in five years as well as violent crime, including murder, which had become the norm in the cocaine markets.

> **Mrs. Hawkins of Florida:** *...Capt. John F. Miller, captain of a police department in the Washington suburbs recently said, "It's like an ocean – everywhere we turn we see cocaine," The statistics bear out this grim assessment. Between 1981 and last year the number of cocaine-related emergency room episodes has increased almost five times! During that period the number of cocaine deaths rose twelve fold. It was five annually. Now it is 61. In Washington as in most places where the drug culture thrives, violence is a way of life. Shootings, robberies, and even murders at many of the 17 cocaine street markets in Washington are part of a everyday ritual for drug pusher and user.* (132 Cong Rec S 12874)

While Mrs. Hawkins highlighted death and murder involving drug users and sellers, Mr. Gilman's statement illustrated how cocaine was linked to threats and death against law enforcement officials.

> **Mr. Gilman of New York***:* *In addition to killing our youth, they are now resorting to kidnapping, murder, bombings, and they have linked up with terrorists throughout the world to facilitate their deadly business activities. Our ambassadors have been threatened, our embassies bombed, our law enforcement agents murdered. A wave of terror radiates throughout the world from the astronomical multibillion-dollar narco-terrorists operations. And just last week, both Time magazine and Newsweek devoted their cover stories to*

> *the global operations and the deadly menace of drug trafficking.* (131 Cong Rec H 1126)

Neither Mrs. Hawkins nor Mr. Gilman's association of death and murder with cocaine were surprising given the deaths that occurred prior to their statements. Mrs. Hawkins spoke before the Senate on September 15, 1986, approximately 3 months after the cocaine related deaths of athletes Len Bias and Don Rogers. Their deaths were media headlines as well as a topic of discussion for the Congressmen. Mr. Gilman made his statement in the House on March 7, 1985, two days after the body of DEA agent Enrique "Kiki" Camarena Salazar was found. Agent Salazar was kidnapped in Guadalajara, Mexico on February 7, 1985 and tortured for two days before he was killed. Of the approximately 500 discussions/documents included in this analysis, Len Bias was mentioned in at least 34 discussions while agent Salazar was mentioned in at least 36 discussions, and independently their mentions represent approximately 7% of the discussions analyzed indicating that the stories of these men captured the attention of the Congressmen. The Congressmen's concerns for Len Bias' death fostered the association of cocaine and death as their concern for agent Salazar's murder fostered their concern about threats to law enforcement and government officials from drug traffickers.

Despite the association between drugs and crimes promoted by the Congressmen from Florida and New York and others; the belief was not shared by all Congressmen. According to Mr. Moynihan drugs, specifically crack, were not the cause of the rising crime rate.

> **Mr. Moynihan of New York**: [reading from a New York Times article "Crack as a scapegoat" by Adam Walinsky] *...The true cause of increasing crime rates is elsewhere. Most street crimes are committed by young men and boys, predominantly from minority groups; the most dangerous years are from the early teens to the early 20's. These young men come increasingly from disintegrating families and*

> *neighborhoods. ...It is long past time that our leaders stop their hysterical grandstanding about new drugs and get to work on the old persistent problems of crime, race and poverty.* (132 Cong Rec S 13741)

Although Mr. Moynihan read the above article on the floor of the Senate, he did not state in his own words that drugs were not the cause of the rising crime rate. However, by reading the article he implied that he agreed with its premise that the increasing crime rate was due to factors other than drugs such as, for Moynihan, disintegrating families, specifically impoverished minority families[23]. Prior to reading the article he stated that drug abuse was increasing and should be a focal concern of the United States. So although he supported halting the growing drug abuse problem, he did not fully support the association between drugs and crime as the major factor in the rising crime rate.

In sum, rather than the expected vilification of Hispanics/Latinos and African Americans due to contentious issues such as reverse discrimination and claims of "welfare queens," cocaine and crack were vilified. Anti-cocaine and crack rhetoric alluding to sickness and proliferation was prevalent throughout the discussions included in this analysis. The drugs were also vilified by associating use with children and the resulting harm, claiming crack was instantaneously addictive, and alleging that the drugs were the cause of the rising crime rate.

---

[23] In the 1965 Moynihan Report ("The Negro Family: The Case for National Action"), Moynihan identified a high unemployment among black males as a major cause of poverty and family disintegration among blacks. While the Report may have been intended as documentation to support the need for federal employment programs it was perceived as an elitist and biased attack against blacks. Depending on how the Report was viewed Moynihan was either a caring supporter or racist. Similarly, how one views Moynihan would influence how his above statement was interpreted.

Race and Class

Due to previous associations of cocaine and blacks at the turn of the 20th Century and the Reagan Administration's lack of support for affirmative action, promotion of ideas regarding reverse discrimination and welfare queens and given that popular belief held that crack cocaine use was associated with the lower classes and minorities while cocaine use was associated with the upper classes and whites, it was assumed that this would foster anti-minority sentiment within the Congressional discussions of the Anti-Drug Abuse Act in that the discussions of the drugs and their penalties would include derogatory comments about African Americans and Latinos/Hispanics and would focus on their use of the drug rather than other segments of the U.S. population. Contrary to expectations, in the Congressional discussions there were few direct references to race. However, subtle allusions to race were made throughout the discussions included in this analysis.

The most explicit reference to race was delivered by Mr. Chiles of Florida in a statement he had inserted into the Record. In the statement he included three articles written by Paul Blythe. In the articles, Blythe stated that crack dealers were usually Black or Hispanic and sold crack in black or interracial neighborhoods.

> **Inserted into the Record by Mr. Chiles of Florida:** [from inserted article "It's cheap, it's available and it's ravaging society" by Paul Blythe] *...Most of the dealers, as with past drug trends, are Black or Hispanic, police said. Haitians also comprise a large number of those selling cocaine rocks, authorities said. That's new and disconcerting, police said, because they previously had not seen Haitians selling drugs. Whites rarely sell the cocaine rocks.*
>
> *Street sales of cocaine rocks have occurred in the same neighborhoods where other drugs were sold in the past: run-down, black neighborhoods from Delray Beach to Fort Pierce.*

> *But the drug market also is creeping into other neighborhoods.*
>
> *An interracial neighborhood east of Howard Park has become one of West Palm Beach's most highly visible cocaine rock areas. Less than a block from where unsuspecting white retirees play tennis, bands of young black men push their rocks on passing motorists, interested or not.*
>
> *...The availability and initial cheapness has caused cocaine use to spread to all levels of society.*
>
> [from inserted article "Police fast being educated about drug" by Paul Blythe] *...Lake Worth Police Sgt. Brad Cummings had undercover officers on bicycles and in taxicabs ride up to dealers to buy drugs and make arrests. He said he "used any excuse," like noting a traffic violation, to stop a car carrying whites out of the black neighborhood where cocaine rock was sold. Then he would check the car for drugs.*
>
> [from inserted article "Rock sellers neither shy nor unavailable" by Paul Blythe] *...Police have encountered several houses where Hispanics and Haitians sold cocaine rocks while surrounded by icons of Santeria, a Caribbean folk religion that mixes Catholicism and traditional African beliefs. ...Although Police said most dealers are Black, cocaine rocks are sold in all types of neighborhoods by all types of people.* (132 Cong Rec S 4668)

Since he submitted the articles for inclusion to the Record it can be assumed that Mr. Chiles agreed with the statements made within them, especially since he offered no additional comments about the articles in his statement. Furthermore, in his statement submitted with the articles he did not specifically state that the dealers or users of crack were usually Black or Hispanic. Therefore, on the one hand he included articles that had racial overtones but on the other he would not directly speak to them. Also of note is that he submitted the articles for inclusion in the Record, he did not read them on the floor of the Senate indicating perhaps that such statements would not be deemed politically correct or maybe more to the point, politically smart.

Although Mr. Chiles submitted his statement for inclusion, a few Congressmen made references to race on the floors of Congress. However, their remarks were not as explicit as that of Mr. Chiles. In the House, Mr. Rangel of New York and Mr. Traficant of Ohio stated that drug abuse was no longer a "minority" or "ethnic" problem, respectively.

> **Mr. Rangel of New York:** *....Drug abuse is not just an urban problem anymore; it is not just an inner city or a minority problem anymore. Drug abuse affects all of us.* (131 Cong Rec H 1126)

> **Mr. Traficant of Ohio:** *...If there is one particular problem that eats and erodes away at the American family, it is this particular phenomenon of drug abuse. It has affected all people. ...This not only an ethnic problem, but it is closely intertwined with American poverty as well, but for us to continue to let foreign imports of narcotics come into this Nation to the tune of 60 metric tons of cocaine per year.* (131 Cong Rec H 1126)

Although not in direct discussion with each other Mr. Rangel and Mr. Traficant made their statements during the same segment of discussions. Neither Representative made a specific association between drug abuse and Blacks or Hispanics instead they referred to its association with minorities or ethnic groups. Given that in this country Blacks and Hispanics are considered minority groups and Hispanics are also considered an ethnic group, avoiding one set of terms while using another is just semantics.

Mr. Rangel and Mr. Traficant's remarks also illustrated another aspect of the anti-minority sentiment in the Congressional discussions. Both Representatives alluded to drug abuse no longer being a minority or ethnic problem but a national one. Although perhaps unintentional on Mr. Traficant's part, the statements suggest that so long as drug abuse was confined to certain segments of society it was tolerable, if not acceptable to the majority of Congress. Given Mr. Rangel's anti-drug history[24], his statements may have been intended to rally the concern of fellow Congressmen by pointing out that drug abuse could no longer be ignored now that it affected all segments of society. Regardless of intention, their statements echoed society's drug mindset regarding opium and marijuana, so long as drug abuse was confined to certain echelons of society it was not an issue but once the drug abuse spread beyond minority or ethnic groups it was deemed a problem that the federal government needed to address.

In the Senate, Mr. Moynihan of New York also made a reference to race that was less direct than Mr. Rangel or Mr. Traficant's.

> **Mr. Moynihan of New York**: *On the other hand, Mr. President, it seems to me that we cannot ignore the fact that when we talk about drug abuse in our country, in the main, we are talking about the consequences it has for young males in inner cities, for whom drug use is an aspect of a generally abused, wasted and ruined life, and indeed, ruinous to those in the community around them. Any society that is really serious*

[24] Mr. Rangel served as the Chairman of the Select Committee on Narcotics Abuse and Control and has been a long time advocate for drug treatment (House.gov, 2008). Since the passage of the 1986 Anti-Drug Abuse Act he has fought for the revocation of the mandatory minimum sentences and advocated for equal penalties for cocaine and crack offenders. As a founding member of the Congressional Black Caucus he has promoted the empowerment of the black community. Thus while his statements in Congress may mention race they were not intended to be derogatory but rather a call to action against drugs.

> *about drug abuse will be serious about that class of young males. It has been growing. It has reached proportions that threaten to bring about the destruction of whole communities and cities across this Nation.*
>
> *I was pleased that a number of very thoughtful commentators, such as Mr. Adam Walinsky -- and Mr. Walinsky was formerly an aide to Robert Kennedy, my distinguished predecessor and friend -- and Ed Yoder, the most perceptive and thoughtful of columnists, have made exactly this point; that if we care about drugs, we would care about the young males in inner cities whose abuse of drugs has made it the focus of national attention once again, as it had been 15, 16 years ago.* (132 Cong Rec S 13741)

In his remarks, Mr. Moynihan made no direct reference to Blacks, Hispanics, minorities or ethnic groups instead he associated drug abuse with young inner city males. In addition he indicated that inner city males abuse of drugs was not a new occurrence, it has also garnered attention in the early 1970's. Similar to Mr. Rangel and Mr. Traficant's remarks, Mr. Moynihan's comment "if we care about drugs, we would care about the young males in inner cities" (132 Cong Rec S 13741) could be taken in a few ways. If the government is going to address drug abuse, it needs to focus on inner cities and the increase in drug abuse by inner city males. Or if drug abuse had not become the focus of national attention the government would not care about young inner city males. How Mr. Moynihan's comment was or is interpreted depends on how he was perceived, caring or prejudiced (see footnote 23 on page 192). Either way, the comments suggest that drug abuse was primarily an inner city problem and popular belief in this country, right or wrong, holds that inner city is synonymous with minorities, specifically Blacks and Hispanics.

Within the Congressional discussions there was also a more subtle implication of the association of drugs with race. As previously mentioned in June of 1986, just four months before the Anti-Drug

Abuse Act was passed, two young athletes died due to drugs. On June 19th Len Bias a 22 year old University of Maryland basketball player drafted to the Boston Celtics died of a heart attack that was later determined to be related to cocaine. Eight days later, on June 27th, the 1984 rookie of the year Cleveland Brown's Don Rogers died of a cocaine overdose. Their deaths, especially Len Bias', garnered media attention in the newspapers and radio and television broadcasts. Their deaths were also mentioned in Congress during the various drug discussions. Mr. Waldon of New York mentioned their deaths in support of his assertion that crack destroyed lives.

> **Mr. Waldon of New York**: *...My colleagues, this is a sad period in the history of America when we hear of young people who are in the prime of their lives as were Len Bias and Don Rogers having their lives snuffed out by this human destroyer which is crack."* (132 Cong Rec H 5939)

In the Congressional discussions included in this analysis Len Bias was mentioned by name in at least 34 discussions as well as being referred to as "the sports athletes" numerous times. With their deaths media and Congressional fodder, Len Bias and Don Rogers became the faces of cocaine, an example of the tragedy that ensues when drugs, specifically cocaine and crack, are abused. Since Len Bias and Don Rogers pictures were all over the news, it is doubtful that anyone failed to notice that they were both African American. Although they were not the only two people to die from cocaine or crack, they were the only two whose names and faces were universally, at least in America, associated with cocaine related death. That Congressmen would hear the stories of the deaths, see the pictures of Len Bias and Don Rogers and then associate cocaine and crack use with African Americans is not unforeseen. For as Gamson et al (1992) noted, "We walk around with media-generated images of the world, using them to construct meaning about political and social issues. The lens through which we receive these images is not neutral...we emphasize the production of images rather than facts or information because this more subtle form of meaning construction is at the heart of the issue" (374). Therefore, even though African Americans were not the only people who suffered cocaine or crack related deaths, since Len Bias and Don Rogers were in the media spotlight, the face of cocaine and crack was African American.

Thus, while Mr. Chiles included explicit racial associations in the Record, on the floor the Congressmen were more circumspect and avoided specific references to race and instead made references to minorities, ethnicity, and young inner city males. In this and in the cases of Len Bias and Don Rogers the racial aspects were much more subtle. While these references to race were rare, slightly more prevalent was associating drug use with class. Mr. Moynihan's assertion that the drug abuse problem was one of primarily inner city males, in addition to alluding to race also alluded to class since popular belief also holds inner city synonymous with lower class and poverty. This association between drug use and the inner city was also made in the House by Mr. Waldon of New York.

> **Mr. Waldon of New York**: *...The use of drugs is no longer an inner city problem. It is so devastating and destructive that nothing short of a declaration of all out war will suffice. ...I believe when there is an understanding of what crack can do in terms of destruction of the human mind and to the human body that America will raise up and begin to attack crack, because it is not respective of any social class. It is not respective of any community and it is extremely devastating and just a killer of all people.* (132 Cong Rec H 5939)

With his remarks, Mr. Waldon asserted that while drug abuse used to be an inner city problem, it had now spread to other communities and social classes. Similar to the statements made by Mr. Rangel and Mr.

Traficant, Mr. Waldon[25] alluded that drug abuse was no longer an inner city problem but a national one suggesting that so long drug abuse was confined to the lower classes it was tolerable for the majority of Congress. However, once the drug abuse spread to other social classes it was deemed a problem that need to be addressed by the federal government.

At the time popular belief held that cocaine was the used by the wealthy while crack cocaine because it was less expensive was used by the lower classes. Thus to an extent cocaine was considered a higher class drug while crack was considered a lower class drug. Mr. Owens of New York and Mr. Dole of Kansas alluded to these distinctions in the House and the Senate, respectively.

> **Mr. Owens of New York:** *...the original exemption became law at a time, unfortunately, when cocaine was viewed as a recreational drug. It is a drug of the white collar set, a drug of the college set. There was an unfortunate assumption made there, an unfortunate view was taken of the drug cocaine. It would seem to be less dangerous than opiates like heroin.*
>
> *...We are speaking today about the problem of drug abuse. It has reached epidemic proportions. Crack has entered the picture and made the price for each use of a drug for a person seeking this kind of gratification cheaper. The volume therefore allows them to sell more of it. It is more widespread. It has become the drug of choice for the people who have little money, as well as the drug of choice for the affluent people who drive about poor neighborhoods in high-*

---

[25] Although Mr. Waldon's comment may have been intended to rally anti-drug support and inform colleagues that the problem of drug abuse could no longer be ignored similar to Mr. Rangel's, since he served less than one year his position on drugs and the meaning behind his statements in Congress are more difficult to interpret and thus for this analysis can only be taken at face value.

> *priced cars and make purchases of these drugs.* (132 Cong Rec H 5939)

> **Mr. Dole of Kansas:** *For years we have lived under the illusion that cocaine is not physically addicting like the lower class drugs of heroin and opium.* (132 Cong Rec S 6528).

Mr. Owens acknowledged that cocaine had previously been considered a recreational drug used by the "white collar set," the upper classes, and the college set, the middle and upper classes. He also stated that crack use was widespread and found in both the lower and upper classes. Mr. Dole added that part of the misperception of cocaine was the assumption that it was not physically addicting and thus a higher class of drug. But with the knowledge that cocaine was addictive it was then more similar to "the lower class drugs" that are physically addicting such as heroin and opium. Thus, class was related not only to the user, but also to the drug itself. Of the two, relating class to that of the user was more prevalent.

Although the Congressmen seemed to make a distinction between race and class, with some referring to the race of the drug dealer or user while others referred to the user's social class, in the United States race and class are not always separate and distinct. The wealthier classes in the United States are primarily white whereas the lower classes have a much greater minority representation. With class and race intertwined, referring to crack as being the drug of the lower classes also implies that its users are minorities while referring to cocaine users as upper class implies that they are white. Although the racial makeup of classes was not discussed in Congress; it may have been widely known and accepted at the time.

More prevalent than the occasional reference to the race and class of drug dealers and users, were the Congressional discussions of the importation of cocaine and the countries involved in international drug trafficking. Approximately 25% of the discussions included in this analysis referred to or discussed international drug trafficking and its effect on the United States. The vast majority of these discussions focused on Mexico, Bolivia and Columbia and the amounts of cocaine manufactured in and/or transported through those countries.

Table 6.4 contains quotes that illustrate the nature of the international drug trafficking discussions in Congress. Given the volume of discussions, the discussions of international drug trafficking addressed a variety of issues but in terms of race the discussions illustrated two themes: the increase in trafficking from Central and South America and the threat to law enforcement. The increase in trafficking from Central and South America was mentioned in both the Senate and the House. In the Senate, Mr. Cochran of Mississippi made general comments about the escalation of drugs without mentioning specific countries.

> **Mr. Cochran of Mississippi:** *The threat of illegal narcotics crossing our borders is escalating dramatically, and there is growing evidence that narcodollars are financing the purchase and shipment of arms to Central and South America.* (132 Cong Rec S 2274)

Whereas Mr. Cochran just stated that the narcotics shipments from Central and South America were increasing, Mrs. Hawkins focused on Mexico.

> **Mrs. Hawkins of Florida**: [as read from "Buried by a tropical storm" from Time] ..*By far the busiest new cocaine alley is the 2,100 –mile Mexican border. "It's a sieve, and we don't have enough fingers to plug all the holes," says Drexel Watson, a senior special agent for the Customs Service. "More drugs than ever are coming in. It's pretty devastating." Mexico has become a conduit for as much as a third of the South American cocaine entering the U.S.* (132 Cong Rec S 2489)

TABLE 6.4 Congressional Discussions Regarding Countries Involved in Cocaine Trafficking

Congressman & State	Quote
Mr. Rangel of New York	"...Unfortunately, Mr. Speakers, in those days, it was really thought that drug abuse was confined to the inner cities and poorer people. Mr. Pepper, then as chairman of the Crime Committee, was trying to point out that this epidemic could spread toward class distinctions, across State lines, and indeed has become an international epidemic. ....Last year we have seen some 10 tons of heroin enter into the United States; some 85 tons of cocaine, and 15 tons of marijuana. From the reports issued by the United Nations, indeed, from the report that supplements it, issued by our own State Department, we expect that this year is going to be even worse. The President has declared war against drugs; can this body do any less? We can see throughout the world our ambassadors being chased out of Columbia and out of Bolivia. That prices are being placed on the heads of our Drug Enforcement administrators and other officers. Indeed, the tragic knowledge that came to our country last night of a dedicated Drug Enforcement agent that had been kidnapped was murdered in cold blood and his partner buried alive. It seems to me that as we see hit squads coming into the United States from South America; as we see threats where our public officials and public buildings are under attack, this is the time to mobilize our strengths.... [approximately two pages later he repeated himself] I do not believe I am exaggerating when I say the United States is at war with international drug traffickers. A DEA agent was kidnapped by drug terrorists in Mexico, last month. His brutally beaten body was reportedly found yesterday. South American drug bosses have placed bounties on top DEA officials, and Colombian hit squads have reportedly been dispatched to the United States to attack DEA agents and bomb Federal buildings." (131 Cong Rec H 1126)
Mr. Coughlin of Pennsylvania	"... The headlines of the past several days leave no doubt about the stakes involved in the war on drug abuse. DEA agent Enrique Camarena Salazar is kidnapped and murdered in Mexico. Nine men and women die in Washington, DC, within days from lethal injections of heroin. The elected Chief of the Turks and Caicos Islands in the Caribbean is arrested in Miami on drug charges." (131 Cong Rec H 1126)

TABLE 6.4 Congressional Discussions Regarding Countries Involved in Cocaine Trafficking (continued)

Congressman & State	Quote
Mr. Fascell of Florida	"... As our distinguished colleagues in this body know, Florida has become a veritable marketplace in recent years for the wares of international narcotics traffickers, particularly those with operations based in several Latin American nations. A tidal wave of violent, narcotics-related crime has inundated South Florida and there is every indication that the sale of illegal substances has resulted in the increased presence of organized crime as well." (131 Cong Rec H 1126)
Inserted by Mr. Rangel of New York:	[New York Times article "United States says smugglers 'overwhelm' borders with record cocaine flow"] "Until about five years ago, he said, three or four Colombian syndicates dominated the processing and transportations of cocaine to the United States. Syndicate agents sold the drug to other Hispanic people, among them a strong Cuban contingent here, who were in charge of the wholesale and, in part, of the retail end of the business. ...Columbians have established a "heavy interaction" with organized crime families in New York City and with Hispanic criminal elements in other cities, especially Los Angeles." (131 Cong Rec E 4231)
Mr. Sheuer of New York	"It became perfectly clear to us that the drugs that emanate from the Southwest, the heroin and marijuana that originate in Mexico and the cocaine that is manufactured in South American countries and transit Mexico, are absolutely crossing our borders freely and spreading death and destruction from our largest cities to the smallest hamlets across the length and breadth of America." (132 Cong Rec H 303)
Mr. DeConcini of Arizona	"...No longer can we afford to sit idly by and be outgunned day in and day out be a well-financed, well-organized army of drug smugglers that is penetrating our borders with record loads of cocaine, marijuana, and heroin. ...Mr. President, if any one of my colleagues doubts the need to go to new and advanced ends to protect our borders from the purge of the drug smuggler, let me suggest that they just read the latest issues of Time and Newsweek; both of which feature a cover story on the cocaine menace that is plaguing this country like never before. And it is difficult to pick up a paper on any given day and not read about another kidnapping, or murder, or execution, or crime that is directly or indirectly the product

TABLE 6.4 Congressional Discussions Regarding Countries Involved in Cocaine Trafficking (continued)

Congressman & State	Quote
	of narcotics. As this bill is being introduced one of our drug enforcement administration agents remains missing following his abduction, presumably by Mexican drug figures, on February 7. The public is outraged and they should be. Letters coming into my office indicate that the people of this nation are sick and tired of illegal narcotics governing the streets and putting them in fear of letting their kids play after dusk; taking a walk with their husbands around the block; or walking to the neighborhood grocery to pick up a carton of milk. …President Reagan, in his State of the Union address of February 6, 1985, again stressed the urgency of establishing a competent military presence in Central and South America." (132 Cong Rec S 2274)
Mr. Cochran of Mississippi	"The threat of illegal narcotics crossing our borders is escalating dramatically, and there is growing evidence that narcodollars are financing the purchase and shipment of arms to Central and South America." (132 Cong Rec S 2274)
Mrs. Hawkins of Florida	[as read from "Buried by a tropical storm" from Time] "..By far the busiest new cocaine alley is the 2,100 –mile Mexican border. "It's a sieve, and we don't have enough fingers to plug all the holes," says Drexel Watson, a senior special agent for the Customs Service. "More drugs than ever are coming in. It's pretty devastating." Mexico has become a conduit for as much as a third of the South American cocaine entering the U.S." (132 Cong Rec S 2489)
Mr. Lungren of California	[reading from "Mexico drug profits flowing to U.S." by Jeff Gerth] "…In recent days some United States law-enforcement officials have harshly criticized Mexico for not prosecuting drug traffickers vigorously enough. Drug enforcement officials here said the use of Mexican banks by Mexican drug rings showed that stopping Mexican drug trafficking was a problem for both countries." (132 Cong Rec H 3414)
Mr. Gekas of Pennsylvania	"…Speaking of the narcotics problem in Mexico, Drug Enforcement Agency Administrator John Lawn told the New York Times last month that "Production is increasing, quantities are increasing, purities are increasing." The Time

TABLE 6.4 Congressional Discussions Regarding Countries Involved in Cocaine Trafficking (continued)

Congressman & State	Quote
	reported in its May 12 edition that United States drug enforcement authorities seized over 10,700 pounds of cocaine as it was being smuggled across the Mexico-California border between October 1, 1985, and March 30, 1986. "That is three times more than was seized along the entire Mexican border during the previous 5 years," the Times stated. The Drug Enforcement Agency his reportedly identified 10 "class 1" drug traffickers in Mexico, giving that country the highest total of these high-volume traffickers in the entire world. ...Tragically, the increase in cocaine trafficking and production in Mexico and other countries has contributed to an increase in suffering here in America." (132 Cong Rec H 4565).
Mr. Owens of New York	"....We have a very serious problem with large amounts of drugs coming in from Mexico, from Southwest Asia, from Turkey, from Iran, from Afghanistan, from Pakistan. All of these countries are not our enemies, they are our allies. They are not Communist countries. There is no great friction between us. They are our allies, and they are often receiving a great deal of aid from us. Surely we can do more to stop the flow of drugs from those countries into this country –Burma, Laos, Thailand, in the Western Hemisphere Columbia, Bolivia, Peru, all of these countries are friendly countries receiving aid from the United States. There should be a way to interdict and prevent a greater quantity of drugs from coming into this country." (132 Cong Rec H 5939)

Mrs. Hawkins focus on Mexico is significant in that the United States has a history of immigration issues with Mexico, specifically the volume of illegal immigrants entering America. As mentioned in Chapter 5, although the United States did not pass immigration laws as strict as the Chinese Exclusion laws it did engage in repatriation in the 1930's and more recently legal deportation. Referring to the Mexican border as cocaine alley fosters the historical tension between the two nations. Although the words were not her own, reading the Time article in the Senate without critiquing it implies that Mrs. Hawkins agreed that Mexico was a major conduit for drugs and thus, was a threat. In addition, since the article was from Time magazine, a mainstream publication with a wide readership, the general public as well as other Congressmen may also have associated Mexico with drug trafficking.

Mr. Gekas of Pennsylvania also focused on Mexico's involvement in drug trafficking but he cited the New York Times rather than Time magazine.

> **Mr. Gekas of Pennsylvania:** *...Speaking of the narcotics problem in Mexico, Drug Enforcement Agency Administrator John Lawn told the New York Times last month that "Production is increasing, quantities are increasing, purities are increasing." The Times reported in its May 12 edition that United States drug enforcement authorities seized over 10,700 pounds of cocaine as it was being smuggled across the Mexico-California border between October 1, 1985, and March 30, 1986. "That is three times more than was seized along the entire Mexican border during the previous 5 years," the Times stated. The Drug Enforcement Agency has reportedly identified 10 "class 1" drug traffickers in Mexico, giving that country the highest total of these high-volume traffickers in the entire world. ...Tragically, the increase in cocaine trafficking and production in Mexico and other countries has contributed to an increase in suffering here in America.* (132 Cong Rec H 4565).

Mr. Gekas not only stated that drug trafficking was increasing; he supported his assertion with data on the volume of drugs. Per the New York Times, in a six month period the cocaine seized along the Mexican border was three times that seized in the previous five years. Similar to the other presentations of data, neither Mr. Gekas nor any other Congressmen questioned the accuracy of the New York Times' information. Furthermore, in the last sentence of his statement he linked the trafficking in Mexico with the drug problems in America implying that Mexico was, in some way, responsible for drug abuse in America.

A second theme in the international drug trafficking discussions was the threat international trafficking posed to law enforcement. Mr. Rangel of New York spoke of the threats against law enforcement officials in the House.

> **Mr. Rangel of New York: ...***Unfortunately, Mr. Speakers, in those days, it was really thought that drug abuse was confined to the inner cities and poorer people. Mr. Pepper, then as chairman of the Crime Committee, was trying to point out that this epidemic could spread toward class distinctions, across State lines, and indeed has become an international epidemic. ....Last year we have seen some 10 tons of heroin enter into the United States; some 85 tons of cocaine, and 15 tons of marijuana. From the reports issued by the United Nations, indeed, from the report that supplements it, issued by our own State Department, we expect that this year is going to be even worse. The President has declared war against drugs; can this body do any less? We can see throughout the world our ambassadors being chased out of Columbia and out of Bolivia. That prices are being placed on the heads of our Drug Enforcement administrators and other officers. Indeed, the tragic knowledge that came to our country last night of a dedicated Drug Enforcement agent that had been kidnapped was murdered in cold blood and his partner buried alive. It seems to me that as we see hit squads coming into the United States from South America; as we see threats where our public officials and public buildings are under attack, this is the time to mobilize our strengths....* [approximately two pages later he repeated himself] *I do not believe I am exaggerating when I say the United States is at war with international drug traffickers. A DEA agent was kidnapped by drug terrorists in*

> *Mexico, last month. His brutally beaten body was reportedly found yesterday. South American drug bosses have placed bounties on top DEA officials, and Colombian hit squads have reportedly been dispatched to the United States to attack DEA agents and bomb Federal buildings.* (131 Cong Rec H 1126)

In his statement Mr. Rangel not only restated that drug abuse which had been associated with inner cities and lower classes had spread to all classes, but also linked its proliferation to international drug trafficking. However, his main focus was on the death threats drug traffickers issued to DEA agents as well as the contracts they put on their lives. He focused on the threat to law enforcement and mentioned a DEA agent who had been kidnapped and killed. Although he did not specify the agent's name, he was referring to Agent Enrique Salazar who as previously mentioned was abducted outside of the U.S. Consulate in Guadalajara, Mexico on February 7, 1985 and tortured for two days before he was killed. His body was not found until March 5th. Although it is unlikely that Agent Salazar was the only drug enforcement officer killed in the line duty during the 99th Congress he was the agent whose death captured the attention of Congress and the media.

On the same day, Mr. Coughlin of Pennsylvania also spoke of Agent Salazar's death as well as other crimes that had made media headlines.

> **Mr. Coughlin of Pennsylvania:** ... *The headlines of the past several days leave no doubt about the stakes involved in the war on drug abuse. DEA agent Enrique Camarena Salazar is kidnapped and murdered in Mexico. Nine men and women die in Washington, DC, within days from lethal injections of heroin. The elected Chief of the Turks and Caicos Islands in the Caribbean is arrested in Miami on drug charges.* (131 Cong Rec H 1126)

In referring to the media headlines, Mr. Coughlin associated drugs with crime, death and murder. Mentioning that Agent Salazar was murdered in Mexico in almost the same breath as the elected official of the Turks and Caicos Islands being arrested on drug charges in Miami reinforces the association between drugs and race. Even though Agent Salazar was a DEA agent he was also Hispanic and killed in Mexico, if bias against Mexicans already existed Agent Salazar's murder may have fostered it. Although the Congressmen rarely verbalized an association between the countries involved in drug trafficking and race, Mr. Rangel of New York submitted an article from the New York Times for inclusion in the Record that did make the connection between international drug trafficking and race in the United States.

> **Inserted by Mr. Rangel of New York:** [New York Times article "United States says smugglers 'overwhelm' borders with record cocaine flow"]
> *Until about five years ago, he said, three or four Colombian syndicates dominated the processing and transportations of cocaine to the United States. Syndicate agents sold the drug to other Hispanic people, among them a strong Cuban contingent here, who were in charge of the wholesale and, in part, of the retail end of the business. ...Columbians have established a "heavy interaction" with organized crime families in New York City and with Hispanic criminal elements in other cities, especially Los Angeles. (131 Cong Rec E 4231)*

Per the Times article, Columbian drug cartels sold their product to "other" Hispanics, specifically Cubans. Since Mr. Rangel did not contest any of the information in the article and he did select it for inclusion, it may be assumed that he agreed with the assertion that Columbians sold their cocaine to "other Hispanics." Although references such as this were rare, they did make the association between international trafficking and race. Given the volume of discussion and newspaper articles submitted regarding international trafficking that these countries are primarily Latin/Hispanic may have influenced how the members of Congress viewed cocaine. It may have influenced them to associate Hispanics/Latinos with selling and using cocaine.

In sum, although contrary to expectations there were few direct references to race, there were more subtle allusions to race throughout the legislative discussions. Rather than directly referring to race, Congressmen made indirect inferences by asserting the drug users, specifically crack, were minorities, "ethnic," from the inner cities or lower class. The focus on the deaths of Len Bias and Don Rogers as well as international drug trafficking in Mexico, Bolivia and Columbia, although more subtle, may have influenced the association of drugs with African Americans and Hispanic/Latino Americans.

Penalties

Since the Anti-Drug Abuse Act of 1986 created increased and in some cases drastically increased penalties, it was assumed that there would be numerous discussions regarding the increased penalties. However, within the Congressional discussions included in this analysis the penalties were only discussed approximately ten times not including when a bill regarding penalties was introduced but not discussed which occurred less often than the discussions of the penalties.

When penalties were mentioned the Congressmen usually stated that the cocaine laws were out of date and urged that stiffer penalties be implemented. Mr. Owens of New York in a long speech before the House argued that although current law did not take cocaine seriously his bill would rectify the mistake.

> **Mr. Owens of New York:** *Current law does not take cocaine seriously. It is not surprising that we have an epidemic now which is heightened by the appearance of a purified form of cocaine which is called crack, because the law has never*

taken cocaine that seriously. Whereas the law requires stiff penalties for other narcotics, the law does not require very stiff penalties in the case of the possession of a considerable amount of cocaine. ...The cocaine preparation called crack is smoked and unpredictably high doses of this drug are absorbed directly into the bloodstream into the lungs. This sometimes has lethal effects. Death by cardiac arrest occurs often and has occurred in some dramatic cases related to some sports celebrities recently.

Current law provides for stiffer penalties for the importation, the manufacturing, the distribution, the dispensing, the sale or possession of over 100 grams of a narcotic drug other than cocaine. Cocaine is made an exception. Cocaine is classified as a schedule I narcotic. Cocaine, you can have much more of that and not receive a stiff penalty.

...the original exemption became law at a time, unfortunately, when cocaine was viewed as a recreational drug. It is a drug of the white collar set, a drug of the college set. There was an unfortunate assumption made there, an unfortunate view was taken of the drug cocaine. It would seem to be less dangerous than opiates like heroin.

...One other thing my bill does, it defines what cocaine really means, the kind of cocaine which becomes crack. The law is very general, current law is very general and there is really no working definition of what they mean. My bill defines 5 grams or more of cocaine, its salts, optical and geometric isomers, or a substance chemically identical thereto.

...This message should be clear and consistent. We should make clear that everybody takes steps to guarantee that everybody understands that cocaine is a killer and that this killer, we will not continue to take a permissible attitude toward this killer. (132 Cong Rec H 5939)

In his speech he highlighted the reasons for increasing the penalties. First, since cocaine was erroneously viewed as a recreational drug it was classified as a schedule I drug while all other narcotics are schedule II drugs receiving harsher penalties for smaller quantities. He also argued for harsher penalties because crack could be lethal. To support the assertion that crack was lethal he mentioned by situation, if not by name, the crack related deaths of athletes Len Bias and Don Rogers.

In response to Mr. Owens speech, Mr. Waldon of New York offered his support of increasing the penalties.

> **Mr. Waldon of New York**: *...certainly I believe that we must take a harder line of approach to enforcement. When we see so many children dying and the purveyors of this death are in a turn-stile justice system, if you will, meaning that after they are arrested they are often on the streets before the police officer can finish the paperwork in court, then something is wrong. I think we look at mandatory sentencing in regard to those who deal in death. I think we should look at making sure that just the possession of a small amount, but when we see a series of actions of the sale of these drugs that these people should be subject to felony punishment and should be prosecuted to the fullest extent of the law.* (132 Cong Rec H 5939)

Per Mr. Waldon mandatory sentencing was needed because with the current drug laws dealers were back on the streets before the paperwork has been processed. Mandatory sentences would prevent the drug dealers from immediately returning to dealing.

Mr. Waldon's remarks also illustrated a previously noted common theme in the Congressional discussions, the harm done to children. Mr. Byrd of West Virginia used the tactic of focusing on the drugs and drug dealers killing children to support the need for harsher penalties.

> **Mr. Byrd of West Virginia:** *...Well, drug pushers are taking innocent lives and drug pushers are making money, billions of dollars, out of taking innocent lives in this country – young lives, kids going to school. ...They are making billions of dollars out of the commission of this crime, killing our young people, destroying lives. And we ought not be softheaded when it comes to dealing with these people.* (132 Cong Rec S 12215)

Although Mr. Byrd did not suggest how the penalties should be changed, he did support increasing them and played on his fellow Congressmen's desire to protect children.

Mr. Byrd's fellow Senators, Mr. Chiles of Florida and Mr. D'Amato of New York, although they did not mention the harm done to children, also advocated for more up to date laws but focused on the differences between cocaine and crack cocaine.

> **Mr. Chiles of Florida**: *But clearly those dealing in rock and crack cocaine should face the stiffest penalties that law allows. Right now a crack dealer faces no greater risk than does a small time pusher. ...One gram of cocaine makes about 20 to 25 rocks. The high concentration of rock and crack warrants that 1 gram receive the stiffest penalty. Some think I am being too harsh with these penalties. I do no have such qualms. My changes are to Federal Law and Federal law is unusually directed at those who deal and traffic in significant amounts of drugs. In my book, if you have 20 rocks on you – you should have the book thrown at you. This is a lethal, potent drug. ...I urge my colleagues to join me in making the penalties the toughest against rock and crack cocaine.* (132 Cong Rec S 7636)

According to Mr. Chiles one gram of cocaine yields approximately 20 to 25 rocks of crack cocaine. Due to the amount of crack produced from one gram of cocaine and the higher potency of crack there should be stiffer penalties. In a statement inserted to the Record Mr. D'Amato added to this line of reasoning.

> **Inserted by Mr. D'Amato of New York**: *...Our laws are seriously out-of-date as applied to cocaine, and absurdly so as applied to crack, or freebase cocaine. An average dose of crack is only 65 milligrams. Under current law, therefore, a crack dealer cannot be subject to the maximum prison term unless he is caught with a kilogram, or more than 15,000 doses, of crack. This simply never happens. As a result, those who traffic in one of the most addictive substances known to man – a substance that is spreading a new crime wave through our cities and towns and our rural and suburban areas – escape the severe punishment they deserve.* (132 Cong Rec S 8091)

Per Mr. D'Amato since the average dose of crack was 65 milligrams but the required a kilogram for the maximum penalty, the law needed to be amended and the penalties increased. Similar to Mr. Byrd's tactic of supporting increased penalties by associating the drugs with harm to children, Mr. D'Amato supported increased penalties by associating crack with rising crime and high addiction.

Although the Congressmen did not provide statistical support for their stance, increasing the drug penalties was supported by the vast majority. Whether their assertions that crack was harmful to children, responsible for rising crime or was instantaneously addictive were correct was moot given that no one challenged their remarks indicating that they may have been widely held.

Despite the overwhelming support for increasing penalties; the sentiment was not shared by all Congressmen. Although Mrs. Hawkins was the most vociferous advocate for the Anti-Drug Abuse Act dominating the discussions in the Senate speaking and submitting statements at a rate of approximately 75 times that of the average

Congressmen during these discussions, she questioned the need for different penalties for cocaine and crack cocaine.

> **Mrs. Hawkins of Florida**: *While it is frightening to behold the accelerated addition and destruction process of crack, we should not be stampeded into forgetting that crack is nothing more than a purified form of cocaine. The dividing line between crack and cocaine is indistinct and arbitrary. And if by some miracle we devised a crack specific defense that worked, who believes that no new form of sophisticated cocaine abuse would rise to take its place. For this reason, I believe we should concentrate our attack on the generic drug, cocaine, rather than be drawn off to concentrate our attack on the current deadly cocaine sideshow of crack. By going after cocaine, we automatically go after crack and any future inventive form of cocaine abuse. I realize that attacking crack is much more palatable politically to the drug culture and those many so-called recreational users of cocaine who might look down on "crack" users. But logic and conviction would dictate an attack on crack through an attack on cocaine itself.* (132 Cong Rec S 9788)

Mrs. Hawkins recommended focusing on cocaine rather than crack, since crack is a derivative of cocaine. In stating this she raised what would become a question after the Act passed. If harsher penalties are placed on crack cocaine than on cocaine, then cocaine dealers can possess greater quantities of cocaine and in turn produce more crack. On the other hand, if cocaine were the focus and had the harsher penalties, by stopping or decreasing the amount of cocaine, crack would also be decreased since it is a derivative of cocaine. As Mrs. Hawkins pointed out, it logically makes sense that by "going after" cocaine the government would also be going after crack. Additionally, in her remarks Mrs. Hawkins alluded to the political aspects of drugs and the difference between cocaine versus crack users. Politically it made more sense to go after crack users who did not have the social standing enjoyed by cocaine users. In spite of her reservations, Mrs. Hawkins continued to be instrumental to the passage of the Act even though it established harsher penalties for crack than cocaine. Thus, although she objected to the penalty decisions she chose to pass the bill rather than dissent. Which raises the question of why she would advocate for a bill with which she had issue? Was she actually concerned with the difference in penalties or was it a political opportunity to make a statement that could be useful in the future?

Despite the seeming agreement among the Congressmen, with the exception of Mrs. Hawkins, that the penalties for cocaine and crack needed to be increased, there was one contentious recommendation that almost prevented the Anti-Drug Abuse Act from passing. Some Congressmen felt that the ramifications of drugs required the harshest penalty possible, the death penalty. The idea of adding the death penalty to the Act fostered more discussion than any other penalty aspect. Whereas the majority of the rare mentions of penalties were statements from Congressmen that brooked no argument or comments, the concept of adding the death penalty fostered a heated 30 page discussion and threats of a filibuster. Mr. Gekas of Pennsylvania introduced the amendment calling for the death penalty on the floor of the House and was immediately opposed by Mr. Edwards of California.

> **Mr. Gekas of Pennsylvania**: *Mr. Chairman, the drug dealer will stop at nothing to further his enterprise. He would poison our populace; he would enslave our children; he would kill a judge; he would kill a prosecutor; he would kill a law enforcement officer; he would kill anybody who would stand in his way. That has beenproved time and time by the history of the issue, in the recent history of this issue. So the amendment I have to offer is society's response to this killer who seems unstoppable at this juncture in our history.*
>
> *...The amendment would offer the jury in a case in which a continuing criminal enterprise concerning drug traffic*

becomes the issue at trial that when an intentional death is caused at the hands of this drug dealer czar kingpin, that that intentional death would result in the possibility of the imposition of the death penalty under the constitutional provisions that have stood the test of the Supreme Court in allowing juries to make that choice.

...There can be no ultimate war on drugs if we do not cast our ultimate weapon: To place the fear of capital punishment in front of the drug czar who does anything he wants as we sit and stand here today.

Mr. Edwards of California: *Mr. Chairman, I think it is a great mistake to bring the death penalty into this bill and to have to debate and vote on it because it is an issue that is very deeply felt by many people throughout the United States and indeed in this body and also whether or not the amendment is approved is not going to make any difference. It is not going to help the war against drugs one tiny, tiny bit. The President understands this. The President and I do not often agree, but we certainly agree on this. It is very divisive and should not be injected into an important bill like this.*

These people do not think they are going to get caught; the people that the gentleman from Pennsylvania refers to, my friend, Mr. Gekas. These are professional dealers and hired killers and they do not really care about the difference between life imprisonment and the death penalty.

Also, if this amendment is adopted, it is going to jeopardize passage in the Senate. There are, in the other body, Members who will filibuster this bill. I assure you, if this amendment is adopted. (132 Cong Rec H 6679)

Mr. Gekas and Mr. Edwards remarks were indicative of the divisive nature of the death penalty discussions. The House was fairly evenly split among those opposing and those supporting the amendment with relatively few remaining neutral. The Congressmen who supported inclusion of the death penalty presented arguments similar to Mr. Gekas' that in order to stop the drug dealers the federal government should utilize its harshest penalty, the death penalty. Since the drug dealers dealt in death they should be eligible for death. On the other side, those who opposed inclusion of the death penalty were willing to go to great lengths, even threatening a filibuster for the entire Anti-Drug Abuse Act, to prevent its inclusion.

The Congressmen who opposed inclusion of the death penalty raised three major arguments against it. First, Mr. Edwards' remarks illustrated the lack of deterrent value of the death penalty in that a punishment does not deter someone from committing a crime when they do not believe they will be caught. Since they do not believe they will be caught, they do not think about the possible consequences before, during or after committing the act. Neither the threat of a life sentence nor the death penalty would prevent professional dealers and assassins from acting. A second argument was raised by Mr. Rodino of New Jersey.

> **Mr. Rodino of New Jersey**: *...There are a number of reasons why even those who favor the death penalty can and should oppose the amendment. First, this amendment will actually drain the resources the Federal Government must use in this war against drugs. In all 37 States that provide the death penalty, that punishment is already authorized for virtually the same crimes covered by this amendment. Under the amendment, the Federal Government would spend millions of dollars prosecuting offenses which are now handled by the States. These capital cases require both complex trials and lengthy appeals and are consequently many times more expensive than noncapital criminal cases. A recent study pegs the cost at $1.8 million for trial and first appeals alone. Time and money spent duplicating State efforts cannot then be spent in areas where the Federal Government can make a unique*

> *contribution, which is the driving force of this bill. And, in States which have not authorized the death penalty for crimes covered by this amendment, Congress would be usurping the States' prerogative to determine punishment under their own criminal laws. In addition, this amendment will add a tremendous burden to the Federal courts, a burden that is now handled by State courts, when Federal courts especially in drug-intensive areas of the country, are already choking on their caseloads.* (132 Cong Rec H 6679)

The second line of reasoning questioned the logic of including a punishment that was already covered by State law and could thus be tried and funded by the State reducing the financial and personnel burden of the federal government. In addition, it raised the question of whether the federal government should usurp one of the powers of state governments which it would if it were to enforce the death penalty in states that did not authorize it. Per Mr. Edwards even for those who personally supported the death penalty in general but perhaps not for inclusion in this bill, the amendment over stepped the federal governments power by infringing on state power.

The third argument against including the death penalty addressed the racial disparity in death penalty sentences. Mr. Rangel of New York referenced Florida's death penalty cases to illustrate racial bias in sentencing.

> **Mr. Rangel of New York**: *...let me tell you about some of my personal concerns about how other people can completely disregard the right to life after birth. That is the way that this bill is written, certain juries can consider who will die for one set of facts and another jury might consider who will die for another set of facts. We recognize that people's value of life vary from community to community. What is shocking to me is that some facts were revealed to me that in the State of Florida during the period of 1976 to 1980 there were 286*

> *blacks that killed white folks in the State of Florida, and during this very same period of time there were 111 white folks that killed some black folks in the State of Florida. When we took a look to examine, when they took a count of who was found eligible or convicted and give the death sentence, the score was: for the whites, zero; for the blacks, 48.* (132 Cong Rec H 6679)

Mr. Rangel acknowledged the racial imbalance that by some would be called racial discrimination and by others racial disparity. While Mr. Rangel raised the issue and presented data that illustrated the racial differences in death penalty sentences, he stopped short of saying that the death penalty has been used to racially discriminate.

Shortly after Mr. Rangel's statement the House voted on the amendment. The vote of 198 for the amendment, 206 against and 27 abstaining indicated that even after 30 pages of discussion the House was still split. However, in the end, the amendment was not passed and the death penalty was not included in the Anti-Drug Abuse Act which was passed 36 days later without a filibuster.

In sum, contrary to expectations the cocaine and crack cocaine penalties outlined in the Anti-Drug Abuse Act were rarely discussed. When they were mentioned it was overwhelmingly in support of increasing the drug penalties for cocaine and crack. Similar to all of the drug discussions in this Congress, the Congressmen supported the need for harsher penalties by mentioning the higher potency and lethalness of crack as compared to cocaine as well as the threat the drugs and drug dealers posed to children. Given that the 100 times difference between cocaine and crack became the most controversial aspect of the Act, it was assumed that Congress would discuss this part of the Act in more depth, however, within Congress the most discussed and controversial penalty was the death penalty. Although the death penalty was not included in the Act, of note is that while some of the Congressmen recognized the potential racial consequences of the death penalty, they did not verbally consider the potential racial consequences of the 100 times difference in amounts of cocaine and crack to incur the same mandatory sentence.

References to Newspaper Stories

Although not necessarily a topic of discussion, during the cocaine and crack cocaine legislation, of note was the volume of references to newspaper stories. Several Congressmen read or submitted newspaper and magazine articles to either make or support a point. In the Senate, Mr. Evans of Washington referred to the media focus on cocaine and crack.

> **Mr. Evans of Washington**: *There has been a lot of focus recently on the drug problem. This is an election year. The national news magazines have recently headlined the drug problem with cover stories. Crack dominates the conversations throughout the country. We have had two tragic deaths of young athletes from cocaine.* (132 Cong Rec S 13741)

In mentioning the volume of media coverage of cocaine and crack he also indirectly acknowledged following the stories. Additionally, by referring to the headlines and claiming that cocaine and crack dominated conversations, he to an extent, justified Congresses focus on the drugs. Among numerous others, Mr. Rangel and Mrs. Hawkins used newspaper articles to inform Congressmen about crack and the prevalence of cocaine.

> **Inserted by Mr. Rangel of New York**: *...I wish to bring to the attention of our colleagues and article by Peter Kerr that appeared in the March 20, 1986, New York Times, entitled "Extra-Potent cocaine: Use Rising Sharply Among Teen Agers." ...Increasing, Mr. Speaker, members are inquiring of the select committee; What is crack/ How is it different from*

> *cocaine? Where is it all coming from? Mr. Kerr answers these questions very succinctly.*
>
> *Crack is purified cocaine in pellet form that sells in vials for as little as $5. Users smoke it, creating a powerful stimulating effect on the nervous system. Unlike regular cocaine, crack takes effect in seconds and induces a greater high, experts say. Compared with users of regular cocaine, crack users experience a stronger yearning for the drug and become addicted more quickly.*
>
> *What is most frightening about crack is that it has made cocaine widely available and affordable for abuse among our youth. ...Mr. Speaker, I am afraid that the crack epidemic will only get worse, before it gets better.* (132 Cong Rec E 944)

> **Mrs. Hawkins of Florida**: *Mr. President, a very disturbing report was featured recently in the Washington Post's Health Magazine. The title says it all: "Drug Use Tops 60's Level." In this article, the results of a recent Washington Post-ABC News nationwide survey, half the individuals between the ages of 18 and 30 said they have tried marijuana and 1 in 5 said the have used cocaine.* (132 Cong Rec H 4565).

Mr. Rangel and Mrs. Hawkins used these references as support for the necessity of the proposed legislation. Perhaps not at the time but in review, their use of the articles in some way makes it seem that they were taking cues from the media. In other words, the media was dictating policy rather than the legislature. Instead of Congress being proactive in its drug policy, it was reacting to the media's anti-drug campaign and perhaps their constituents' reaction to the media's campaign.

Since several Congressmen referred to and read newspaper articles during the Congressional discusses or submitted them for inclusion in the Record and few, if any, questioned their inclusion, it appears to have been a common or at least acceptable practice. People may be influenced by what is written in newspapers, but the extent of the influence on the Congressmen was surprising. Depending on the quality of the publication, a newspaper can be a source of information, but is it acceptable for newspapers to be essentially the only source of information? Mrs. Hawkins previously mentioned remarks in the Senate as the educational value of the media's coverage of the drug problem indicated that at least for her and potentially others, newspapers and televised news broadcasts were a primary source of information.

> **Mrs. Hawkins of Florida:** *The media, local and national, from one end of the country to the other have been doing their job. They have been educating the public to the scope and nature of the threat. Two of the major networks, CBS and NBC, have aired documentaries on cocaine. The news magazines – Time, Newsweek, and U.S. News & World Report – have run cover stories on cocaine, and its chemical cousin, crack.* (132 Cong Rec S 12599)

It was assumed that if an argument was presented as to why legislation was necessary, it would be accompanied by statistical data and/or scientific research. However in the case of the cocaine and crack cocaine legislation although there was some data and scientific documentation presented its accuracy and authenticity were never questioned. Given that some of the data that was presented was not supported by the National Household Survey of Drug Abuse or Monitoring the Future data is cause for concern. As previously noted only Mr. Rockefeller commented on the lack of data on crack.

> **Mr. Rockefeller of West Virginia**: *...My distinguished colleagues have just talked about "crack," freebase cocaine. National data still needs to be developed on the scope of the use of this drug, but we don't need studies to know that "crack" has made its way to small communities as well as*

> *large cities and that it has come to our schools.* (132 Cong Rec S 10425) August 5, 1986

That his call for national data on crack was coupled with a claim that studies were not needed to know that crack use had spread is disconcerting and raised the question of where his information came from if not studies. Given the volume of articles presented in Congress and Mrs. Hawkins assertions as to the educational aspect of the media coverage, the most probable source of information was the media. Without scientific evidence linking cocaine and crack cocaine use with crime and addiction or indicating that young people were the primary users, how did the Congressmen differentiate between fact and fiction?

On September 26, 1986, twenty one days before the Anti-Drug Abuse Act was passed, Mr. Evans of Washington in referring to a Washington Post article highlighted the major issue with referencing newspapers as support without critique.

> **Mr. Evans of Washington**: *...I would point out, in addition, that a recent article, I believe yesterday, in the Washington Post, quoting the 3-month survey by the Federal Drug Enforcement Administration has found that crack, in their view, is not the drug of choice for most users and that its prevalence has been exaggerated by heavy media news attention.* (132 Cong Rec S 13741)

Mr. Rockefeller was not the only person who saw the necessity for studies on crack cocaine; the DEA not only saw the need but completed a three month study. The DEA's results highlighted why the Congressmen should have been more critical of the newspaper articles submitted and the information presented as support, the DEA findings indicated that the prevalence of crack had been exaggerated. Utilizing sources such as the National Household Survey of Drug Abuse and Monitoring the Future would have yielded similar results. The Congressmen's over reliance on the media for information and to support their position while not questioning its accuracy does not speak highly of them making informed decisions.

CONCLUSION

The analysis of the Anti-Drug Abuse Act of 1986, specifically the cocaine and crack penalties, and the Congressional discussions addressed the research questions discussed in Chapter Three. The second research question addressed the content of the laws and whether they were racially biased or race neutral in their wording. The Anti-Drug Abuse Act made no mention of African Americans, Hispanics/Latinos or any other racial or ethnic group and in general referred to people using the neutral phrase "such person." Therefore, the content of the wording of the Anti-Drug Abuse Act of 1986 was race neutral.

The fifth research question asked how minority groups were vilified during the period leading up to the enactment of the drug legislation. Although anti-minority sentiment may have been voiced in the press and by private citizens, within the Congressional discussions regarding and surrounding the Anti-Drug Abuse Act there were few direct overtly negative associations of minorities to cocaine and crack. Rather than directly associating drug use with Blacks or Hispanics, the Congressmen made indirect associations by asserting that drug users were minorities, "ethnic," inner city males, or lower class. Also embedded within the Congressional discussions were the more subtle racial nuances of international drug trafficking and the deaths of Len Bias and Don Rogers. While rarely specifically stated, associations were made between Mexico, Columbia and Bolivia's involvement in drug trafficking and Hispanic drug use in America. Furthermore, using the deaths of Len Bias and Don Rogers as illustrations of the evils of cocaine and crack use fostered the association of African Americans and drug abuse. Thus, although African Americans and Hispanics were not overtly vilified in the discussions they were connected to drug use and abuse.

Rather than a minority group being overtly vilified, cocaine and crack were vilified by referring to them as an epidemic and a scourge. The drugs were also vilified by associating their use with causing people to commit crimes and deplete financial resources. Crack was maligned by allegations of instantaneous addiction; one puff and people were hooked. The evilness of crack was further solidified by claiming children, specifically high school students, were using it more frequently due to its low cost and availability near schools[26]. Thus, contrary to expectations the drugs more than minority groups were vilified during the legislative process.

Research questions three and four asked whether the discussions surrounding the 1986 Anti-Drug Abuse legislation impacted their passage and whether competition for economic and political resources affected the drug laws. Although the United States during the Reagan Administration experienced an affirmative action backlash and a recession in the early 1980's, there were relatively few references to job competition, reverse discrimination or welfare queens and no references to political competition. Instead of referring to job competition with African Americans and Hispanics/Latinos, the rare discussions focused on job competition with foreign countries and the comparable worth of men and women's wages. Similarly, rather than associating the term welfare queen with black women who live off of welfare instead of working, the term was associated with defense contractors bilking the federal government. The few references to reverse discrimination that related to affirmative action indicated that Congress supported affirmative action and did not deem goals reverse discrimination as the Reagan Administration did. Within these rare discussions of reverse discrimination minorities, specifically African and Hispanic Americans were not referred to in a derogative manner. Perhaps, this was the case because affirmative action, job competition,

---

[26] These findings are similar to those of Reinarman and Levine's (1997) analysis of the media accounts of cocaine and crack use in America, fostering the question as to the extent that Congressmen were influenced by the media and how much of their information was obtained via the media.

reverse discrimination and welfare queens were a focal point in the early 1980's and by the 99th Congress in 1985 and 1986 Congress and the United States had moved on to new concerns, specifically drugs. Since there were relatively few references and most of them were contrary to expectations, the surrounding discussions had little, if any impact on the anti-drug abuse legislations.

Finally, the first research question asked whether racism had been embedded in our drug laws. Without knowing the actual intent of the Congressmen this question cannot be definitively answered. However, sometimes a Congressmen's beliefs, if not intent, can be ascertained through analyzing the content of their Congressional discussions. Although the Anti-Drug Abuse Act of 1986 did not specifically reference African Americans, Hispanics or any other racial group, the inclusion of the 100 times difference in the amount of crack and cocaine to incur the same mandatory sentence may have indirectly targeted minorities given that the Congressmen associated the use of crack with Blacks, minorities, ethnic groups, inner city males and the lower classes all of which can and have been at some time synonymous with Blacks or Hispanics.

Furthermore, when on the rare occasions they mentioned the penalties established in the Act, there were few explanations provided for the differing amounts for cocaine and crack other than prevalence of crack was rapidly increasing, children could afford and were using crack, it was instantaneously addictive, and the violence and death associated with the drugs. While at face value these are all legitimate reasons for harsher penalties, were they actual documented issues or a result of the "war on drugs" hype proliferated by the media and Congressmen? Per data from the National Household Survey on Drug Abuse, Monitoring the Future and the DEA the prevalence of crack was exaggerated in the media and by the Congressmen; it was presented as a perilous drug when in reality a small percentage of drug users used crack and it was not instantaneously addictive.

The data that was presented in Congress varied widely in terms of percentage of users, yet none of the Congressmen questioned the varying results. Furthermore, while Mr. Rockefeller, on the one hand, acknowledged the need for data to ascertain the prevalence of crack, he also claimed that studies were not needed to know that the use of crack had spread. The reliance on data that was not questioned or authenticated (and was not supported by the above referenced three studies) combined with the over reliance on newspaper and magazine articles for information and support raises a few questions. If the scarcity of data on crack necessitated studies, how did the Congressmen know crack use had spread? Where did they obtain their information? And if they did lack information, why would they pass the legislation? Given the volume of newspaper and magazine articles whether read or referred to in Congress and submitted to the Record, it is highly likely that for many of the Congressmen the media was their source of information. With newspaper and magazine articles being addressed in over a third of the discussions, the media's campaign may have affected the Congressmen's decisions in at least two ways. The media's campaign may have directly influenced the Congressmen's willingness to pass legislation without accurate information. Or the press may have energized the public's anti-drug stance and constituents' voiced concerns in turn may have generated pressure for legislators to pass anti-drug legislation.

As previously indicated, the actual intention of the Congressmen is difficult, if not impossible, to ascertain. Nevertheless, their focus on children's use of cocaine and crack, the addictiveness of crack, and how cocaine and crack use and dealing led to criminal behavior indicate that for some of the Congressmen the law targeted these issues rather than Blacks or Hispanics. However, the discussions were also laced with subtle racial nuances that ranged from a few explicit associations of crack dealing and use with Blacks, to more indirect references to class, to Congressmen making subtle connections between foreign countries, particularly Mexico's, involvement in international drug trafficking and Hispanics in the United States or the images of Len Bias and Don Rogers and their cocaine/crack related deaths and African American's use of crack. With the Len Bias and international drug trafficking accounting for approximately 25% of the discussions it can be concluded that for some of the Congressmen race may have been a factor in the creation and passage of the differing cocaine and crack penalties. It could be argued that some of the racial nuances were too subtle to have an effect, however, Mrs. Hawkins, the most vociferous advocate for the Anti-Drug Abuse Act questioned the differing penalties and insinuated that it would be more politically acceptable to focus on crack users than cocaine users.

> **Mrs. Hawkins of Florida**: *While it is frightening to behold the accelerated addition and destruction process of crack, we should not be stampeded into forgetting that crack is nothing more than a purified form of cocaine. The dividing line between crack and cocaine is indistinct and arbitrary. And if by some miracle we devised a crack specific defense that worked, who believes that no new form of sophisticated cocaine abuse would rise to take its place. For this reason, I believe we should concentrate our attack on the generic drug, cocaine, rather than be drawn off to concentrate our attack on the current deadly cocaine sideshow of crack. By going after cocaine, we automatically go after crack and any future inventive form of cocaine abuse. I realize that attacking crack is much more palatable politically to the drug culture and those many so-called recreational users of cocaine who might look down on "crack" users. But logic and conviction would dictate an attack on crack through an attack on cocaine itself.* (132 Cong Rec S 9788)

Mrs. Hawkins acknowledged that while there is not much difference between cocaine and crack cocaine there is a difference in how their users are perceived; the drug culture originally designated cocaine as a recreational drug of choice for upper class whites where as crack was designated as a lower class drug used by Blacks and Hispanics. Given that there were no responding comments to her remark, it is probable that she was not alone in her knowledge that the penalties targeted crack users. Therefore, given all of the above while it can not be said that race was the sole factor or even the most important factor in the creation of the 100 times difference in the cocaine and crack penalties, it is probable that racism was embedded in the Narcotics Penalties and Enforcements Act of the Anti-Drug Abuse Act of 1986.

CHAPTER 7

Conclusions

This research investigated whether there is a connection between the social climate and the advent of some federal drug laws. It examined the content of Congressional discussions to ascertain if we have and perhaps continue to institutionalize racism in our federal drug laws. It investigated the extent to which racism was institutionalized in our federal drug laws, specifically the 1880, 1887, 1890 and 1909 opium laws, the Marihuana Tax Act of 1937 and the Anti-Drug Abuse Act of 1986.

Before addressing the research questions, there were a few notable differences in the Congressional discussions over time. First, the volume of the discussions increased over the years. For the opium and marijuana legislation the data was a couple hundred pages each with marijuana consisting almost entirely of committee hearings. The volume of discussion increased exponentially for the 99th Congress, the cocaine and crack laws, to literally thousands of pages. Although not addressed in this research, the increase may have been due in part to the growth of the United States and the subsequent increase in the number of members of Congress. Second, for the opium and marijuana laws relatively few Congressmen participated in the discussions, while in the 99th Congress almost every Congressman spoke at least one time during the discussions. Furthermore, the nature of the discussions shifted from actual discussions to "prepared" speeches that did not necessarily relate to those immediately before or after. This may be due to technological changes in our society, specifically television. While the opium and marijuana discussions were recorded in the Record and may have occasionally been reported in the newspapers, the 99th Congress was televised live via CSPAN which may have prompted the Congressmen to be more vocal to garner more camera time and more aware of their audience. While this difference was noted, it was not within the scope of this research. However, the effect of CSPAN on congressional discussions could be researched in the future. Third, the volume of submissions to the Record also increased exponentially in the 99th Congress. Although not specifically addressed in this analysis, it seemed the more potentially controversial a statement the more likely it was to be inserted into the Record rather than stated on the floor of Congress. An analysis of these insertions and how they differ from statements on the floor may add to future analyses of the connection between social climate and the advent of drug legislation.

The analysis of the drug laws and the Congressional discussions addressed the research questions discussed in Chapter Three. The second research question addressed the content of the laws and whether they were racially biased or race neutral in their wording. Of the opium laws, only the 1887 law that created harsher penalties for Chinese was not race neutral in its wording. The wording of the 1880 opium law which was a treaty between the United States and China in which each nation prohibited only the citizens of the other nation from importing opium was race neutral. Although the 1890 and 1909 opium laws focused on smoking opium which was generally associated with the Chinese, they were also race neutral in their wording. Since both the Marihuana Tax Act of 1937 and the Anti-Drug Abuse Act of 1986 only referred to people as "any person" and "such person," respectively, they were also race neutral in their wording. Therefore with the exception of the 1887 opium law, over time the drug laws were race neutral in their wording.

The fifth research question asked how minority groups were vilified during the period leading up to the enactment of the drug legislation. Of the drug laws, the opium laws presented the clearest and most overt illustrations of vilification. Anti-Chinese sentiment and rhetoric were present in all the Congresses included in the analysis referring to the Chinese as evil and a curse as well as alluding to their depravity and criminality. Even though the anti-Chinese sentiment was overt, it was not held by everyone, but that the sentiment was for the most part uncontested suggests that it may have been a popular viewpoint.

While the vilification of and anti-minority sentiment during that time period was clear and recognizable, the anti-minority sentiment in the mid 1980's was not. Within the Congressional discussions for the cocaine and crack laws references to Blacks and Hispanics were rarely overt and direct, instead of referring to specific racial groups the Congressmen referred to minorities, ethnicity, inner city males and the lower classes as using drugs. There were also more subtle racial nuances made by linking Mexico, Columbia and Bolivia's involvement in international drug trafficking to Hispanic drug use in America as well as by linking the cocaine/crack related deaths of Len Bias and Don Rogers to the association of African Americans and drug use, implying that most crack users were African American. Therefore, although African Americans and Hispanics were not overtly vilified as the Chinese were, within the discussions they were connected to drug use.

Whereas in the discussions surrounding the opium, cocaine and crack legislation did have racial overtones, Mexicans were only mentioned a few times during the Congressional discussions regarding and surrounding the Marihuana Tax Act and did not constitute vilification. Thus, of the three sets of laws, the Chinese were vilified prior to the passage of the opium laws, the Mexicans were not vilified prior to the passage of the opium laws and African Americans and Hispanics although negatively associated with crack use were not vilified to the extent of the Chinese. Given the above while periodically present there is not a consistent pattern of vilification of minority groups during the period leading up to the enactment of drug legislation.

While the Chinese were vilified in the opium legislation discussions, the drugs themselves were vilified during the marijuana and cocaine and crack legislation discussions. Rhetoric was used to vilify the drugs. Marijuana was referred to it as an evil and a menace while cocaine and crack were an epidemic and a scourge. The drugs were further vilified by associating their use with causing people to commit crime and with children, specifically high school students, and the resulting harm. Marijuana was also vilified by associating its use with insanity while crack was considered instantaneously addictive. Thus, over time there was a shift from overtly vilifying a minority group to vilifying the drugs. Also of note is the pattern of vilifying the drug by associating it with crime and harm done to children that emerged during the marijuana legislation and continued during the cocaine and crack legislation[27].

Research questions three and four asked whether the discussions surrounding the drug legislation impacted their passage and whether competition for economic and political resources affected the drug laws. During each of the three time periods the United States experienced an economic recession and the resulting competition for jobs. Prior to and/or during the opium and marijuana legislation, the United States experienced an influx of Chinese and Mexican immigration, respectively. Despite these similarities, the content of the Congressional discussions differed. As expected, discussions regarding Chinese immigration and the labor competition between Chinese immigrants who would work for lower wages and white laborers occurred before, during and after the enactment of the opium laws. Although immigration and labor issues were not specifically mentioned during the opium legislation discussions, since these issues completely surrounded the opium discussions they may have affected the opium

---

[27] As previously stated in footnote 26, these findings are similar to those Reinarman and Levine's (1997) analysis of media accounts of cocaine and crack cocaine. Given the similar findings, future analysis could address the media's role in legislation.

legislation, especially since all of the opium legislation focused in some way on the Chinese and excluded almost everyone else.

While economic competition was prevalent throughout the opium legislation, it was not prevalent during the marijuana or the cocaine and crack legislation. Even though the United States was in the midst of the Great Depression and there had been an influx of Mexican immigration until approximately 1930, there were no references to economic competition surrounding the marijuana discussions. This may have been due to the repatriation of hundreds of thousands of Mexicans in the 1930's and therefore by 1937 the Mexican population had already been substantially diminished thus decreasing job competition as well. Similarly, during the Reagan Administration there was an affirmative action backlash with the Reagan Administration failing to support affirmative action and accusations of reverse discrimination as well as a recession in the early 1980's. Although job competition and reverse discrimination were mentioned within the Congressional discussions, contrary to expectations, job competition was discussed in terms of foreign competition and comparable wages for men and women while reverse discrimination only occasionally referred to affirmative action. Even in the few references to affirmative action, the discussion was about goals not constituting reverse discrimination with no derogatory inferences to racial or minority groups. Given that there was no mention of economic competition during the marijuana legislation and it was barely mentioned in the cocaine and crack legislation, it is unlikely that economic competition impacted this drug legislation.

The findings for political competition mirrored those of economic competition. Political competition while present during the opium discussions was only mentioned a few times and remained a localized concern in that it was only voiced by the California Congressmen. Given the number of Chinese in America at the time, it was a perceived rather than actual threat. Since political competition remained localized and was barely mentioned it is unlikely that it affected the opium legislation. While there was some mention of political competition during the opium legislation, there was no mention of political competition during either the marijuana or the cocaine and crack legislation. Therefore, it is unlikely that political competition affected this drug legislation.

Although it was concluded that it was unlikely that economic and political competition affected the marijuana and cocaine and crack legislation, there were differences in the Congressional discussions included in the opium legislation analysis as compared to those included in the analysis of the marijuana and cocaine and crack legislation. Given that there were four opium laws over a number of years, discussions from nine Congresses were included in the opium analysis. Since there was only one marijuana law, fewer Congresses, two, were included in that analysis. The discussions regarding and surrounding the Anti-Drug Abuse Act were limited to the 99th Congress due to the voluminous nature of the Congressional Record. Given that the Congressional discussions included in the opium analysis yielded support for economic competition affecting the drug legislation, a case can and in the future should be made for continuing to research the effect of competition on legislation. Future research may build a plausible case for the presence of economic and/or political competition affecting the marijuana and cocaine and crack legislation that this research did not support by expanding the number of Congresses included in the analysis. For marijuana, including Congresses back to 1930 or earlier might yield more discussions regarding Mexican immigration and job competition between Mexicans and whites. In regard to cocaine and crack, since the War on Drugs began years, even decades, before 1985, including Congresses back to 1980 or earlier might yield more discussions regarding issues of affirmative action and job competition that may have affected the Anti-Drug Abuse legislation.

Finally, the first research question asked whether racism had been embedded in our drug laws. Although this question cannot be definitively answered since the actual intent of the Congressmen cannot be ascertained. However, sometimes a Congressmen's beliefs, if not intent, can be inferred through analyzing the content of their Congressional discussions. A plausible case can be made that the 1887, 1890 and 1909 opium laws at least represent indirect institutional discrimination. The 1887 law created harsher penalties for the Chinese than for Americans that may have yielded negative outcomes. Although the 1890 and 1909 laws did not specifically reference the Chinese, they did focus on smoking opium which was generally associated with the Chinese. The focus on smoking opium can not be justified by public health or addiction concerns because the available addiction studies indicated that smoking opium did not have the highest addiction rates. If public health was the concern then the focus should have been on opium, laudanum, and morphine. When the focus on the Chinese and smoking opium is combined with the anti-Chinese immigration and labor competition discussions it indicates that the laws, at the least, indirectly targeted the Chinese. Therefore, racism was embedded in the 1887, 1890 and 1909 opium laws.

While the opium laws seemed to present the ideal example of racism being embedded in drug laws, the same cannot be said of the Marihuana Tax Act or the Anti-Drug Abuse Act of 1986. Given that there were few references to Mexicans within the one hundred and fifty pages of committee hearing testimony and Congressional discussions and that the majority of the discussions related to Congress's power to pass the legislation, the protection of the legitimate commercial uses of cannabis and how much people should be taxed, the analysis did not support racism being embedded in the Marihuana Tax Act. Whereas racism was embedded in the opium laws but not in the marijuana law, the Anti-Drug Abuse Act fell somewhere between the two. The Congressmen in the 99th Congress focused on children's increasing use of cocaine and crack, the addictiveness of crack and how cocaine and crack use led to criminal behavior. Any of those issues may have influenced individual Congressmen to pass the legislation. However, there were also a few direct and numerous more subtle references to the race of dealers and users that also may have influenced individual Congressmen to endorse and ultimately pass the legislation creating the differing penalties for cocaine and crack. Therefore, it cannot be said that racism is not embedded in the legislation. Nor can it be said that race was the sole factor or even the most important factor in the creation of the 100 times difference in the cocaine and crack amounts to incur the same penalty, however, it is probable that racism was embedded in the Narcotics Penalties and Enforcements Act of the Anti-Drug Abuse Act of 1986.

In addition to addressing the issues of racism and economic and political competition, although not actual topics of discussion in Congress, this analysis found that the themes of lack of discussion, lack of knowledge and reliance on the media for information and support were also present in the Congressional discussions. A lack of discussion of the legislation in Congress was noted for all the drugs but in varying degrees. There were no discussions in Congress of either the 1880 treaty or the 1890 opium legislation. The 1887 opium legislation was merely read in Congress and referred to as necessary to execute the 1880 treaty as requested by the President. If there were any additional discussions they may have occurred in committee but there was no mention of committee reports. Although the 1880 treaty and the 1887 and 1890 opium legislation were passed with essentially no discussion in Congress, the 1909 law was discussed in both the House and the Senate albeit briefly.

Although seemingly difficult to achieve, within the Congressional Record the volume of discussion on the marijuana legislation was less than that of the early opium laws. During the 74th and 75th Congresses, with the exception of one day, marijuana was only mentioned in Congress to say that a bill had been referred to a committee – a few sentences buried within thousands of pages of the Congressional Record. Even on the one day the Marihuana Tax Act was discussed in the House of Representatives the discussion comprised only approximately a page and a half of the Congressional Record whereas the verbatim reading of the bill itself constituted approximately 2 and a half pages of the Record.

Even though the volume of "discussions" in the Congressional Record increased exponentially in the 99th Congress for the cocaine and crack legislation, there was still an over all lack of discussion. As previously noted, by the 99th Congress there had been a shift from actual discussions to "prepared" speeches that did not necessarily relate to those immediately before or after resulting in relatively few questions or exchanges of ideas, the most notable exception being the unusual (for these "discussions") 30 page debate over the death penalty. Thus in all three time periods there was a noteworthy lack of discussion on the floor of Congress.

In addition to the lack of discussion, there was also a lack of knowledge apparent during both the marijuana and cocaine and crack legislation. For the Marihuana Tax Act the lack of knowledge of the proposed legislation and marijuana, itself, was evident in both the committee hearings and Congress. Despite articles, editorials and cartoons about marijuana in the press, the 1936 depiction of marijuana in Reefer Madness, and Commissioner Anslinger's public campaign (in the form of articles and public speeches) against it, some of the committee participants and even some of the hemp manufacturer representatives did not understand what marijuana was. Even though the committee hearings encompassed approximately four days and roughly 145 pages of text, there was essentially no scientific documentation presented regarding the prevalence of marijuana or its effect on criminal behavior. Moreover, only one person, who was not a Congressman, seemed to object to this lack of evidence. Furthermore, discussion of the Marihuana Tax Act in the House of Representatives was delayed not only due to lack of time, but also because the Representatives had little knowledge of the bill. Even given four days to familiarize themselves with the bill and the Ways and Means' report, the Representatives had little knowledge of what constituted marijuana indicating that, at least, some of them did not read the information.

The lack of knowledge, although present, was different during the cocaine and crack legislation. While the Congressmen had basic information about the drugs, they failed to critically assess the available data. Regardless of type of statistics presented, they were not questioned. None of the Congressmen asked who did the study if the information was not provided, how the statistics were generated, or questioned the numbers presented. Essentially, if a Congressman presented statistics or numbers of any sort to support his/her argument, their authenticity was assumed. Moreover the data provided by the Congressmen indicated use percentages much higher than those indicated by the National Household Survey on Drug Abuse or Monitoring the Future. Therefore, while support was provided, its accuracy was neither questioned nor confirmed. Furthermore, although the lack of data on crack cocaine was noted by one Congressman, he also claimed that studies were not needed to know that the use of crack had spread and that crack was being used in schools. Thus, in the last two time periods, 1935-1937 and 1985-1986, of this analysis there was a lack of knowledge of the drugs and/or legislation.

A third theme that was noted during the legislative discussions of all the drugs was the references to newspaper stories. Although the Congressmen only occasionally referred to newspaper articles to support their point during the opium legislation the volume of references increased during both the marijuana and cocaine and crack legislation. During the opium discussions only a few of the Congressmen mentioned newspaper stories but they rarely, if ever, read the article in Congress, however, during the 75th and 99th Congresses newspaper articles were mentioned as well as read in part and whole. During the Marihuana Tax Act legislation several committee participants quoted newspapers, especially editorials, to support the necessity of the legislation. Additionally, for some of the Congressmen newspapers were their primary source of information on marijuana. By the 99th Congress the volume of references to newspaper and magazine articles had increased exponentially from several during the Marihuana Tax Act to encompassing more than a third of the Anti-Drug Abuse Act discussions included in the analysis. Numerous Congressmen read or submitted newspaper and magazine articles to either make or support a point. Some of the Congressmen highlighted the media's focus on cocaine and crack indirectly acknowledging following the stories as well as justifying Congress's focus on the drugs. The Congressmen also used newspaper articles to inform fellow Congressmen about crack, cocaine and their prevalence. Thus during the Congressional discussions for all of the drug legislation, Congressmen utilized newspaper accounts to support the necessity of the legislation and sometimes as a source of information about the drug.

Individually and especially when combined the lack of discussion, lack of knowledge and the reliance on the media raises questions regarding the legislative process. How and why was legislation passed when there was a lack of discussion and/or a lack of knowledge? More specifically, in regard to the 1880, 1887 and 1890 opium laws, since there was essentially no discussion of these three laws and anti-Chinese concerns appear to have been localized to the Pacific Coast, how did the laws garner enough support for passage? In regard to the Marihuana Tax Act, if the Congressmen did not know what the bill was and they were unclear as to what constituted marijuana, why was the legislation passed, let alone put to a vote without more discussion? Furthermore, since no scientific or statistical documentation on marijuana was presented, on what did they base their decisions? Per the Anti-Drug Abuse Act, if the scarcity of data on crack cocaine necessitated studies, how did the Congressmen know crack use had spread? Where did they obtain their information? Without scientific evidence linking cocaine and crack cocaine use with crime and addiction or indicating that young people were the primary users, how did the Congressmen differentiate between fact and fiction? And if they did lack information, why would they pass the legislation?

The 1880, 1887 and 1890 opium laws may illustrate how legislation is passed when there is a lack of discussion. With the 1880, 1887 and 1890 opium laws there was essentially no discussion and anti-Chinese concerns appeared to have been localized to the Pacific Coast, yet the laws garnered enough support for passage. Since the 1880 law was a treaty between the United States and China and the 1887 legislation enforced the treaty, that both were supported or requested, respectively, by the President may have been sufficient motivation for Congressmen to support their passage. The 1890 legislation which raised a tariff on the manufacturing of only smoking opium, however, was not related to the 1880 treaty nor was it specifically requested by the President, yet it still passed with no discussion indicating that perhaps the Pacific Coast Congressmen bargained with other Congressmen for their support of this legislation in exchange for support on other legislation. Since there were no discussions of the 1890 legislation on the floor of Congress, any conversations would have occurred outside of Congress in the halls or offices for which there is no record and can only be assumed. Thus it can only be assumed that the practice of logrolling may have occurred and been a factor in the passage of at least the 1890 opium law.

While the main legislative process question for the opium laws was how a seemingly localized issues garnered support, the Marihuana Tax Act and the Anti-Drug Abuse Act raised questions of how legislation for which the Congressmen lacked knowledge could be passed. It was assumed that if an argument was presented as to why legislation was necessary, it would be accompanied by statistical data and/or scientific research. However, in the case of the marijuana there was essentially no scientific data presented and the available cocaine and crack data was not critically assessed. Without scientific evidence linking marijuana use with crime and insanity and cocaine and crack to crime and addiction or indicating for both that young people were the primary users, how did the Congressmen differentiate between fact and fiction? On what did the Congressmen base their decisions? In the case of marijuana, it appears from some of the Congressmen's comments that newspapers were their source of information. Given the volume of newspaper and magazine articles whether read or referred to in Congress and submitted to the Record during the 99th Congress and Mrs. Hawkins comments among others, it is highly likely that for many of the Congressmen the media was also their source of cocaine and crack information. Since several people referred to and read newspaper articles and editorials during the marijuana committee hearings as well as the cocaine and crack discussions and few, if any, questioned their inclusion, it appears to have been a common or at least acceptable practice. People may be influenced by what is written in newspapers, but the extent of the influence on the Congressmen was surprising. Depending on the quality of the publication, a newspaper can be a source of information, but is it acceptable for newspapers to be essentially the only source of information? The Congressmen's over reliance on the media for information and to support their position while not questioning its accuracy does not speak highly of them making informed decisions and to an extent caring about making informed decisions. Perhaps not at the time but in review, their use of the articles in some way makes it seem that they were taking cues from the media. In other words, the media was dictating policy rather than the legislature. Instead of Congress being proactive in its drug policy, it was reacting to the media's anti-drug campaign and perhaps their constituents' reaction to the media's campaign.

Although it is beyond the scope of this research to address in any depth, if Congress's drug policy was reactive rather than proactive, then the media's anti-drug campaigns may have influenced the Congressmen's willingness to pass legislation without accurate information and/or adequate discussion. Regardless of the accuracy of the information, the press can generate public concern and fear about issues of drug use and abuse. For marijuana and cocaine and crack newspaper and/or magazine articles repeatedly associated the drugs with crime, use by young people, addiction (for crack) and insanity (for marijuana). Whether the associations were accurate they could and did generate public concern that constituents' in turn may have voiced to their Congressmen. In order not to be perceived as unconcerned or "soft" on drugs the Congressmen rather than questioning the accuracy of the media's anti-drug campaign may have jumped on the band wagon, so to speak. The more press generated on the evils of the various drugs in regard to crime and harm to children the more difficult it becomes for Congressmen to oppose or even question the legislation. Thus, the media may have been more of a force than any one person in the passage of the legislation. Although beyond the scope of this research, future analysis could address the media's role in legislation.

Future research could also address the possibility of the media's role in whether racism was embedded in the drug legislation. As previously mentioned although this analysis did not support racism being embedded in the Marihuana Tax Act and found that it was probable that racism may have been embedded in the Anti-Drug Abuse Act of 1986, an analysis of the media published before and during the legislation of the two laws may find racial bias in the press. Racial bias may have originated with the press creating and/or amplifying an issue that the legislators reacted to either to placate constituents or to increase their political capital. For example, during the marijuana legislation, due in part to Anslinger's anti-marijuana campaign, newspapers did contain anti-Mexican sentiment that may have influenced the Congress. Even though the newspapers read during the hearings made few references to Mexicans it is unknown what articles the Congressmen read on their own and how they may have been influenced by them. With the increased references to news articles in the 99th Congress, the press may have been even more influential. Given that many of the articles read in Congress or inserted into the Congressional Record directly associated drug selling and use, especially crack, with minority males, the racial bias in the articles may have influenced some of the Congressmen's decisions. However, determining how the media and racial bias within the media may have influenced the Congressmen and thus the legislation was beyond the scope of this research.

In sum, although consistent patterns did not develop over the three time periods of the opium, marijuana and cocaine/crack laws, given that the opium laws presented the ideal case of racism embedded in drug laws and the Anti-Drug Abuse Act provided if not a definitive answer, the probability of racism embedded in drug laws, the research did develop a plausible case that racism has and could be embedded in our drug laws. Similarly, while economic and political competition were not prevalent during the marijuana and cocaine/crack legislation, economic and to an extent political competition were present during and at least the former may have affected the opium legislation, thus it is plausible that competition may affect legislation. While consistent patterns over time were not found for economic and political competition or racial biases, more consistent patterns did develop for lack of discussion, lack of knowledge and reliance on newspaper articles for information and support. Since the effect of these on the legislative process was for the most part beyond the scope of this research, future research should address this as well as the media's role in racial bias. As previously suggested, further research should focus on expanding the number of Congresses included in the analysis of the drug laws to allow more time for the issues surrounding economic and political competition and racial biases to develop as they did in the Congresses included in the analysis of the opium laws. Ideally, future analysis would also include more drugs and laws rather than just three, which would aid in determining if patterns were emerging over time.

APPENDIX

Methodology

DATA: THE CONGRESSIONAL RECORD

The Congressional Record Indexes were used to search for all discussions of the proposed legislation regarding opium and the Marihuana Tax Act. The LexisNexis online search engine for the Congressional Record was used to search for discussions of the Anti-Drug Abuse Act of 1986.

Although required by the Constitution, the United States government did not officially publish Congressional proceedings for the first 41 congresses (McKinney, 2005; Danner, 2003; Amer, 1993). Commercial publishers, usually newspapers, did provide a partial record of Congressional proceedings to the extent available given column space (McKinney, 2005). These early recordings of the proceedings were not verbatim and the accuracy depended on the reporter's shorthand abilities as well as the ability to hear the discussions from the gallery. In addition to these challenges to the accuracy of the record of the proceedings, what was published was subject to the political views of the editors of the commercial publications.

The Annals of Congress cover Congress from 1789 to 1824, the first 18 Congresses (McKinney, 2005). The Annals are the compilation of the early commercial publisher's summaries of Congressional debates and actions. Although the Annals are recognized as the best source of Congressional proceedings for the first 18 congresses, they are not complete. They include the summaries that Joseph Gales and William Seaton, the commercial publishers, located and selected for inclusion.

Gales and Seaton also published the Register of Debates in Congress (McKinney, 2005). The Register covers the proceedings of the 18th to the first session of the 25th Congress (1824-1837). Compilation of the content of the Register began ten years after the 18th Congress in approximately 1834. Similar to the Annals it is also not a verbatim record of Congressional proceedings. Although some selected reporters, not all, were allowed on the floor of Congress and were better able to hear the proceedings, they still had to rely on their shorthand abilities. In addition, some speeches and/or debates that were deemed not of interest were omitted and members of the House and Senate were able to revise their remarks prior to publication.

The Register of Debates slightly overlaps the Congressional Globe which covers congressional proceedings from the 23rd through the 42nd Congress (1833-1873) (McKinney, 2005). The Congressional Globe published by Francis Preston Blair and John Cook Rives is also not a verbatim record. Even though both were commercially published, the Globe was considered more partisan than the Register partially due to Blair and Rives appointment by President Andrew Jackson (McPherson, 1942). Members of both parties complained of being misrepresented or their statements not reported. Regardless of issues of partisanship, members could submit copies of their speeches to be included in the appendix that was published at the end of the Congressional session (McKinney, 2005). By the middle of the century, the accuracy of the Globe was increased due to the Senates' 1848 and the Houses' 1850 adoption of Issac Pitman's phonetic shorthand method (McPherson, 1942).

At the end of the 42nd Congress, Blair and Rives contract ended and Congress decided to publish its own proceedings (McKinney, 2005; McPherson, 1942). The Government Printing Office (GPO) began publishing the Congressional Record with the first session of the 43rd Congress (December 1873) and continues to publish it today (McKinney, 2005). Therefore, all the research for this book was conducted using the Congressional Record published by the Government Printing Office.

Since 1873 the format of the Congressional Record has changed from two columns to three as has the volume of the record (from 5500 pages for the first session of the 43rd Congress to over 30,000 pages for more current sessions) (McKinney, 2005). "The Congressional Record contains House and Senate floor proceedings, substantially verbatim transcripts of floor debate and remarks, notice of all bills introduced, full text of all conference committee reports, notices of committee and Presidential actions and communications, and statements or documents submitted by members of Congress for publication" (McKinney: 4). Members can make non-substantive changes to their statements prior to the publishing of the daily edition (which is published by the next day) and again prior to the publishing of the hardbound permanent edition (which is published on average five years after the session ends). All revisions, extensions of remarks or insertions not delivered on the floor of Congress appear in capital letters. Although conference committee reports are usually, but not always, published in the House proceedings, standing committee hearings and reports are not printed in the Congressional Record.

Included with the Congressional Record is an Index and Appendix. The Index is usually printed at the end of the last session of a Congress and is published several years after the end of the session (McKinney, 2005). The Index is organized alphabetically by subject and provides the page number and sometimes depending on the year whether it occurred in the Senate or the House. More recent Indexes including the 99th Congress (1985-1986) are organized alphabetically by subject and then within each subject by type of proceeding (i.e. addresses, amendments, analyses, appointments, articles and editorials, bills and resolutions, remarks in House, remarks in Senate, reports, statements, etc.). Thus, over the years, the Index has become more organized making the Congressional Record more accessible. Additionally, the Index from 1983 to present is available online via the GPO Access website.

The Congressional Record is available in a few formats depending on the year of publication and the physical location of the collection. The source of the Congressional Record for the research on opium laws and the Marihuana Tax Act was the Law Library of the William and Mary Marshall-Wythe School of Law. In this library the Annals of Congress, the Register of Debates, the Congressional Globe and the Congressional Record prior to the 1980's are available in bound volumes. Beginning with the Congressional Sessions in the 1980's the library stopped carrying the Congressional Record in bound volumes and switched to microfiche. Even though the Congressional Record after 1980 was only available on microfiche, the Index was available in bound volumes. However, due to the nature of conducting research with microfiche, the LexisNexis online search engine was used to conduct research on the Anti Drug Abuse Act of 1986. Beginning with the 99th Congress and continuing to the present LexisNexis has the Congressional Record available on line. The format is different than the bound version in that the search engine pulls up only discussions that pertain to the search term rather than providing a volume and page number as the Index does for the bound volumes. Nevertheless, it is a verbatim account of the bound Congressional Record.

Recording and Accuracy of the Congressional Record

Congressional proceedings were first recorded by reporters who were only allowed in the gallery (McKinney, 2005). Their ability to accurately capture the proceedings depended on their ability to hear the proceedings, how fast they could write and when they were present. Even if they could capture close to a verbatim account, the publishers often selected what would be published based on their political beliefs and column space. The accuracy of the record of Congressional proceedings increased when the House and Senate adopted Isaac

Pittman's phonetic shorthand method in 1850 and 1848, respectively (McPherson, 1942). The accuracy of the Congressional Record has also increased with advancements in technology. In the Senate, a team of seven stenographers work on the floor in ten minute shifts moving among the Senators recording every word and business transaction using stenographic machines and shorthand if necessary (McKinney, 2005). Immediately after their ten minute shift, the stenographers transcribe and edit their notes and then make them available to the Senators involved in the proceedings. The House also has a team of stenographers who operate the same way the Senate does except that the stenographer's transcript is only given to the House member in charge of the floor for the duration of the transcript to review. The House member in charge of the floor distributes the transcript to the House members involved at his/her discretion. Even with Congressional member's ability to review the transcripts and make non substantive changes, that days proceedings are transcribed, edited, typeset, printed and made available before Congress convenes on the next day.

Since the GPO began publishing the Congressional Record with the 43rd Congress, Congressional members have been able to revise their comments. Although they are not allowed to make substantive changes nor can they alter anything but their own comments, members can alter the wording of their comments. In essence they have the opportunity to remove or rewrite remarks, such as profanity and racially biased or any salacious comments that may be offensive to someone reading or reporting from the Record. Additionally, as previously mentioned, members of Congress have been able to make submissions for publication in the Appendix since the Register of Debates, this practice was continued with the Congressional Record. The Appendix contains the extension of remarks and insertions that were not delivered on the floor of Congress (McKinney, 2005). Submissions can be made for both the daily and bound versions, giving members ample time to alter their remarks. Although these remarks and insertions are included it does not necessarily mean that they were read by members of Congress. Therefore, although the extended remarks may provide more insight into individual Congressional member's motives or thoughts regarding the legislation, what is said on the floor is more important due to how it may influence other Congressional members.

Coding

The Congressional Record discussions were coded for latent content. This assesses the underlying meaning of the discussions providing a more in depth overall assessment rather than quantifying how many times specific words or phrases occurred. A provisional "start list" (Miles & Huberman, 1994: 58) of codes prior to data collection were based on the research questions. During analysis of opium law discussions initial codes included anti-Chinese sentiment, railroads (economic advancement of Chinese), and vilification of Chinese (references to savagery/brutality while using opium). The "start list" codes (start codes) varied slightly for each drug law. For marijuana, the codes included Mexican immigration/migration, Mexicans in the workforce, vilification of Mexicans, and origin of the drug. The Anti Drug Abuse Act of 1986 start codes were vilification of Latinos/Hispanics and blacks, reverse discrimination/competition for jobs, and "welfare queens". Due to the nature of the research some of the start codes were retained and new codes were developed as patterns emerged during analysis.

Although not included in the time periods proposed, an example of vilification of a minority group occurred during testimony for a House of Representatives committee in 1910:

> The colored people seem to have a weakness for it {cocaine}.... They have an exaggerated ego. They imagine they can lift this building, if they want to, or can do anything they want to. They have no regard for right and wrong. It produces a kind of temporary insanity. They would just as

> leave rape a woman as anything else and a great many of the southern rape cases have been traced to cocaine (Morgan, 1981: 93).

During his lobbying and testifying for the Hatch Bill, which eventually was passed as the Marihuana Tax Act of 1937, Harry Anslinger made references to the dangers of Mexican's and blacks while under the influence of marijuana using derogatory racial slurs (Lusane, 1991). Although these two examples do not constitute proof, they do lead me to believe that they will not be the only legislative discussions with racial overtones.

One of the goals of this research is to build a plausible case that there is a connection between the social climate and legislation. The start codes for each time period include codes for competition for resources as well as vilification which is one way for a dominant group to maintain power over a minority group. With the passage of opium laws, the Marihuana Tax Act and the mandatory drug sentencing guidelines following economic recessions, perceived or actual increased job competition, and vilification of one or more minority groups in reference to the drug, it is plausible that competition for scarce resources (the social climate) is connected to drug legislation.

<u>Opium Legislation Search Terms and Coding</u>:
The start codes for analysis of the opium law discussions were anti-Chinese sentiment, railroads (job competition), and vilification of Chinese. Given the increase in Chinese immigration I assumed that the influx of Chinese immigrants would foster anti-Chinese sentiments such as references to evil, female prostitution, and lack of Christianity, within the Congressional discussions of the opium laws. A second assumption, given that the discussions of the opium laws began towards the end of the Gold Rush and during the building of the railroads (Kennedy, 1990; Musto, 1999), was that the Congressional discussions would also include references to job competition, specifically discussions of Chinese, especially coolie, immigrants

taking jobs away from white workers because they were willing to work for less money. The third start code of vilification of Chinese was used due to the assumption that Congressional discussions of opium would include references to Chinese savagery or brutality while using opium. Due to the nature of the research some of the start codes were sustained and new codes were developed as patterns emerged during analysis.

During analysis the start codes of anti Chinese sentiment and vilification of the Chinese were retained. The start code of railroads (job competition) was amended to labor competition to encompass all forms of labor, especially mining, rather than restricting the code to railroads. Three additional codes were added, political competition, localization and smoking opium. Political competition denotes discussions regarding the political power of Chinese immigrants. Localization represents the extent to which Congressional members from one location dominated the discussions and to an extent indicated that the issue may be one of local concern rather than a national concern. The smoking opium code was used to designate when the discussion and/or legislation focused on smoking opium rather than opium in general.

The Congressional Record Indexes were used to locate all discussions related to the opium legislation in 1880, 1887, 1890 and 1909. Each search was begun in the year that a law regarding opium was passed and then I worked backwards in time to the introduction of the bill and/or discussions regarding the need for such a bill. On average from inception to passage the time frame for a law to be enacted was two years or less.

The 43rd and 44th Congress (1873-1876) were examined because San Francisco passed the first opium ordinance in 1875 (Gray, 2000) and it was assumed that given the passage of the city ordinance there may have been some discussion of opium in Congress. The 43rd Congress's (December, 1873 – March, 1875) Indexes were used to find discussions relating to the opium legislation. The Volume 2 Index did not contain the terms: China, Chinese, cocaine, drugs, immigration, imports, labor, opium or smoking opium. A search under the California Senators John Hager and Aaron Sargent did yield references to the Chinese, Chinese labor and Chinese intoxication. In the Senate Index of Volume 3 there was no reference to the following search terms: China, Chinese, drugs, opium, smoking opium, labor, or imports. The House Index of Volume 3 also did not reference the terms China, Chinese, labor, opium or smoking opium. It did however contain references to drugs and perfumery repeal taxes, immigration and imports. The Index was also searched for references to the Senators (John Hager and Aaron Sargent) and Representatives (Charles Clayton, Sherman Hohton, John Luttrell, and Horace Page) of California because California had the highest volume of Chinese immigration and San Francisco was the city to pass the first opium ordinance in 1875, therefore it was assumed that the California Congressmen would be the most active in discussing opium legislation.

The 44th Congress's (1875-1876) Index was searched for the same terms as the 43rd Congress as well as the additional terms: California, China, Chinese, coolie, drugs, immigration, importation, labor, opium, San Francisco, and smoking opium. The Index was also searched for references to the Senators (Newton Booth and Aaron Sargent) and Representatives (John Luttrell, Horace Page, William Piper and Peter Wigginton) of California. Neither the Senate nor the House Index referenced opium or smoking opium.

The 46th Congress (March, 1879 – March, 1881) was examined because of the passage of the American-Chinese treaty of 1880, a commercial treaty, which prohibited Chinese citizens residing in the United States from importing smoking opium (Wright, 2002). The 46th Congress's Index was searched for the terms: American, China, Chinese, employment, immigration, importation, labor, opium, smoking opium, and treaty. The Index was also searched for references to the Senators (Newton Booth and James T. Farley) and Representatives (Cambell P. Berry, Horace Davis, and Romualdo Pacheco and Horace Page) of California.

The 49th Congress (March 1885 – March, 1887) was examined due to the enactment of a law prohibiting the importation of opium and smoking opium among the Chinese (Szasz, 2003; Lusane, 1991). The 49th Congress's Index was searched for the terms: China, Chinese, drugs, employment, immigration, importation, labor, opium, and smoking opium. The Indexes were also searched for references to the Senators (George Hearst, John F. Miller, Leland Stanford and Abram P. Williams) and Representatives (Charles N. Felton, Barclay Henley, J. A. Loutit, H. H. Markham, Joseph McKenna, and W. W. Morrow) of California.

The 50th, 51st and Special Session of the 51st Congresses (December 1887- March 1891) were examined because of the passage of the 1890 law that restricted the manufacturing of smoking opium (Szasz, 2003; Lusane, 1991). The Indexes for both Congresses were searched for the terms: California, China, Chinese, drugs, immigration, imports, labor, manufacturing, opium, and smoking opium. The Special Session of the 51st Congress (March 1889) Index did not reference China, Chinese, opium or smoking opium. The Indexes were also searched for references to the Senators (George Hearst and Leland Stanford) and Representatives (Marion Biggs, Thomas J. Clunie, John J. De Haven, Charles N. Felton, Thomas J. Geary, Joseph McKenna, W. W. Morrow, T. L. Thompson and William Vandever) of California.

The 60th and 61st Congresses were examined due to the passage of the 1909 Smoking Opium Exclusion Act. The second session of the 60th Congress (December, 1908 – March, 1909) and the first and second sessions of the 61st Congress (March, 1909 – June 1910) Indexes were searched under the following terms: China, Chinese, drugs, food and drugs, immigration, importation, labor, manufacturing, opium and smoking opium. Even though the first and second sessions of the 61st Congress were held after the passage of the 1909 Smoking Opium Exclusion Act, the Index was searched and it verified that there were no more discussions of China, Chinese, opium or smoking opium; none of these terms was included in the subjects of the Index. The Indexes for both Congresses were also searched for references to the

California Senators (Frank Flint and George Perkins) and Representatives (William Englebright, Everis Hayes, Julius Kahn, Joseph Knowland, Duncan McKinlay, James McLachlan, James Needham and Sylvester Smith).

For the each of the Congressional Sessions and search terms referenced in the Indexes, I noted all the documents and page numbers referenced. Each reference to the search terms denoted by Congressional Record page number was located, relevance assessed and analyzed regardless of length of mention[28]. In addition to page citations, the Index also provided a history of bills. I traced the history of each bill that was related to opium and verified that all the pages referencing those bills had been assessed.

Marihuana Tax Act Search Terms and Coding:

The start codes for analysis of the Marihuana Tax Act discussions were anti-Mexican sentiment, job competition, vilification of Mexicans and origin of marijuana. Given the increase in Mexican immigration and the migration of Mexican immigrants to the Midwest I assumed that the influx of Mexican immigrants would foster anti-Mexican sentiments within the Congressional discussions of the Marihuana Tax Act. A second assumption, given that the Marihuana Tax Act was created, discussed and passed during the Great Depression, was that the Congressional discussions would also include references to job competition, specifically discussions of Mexican immigrants taking jobs away from white workers because they were willing to work for less money. The third start code of vilification of Mexicans was used due to the assumption that similar to the opium law discussions, Congressional debates of marijuana would include references to

---

[28] Some references were mere statements that a bill had been sent to a committee or was still in a committee. Although these references were read, due to the nature and the volume of such references they were determined to have little relevance to the actual discussion of the laws and are not included in the analysis of the legislative discussions.

Mexican savagery or brutality while using marijuana. For the final start code, origins of marijuana, it was assumed that discussions would include references to Mexico and the Southwestern states, specifically those bordering or closest to Mexico. Due to the nature of the research some of the "start list" codes were sustained and new codes were developed as patterns emerged during analysis.

During analysis the start codes were amended to Mexicans/Mexico, hemp manufacturing and/or commercial use, tax and taxing ability, the vilification of marijuana, lack of knowledge/lack of discussion, and newspapers. The Mexicans/Mexico code was used to designate references to Mexicans and their use of marijuana and Mexico as the source of the drug. Hemp manufacturing and/or commercial use refers to the discussions of how the legislation would affect the hemp manufacturers and how commercial use might change. Tax and taxing ability denotes discussions centered on how the legislation could and would be enforced. The vilification of marijuana code was used to indicate discussions about negative consequences of marijuana use. This code was split into the three sub codes of children (for discussions focusing on the concern about children's use of marijuana), crime (for stories about heinous crimes committed while under the influence of marijuana) and insanity (for comments about marijuana use causing insanity). The code lack of knowledge/lack of discussion was used to designate remarks indicating Congressional members' lack of knowledge and/or discussion of marijuana or the legislation. The final code of newspaper was added to indicate when newspaper accounts were used to support views.

The Congressional Record Indexes for the 74th and 75th Congresses were used to search for all discussions of and references to the proposed marijuana legislation. Based on the start codes, the search terms used were Harry Anslinger, cannabis, drugs, hashish, Hatch bill (the previous name of the Marihuana Tax Act legislation), labor, marijuana/marihuana, Mexicans, narcotics and the names of southwestern congressmen. It was assumed that since the southwestern states were the closest to Mexico, the purported source of marijuana, and experienced the highest levels of Mexican immigrants that the southwestern congressmen would be the most active in the marijuana legislation discussions. During the first session of the 74th Congress (January, 1935 – August, 1935) there was no reference to Harry Anslinger, drugs, hashish or marijuana and only a brief reference to cannabis and the Hatch bill. There was also no mention of hashish, cannabis or marijuana during the second session of the 74th Congress (January, 1936 – June, 1936). The Index for the first session of the 75th Congress (January, 1937 – August, 1937) did not include the search terms Harry Anslinger or Hatch bill, but did include marijuana and cannabis. Although the second session of the 75th Congress (November, 1937 – December, 1937) was held after the passage of the Marihuana Tax Act, I did search the Index to verify that there were no more discussions of cannabis or marijuana; neither of those terms was included in the subjects of the Index.

For the search terms referenced in the Indexes, I noted all the documents and page numbers referenced. Each reference to the search terms denoted by Congressional Record page number was located and analyzed regardless of length of mention. In addition to page citations, the Index also provided a history of bills. I traced the history of each bill that was related to marijuana or cannabis and verified that all the pages referencing those bills had been assessed.

Anti Drug Abuse Act Search Terms and Coding:

The start codes for analysis of the Anti Drug Abuse Act of 1986 discussions were vilification of Latinos/Hispanics and African Americans, reverse discrimination (job competition) and welfare queens. Given that popular belief held that crack cocaine use was associated with the lower classes and minorities while cocaine use was associated with the upper classes and whites, it was assumed that the discussions about these drugs and their penalties would include derogatory comments about African Americans and Latinos/Hispanics and would focus on their use of the drug rather than other segments of the U.S. population. A second assumption, given that the Anti Drug

Abuse Act was created, discussed and passed after the economic recession of the early 1980's and following the California v. Bakke decisions, was that the Congressional discussions would also include references to reverse discrimination and job competition. The third start code of welfare queens was used due to the assumption that similar to reverse discrimination, since there were ongoing debates about the welfare system and welfare queen was a term used in reference to black women, the Congressional debates about the Anti Drug Abuse Act would include references to welfare queens. As with opium and the Marihuana Tax Act, due to the nature of the research some of the "start list" codes were sustained and new codes were developed as patterns emerged during analysis.

During analysis the start codes were amended to vilification of cocaine and crack, race, class, penalties, and newspapers. The vilification of cocaine and crack code was used to indicate discussions about the negative consequences of cocaine and crack use. This code was split into the three sub codes of children (for discussions focusing on the concern about children's use of cocaine and crack), addiction (for comments about cocaine and more specifically crack's addictiveness) and crime (for discussions focusing on cocaine and crack's association with crime). Race denotes references to racial minority members, specifically African American and Hispanic/Latino, and their use of drug as well as the Hispanic/Latino countries involved in international trafficking of cocaine. The class code was used to designate references to the social class of cocaine and crack users and dealers. Penalties refer to the discussions focusing on the penalties for use/possession of cocaine and crack. The final code of newspaper was added to designate when newspaper and/or magazine accounts were used for information and to support views.

Given the sheer volume of the Congressional Record for each Congress in the 1980's (approximately 30,000 pages per Congressional session with usually two sessions per Congress), a sampling frame was designed. Since the Anti Drug Abuse Act was enacted in 1986, I decided to limit the data to the 99th Congress (January, 1985 – October,

1986) which would still allow for approximately two years of data. To further narrow the scope of the data, I chose to focus on the discussions regarding cocaine and crack cocaine since the most controversial aspect of the Anti Drug Abuse Act has been the 100 times difference in the amount of crack cocaine and cocaine to receive the same 5 year penalty. Narrowing the scope of the data to these discussions also allowed for analysis of all the discussions and proceedings regarding cocaine and crack cocaine rather than a systematic sampling of the discussions with which valuable data may have been left out. The discussions regarding cocaine and crack cocaine were found through the online LexisNexis Congressional database search engine. The search terms used and the number of documents found are listed in Table Appendix.1. Multiple search terms were used to ensure that all discussions and proceedings regarding cocaine and crack cocaine were captured. The lists of documents from each search were cross checked and resulted in approximately 500 documents in total ranging from a few sentences to a couple hundred pages. In addition to searching by term, the LexisNexis Congressional database can provide a history of bills. I traced the history of each bill that was related to Anti Drug Abuse Act and verified that all the dates and citations referencing those bills had been assessed.

TABLE Appendix.1 Anti Drug Abuse Act of 1986 Search Terms and Number of Documents

Search Terms	Number of documents
Anti Drug Abuse Act of 1986	95
Anti Drug Abuse Act	105
Cocaine	487
Crack cocaine	67
Job competition	5
Reverse discrimination	30
Welfare queen	17
Mandatory minimum, drug	50
Mandatory minimum, cocaine	26
Mandatory minimum, crack	21
Sentencing guidelines, drug	23

References

Abadinsky, Howard. (2008). Drug Use and Abuse: A Comprehensive Introduction. Belmont, CA: Thomson Wadsworth.

Aguirre, Adalberto, Jr. & Turner, Jonathan H. (1995). American Ethnicity: The Dynamics and Consequences of Discrimination. New York: McGraw-Hill.

Alba, Richard, and Nee, Victor. (2003). Remaking the American Mainstream: Assimilation and Cotemporary Immigration. Cambridge, MA: Harvard University Press.

Albonetti, Celesta. (1997). "Sentencing under the Federal Sentencing Guidelines: Effects of Defendant Characteristics, Guilty Please, and Departures on Sentence Outcomes for Drug Offenses, 1991-1992." Law & Society Review 31: 789-822.

Alvarez, Jose Hernandez. (1966). "A Demographic Profile of the Mexican Immigration to the United States, 1910-1950." Journal of Inter-American Studies 8(3): 471-796.

Apostle, Richard A., Glock, Charles Y., Piazza, Thomas & Suelzle, Marijean. (1983). The Anatomy of Racial Attitudes. Berkeley, CA: University of California Press.

Balderrama, Francisco E. (2005). "The Emergence of Unconstitutional Deportation and Repatriation of Mexicans and Mexican Americans as a Public Issue." Radical History Review 93: 107-110.0

Barrera, Mario. (1979). Race and Class in the Southwest. Notre Dame, IN: University of Notre Dame Press.

Batten, James Hoffman. (1930). "New Features of Mexican Immigration: The Case Against Further Restrictive Legislation." Pacific Affairs 3(10): 956-966.

Blalock, Hubert M. (1967). Toward a Theory of Minority-Group Relations. New York: Wiley.

Blauner, Robert. (1972). Racial Oppression in America. New York: Harper & Row.

Bloch, Louis. (1929). "Facts About Mexican Immigration Before and Since the Quota Restriction Laws." Journal of American Statistical Association 24(165): 50-60.

Bonacich, Edna. (1972). "A Theory of Ethnic Antagonism: The Split Labor Market. American Sociological Review 37(5)" 547-559.

Bonilla-Silva, Eduardo. (2001). White Supremacy & Racism in the Post-Civil Rights Era. Boulder, CO: Lynne Rienner Publishers Inc.

Bonnie, Richard J. & Whitebread, Charles H. II. (1999). The Marijuana Conviction: A History of Marijuana Prohibition in the United States. New York: The Lindesmith Center.

Bositis, David A. (2004). "Blacks and the 2004 Republican National Convention." Washington, D.C.: Joint Center for Political and Economic Studies.

Bositis, David A. (2005). "The Black Vote in 2004." Washington, D.C.: Joint Center for Political and Economic Studies.

Bourgois, Phillippe. (1995). In Search of Respect: Selling Crack in El Barrio. Cambridge, UK: Cambridge University Press.

Brodie, Mollyann; Parmelee, Lisa Ferraro; Brackett, April & Altman, Drew E. (2001). "Polling and democracy: the will of the people." Public Perspective July/August: 10-14.

Bureau of Justice Statistics. (2003). "Drug and Crime Facts." (www.ojp.usdoj.gov/bjs/).

Bureau of Justice Statistics. (1994). "Drug and Crime Facts, 1994." (www.ojp.usdoj.gov/bjs/).

Chambliss, William J. (1964). "A Sociological Analysis of the Law of Vagrancy." Social Problems 12(1): 67-77.

Chambliss, William J. (1978). "The political economy of smack: opiates, capitalism and law." Research in Law and Sociology 1:115-141.

Chen, Jack. (1996). "Linking a Continent and a Nation." Pg. 23-37 in Exploring America's Past: Essays in Social, Political, and Cultural History, 1865-Present. Lanham, MD: University Press of America, Inc.

The Chinese in California, 1850-1925. (2008). http://memory.loc.gov/ammem/award99/cubhtml/chron/html.

Chiricos, Theodore G. & Bales, William D. (1991). "Unemployment and Punishment: An Empirical Assessment." Criminology 29:701-724.

Congress.org. (2010). http:congress.org/congressorg/directory/demographics.

Congressional Record (for the 43rd, 44th, 46th, 49th-51st, 60th, 61st, 74th, 75th and 99th Congresses). Government Printing Office.

Cotterrell, Roger. (1998). "Why Must Legal Ideas Be Interpreted Sociologically?" Journal of Law and Society 25(2): 171-92.

Courtwright, David T. (2001). Dark Paradise: A History of Opiate Addiction in America. Cambridge, MA: Harvard University Press.

Dickerson, Donna L. (2003). The Reconstruction Era: Primary Documents on Events from 1865-1877. Portsmouth, NH: Greenwood Press.

Doob, Christopher Bates. (1996). Racism: An American Cauldron. HarperCollins College Publishers.

Downs, Anthony. (1970). Racism in America and How to Combat It. Washington, DC: U.S. Commission on Civil Rights.

Edsall, Thomas Byrne & Edsall, Mary D. (1992). Chain Reaction: the Impact of Race, Rights, and Taxes on American Politics. New York: Norton.

Fagan, Jeffrey & Chin, Ko-lin. (1991). "Social Processes of Initiation into Crack." Journal of Drug Issues 21: 313-343.

Feagin, Joe R. & Feagin, Clairece Booher. (1978). Discrimination American Style. New Jersey: Prentice-Hall, Inc.

------- (1993). Racial & Ethnic Relations. Englewood Cliffs, NJ: Prentice-Hall. Fourth Edition.

---- (1999). "Theoretical Perspectives in Race and Ethnic Relations" Pp. 41-59 in Race and Ethnic Conflict: Contending Views on Prejudice, Discrimination, and Ethnoviolence. Boulder, CO: Westview.

Feagin, Joe R. & McKinney, Karyn D. (2003). The Many Costs of Racism. Lanham, MD: Rowman & Littlefield Publishers, Inc.

Feagin, Joe R. & Vera, Hernan. (1995). White Racism. New York: Routledge.

Fernandez, Humberto. (1998). Heroin. Center City, MN: Hazelden.

Glazer, Nathan. (1975). Affirmative Discrimination: Ethnic Inequality and Public Policy. New York: Basic Books, Inc.

Grana, Sheryl & Ollenburger, Jane C. (1999). The social context of law. New Jersey: Prentice-Hall.

Gray, Mike. (2000). Drug Crazy: How We Got Into This Mess and How We Can Get Out. New York: Routledge.

Hacker, Andrew. (2003). Two Nations: Black & White, Separate, Hostile, Unequal. New York: Scribner.

Handman, Max Sylvius. (1930). "Economic Reasons for the Coming of the Mexican Immigrant." The American Journal of Sociology 35(4): 601-611.

House.gov (2008). http://www.house.gov/

Human Rights Watch. (2002). "Punishment and Prejudice: Racial Disparities in the War on Drugs." Vol. 12, No. 2.

Inciardi, James A. (1992). The War on Drugs II. Mountain View, CA: Mayfield Publishing Company.

James, Joy. (1998). The Angela Y. Davis Reader. Malden, MA: Blackwell Publishers Ltd.

Johnson, Allan G. (1995). The Blackwell Dictionary of Sociology. Malden, MA: Blackwell Publishers, Inc.

Johnson, Bruce D., Golub, Andrew, and Fagan, Jeffrey. (1995). "Careers in Crack, Drug Use, Drug Distribution, and Nondrug Criminality." Crime and Delinquency 41(July): 275-95.

Johnson, Kevin R. (2005). "The Fifteenth Annual Dyson Distinguished Lecture: The Forgotten "Repatriation" of Persons of Mexican Ancestry and Lessons for the "War on Terror."" Pace Law Review 26(1): 1-26.

Katz, Michael B; Stern, Mark J., and Fader, Jamie J. (2007). "The Mexican Immigration Debate: The View from History." Social Science History 31(2): 157-189.

Kennedy, Stetson. (1990). Jim Crow Guide: The Way It Was. Boca Raton, FL: Florida Atlantic University Press.

Kozol, Jonathan. (1991). Savage Inequalities: Children in America's Schools. New York: Crown Publishers, Inc.

Levenstein, Harvey A. (1968). "The AFL and Mexican Immigration in the 1920's: An Experiment in Labor Diplomacy." The HispanicAmerican Historical Review 48(2): 206-219.

Li, Tien-Lu. (1916). Congressional Policy of Chinese Immigration or Legislation Relating to Chinese Immigrants to the United States. Nashville, TN: Publishing House of the Methodist Episcopal Church.

Liska, Ken. (2004). Drugs and the Human Body: With Implications for Society. Upper Saddle River, NJ: Pearson Prentice Hall.

Lusane, Clarence. (1996). No Easy Victories: Black Americans and the Vote. New York: Franklin Watts, A Division of Grollier Publishing.

Lusane, Clarence. (1991). Pipe Dream Blues: Racism & the War on Drugs. Boston, MA: South End Press.

Lyman, Stanford M. (1974). Chinese Americans. New York: Random House.

Massey, Douglas S. & Denton, Nancy A. (1993). American Apartheid: Segregation and the Making of the Underclass. Cambridge, MA: Harvard University Press.

Mauer, Marc. (2009). "Testimony on Racial Disparities in the Criminal Justice System." www.sentencingproject.org.

McInturff, Bill & Weigel, Lori. (2001). "Servants of the people: political leadership and the public voice." Public Perspective July/August: 32-35.

Miles, M. & Huberman, A.M. (1994). Qualitative Data Analysis. Thousand Oaks, CA: Sage.

Molina, Natalia. (2006). "Medicalizing the Mexican: Immigration, Race, and Disability in the Early-Twentieth-Century United States." Radical History Review 94: 22-37.

Morgan, H. Wayne. (1974). Yesterday's Addicts: American Society and Drug Abuse 1865-1920. Norman, OK: University of Oklahoma Press.

----- (1981). Drugs in America: A Social History, 1800-1920. Syracuse, NY: Syracuse University Press.

Musto, David F. (1999). The American Disease: Origins of Narcotic Control (3rd ed.). New York: Oxford University Press.

----- (2002). Drugs in America: A Documentary History. New York: New York University Press.

Myers, Martha. (1989). "Symbolic Policy and the Sentencing of Drug Offenders." Law & Society Review 23: 295-315.

Oliver, Melvin L. & Shapiro, Thomas M. (1997). Black Wealth/White Wealth: A New Perspective on Racial Inequality. New York: Routledge.

Parsons, Talcott. (1962). "The Law and Social Control" in Law and Sociology, edited by William Evan, pp. 56-72.

Pohlman, Marcus D. (1999). Black Politics in Conservative America (2nd ed.). New York: Longman.

Pound, Roscoe. (1908). "Mechanical Jurisprudence." Columbia Law Review 8(8): 605-623.

Provine, Doris Marie. (2007). Unequal Under the Law: Race in the War on Drugs. Chicago: The University of Chicago Press.

Ray, Oakley & Ksir, Charles. (1993). Drugs, Society, & Human Behavior. St. Louis, MO: Mosby-Year Book, Inc.

Reinarman, Craig & Levine, Harry G. (1997). "The Crack Attack: Politics and Media in the Crack Scare" in Crack in America: Demon Drugs and Social Justice ed Craig Reinarman and Harry G. Levine. Berkley, CA: University of California Press.

Ringer, Benjamin B. (1983). "We the People" and Others: Duality and America's Treatment of its Racial Minorities. New York: Tavistock Publications.

Robinson, Michael J. (1999). "The genius of our success." Public Perspective October/November: 3-7.

The Roper Center. (2001a) "Government by the people."

----- (2001b). "People, Opinions & Polls. An American Dilemma (Part II)." Public Perspective February/March: 19-42.

Sedlacek, William E. & Brooks, Glenwood C. (1976). Racism IN American Education: A Model for Change. Chicago: Nelson-Hall.

Senate.gov. (2010). www.senate.gov/artandhistory/history/common/briefing/minority_senators.

The Sentencing Project. (1993). (**http://www.sentencingproject.org**).

The Sentencing Project. (2010). (**http://www.sentencingproject.org**).

Seward, George F. (1970). Chinese Immigration: Its Social and Economic Aspects. New York: Arno Press, Inc.

Sloman, Larry. (1979). Reefer Madness: The History of Marijuana in America. New York: St. Martin's Griffin.

Spohn, Cassia & Spears, Jeffrey. (2002). "Sentencing of Drug Offenders in Three Cities: Does Race/Ethnicity Make a Difference?" in Crime Control and

Criminal Justice: The Delicate Balance ed. Darnell F. Hawkins, Samuel L. Meyers Jr., and Randolph N. Stone. Westport, CT: Greenwood.

Sutton, John R. (2001). Law/Society: Origins, Interactions, and Change. Thousand Oaks, CA: Pine Forge Press.

Szasz, Thomas. (2003). Ceremonial Chemistry: The Ritual Persecution of Drugs, Addicts, and Pushers (Revised Edition). New York: Syracuse University Press.

Taylor, Paul S. (1930). "Some Aspects of Mexican Immigration." The Journal of Political Economy 38(5): 609-615.

Taxation of Marihuana: Hearings before the Committee on Ways and Means, House of Representatives, Seventy-Fifth Congress First Session on H.R. 6385. (1937a). Washington: United States Government Printing Office.

Taxation of Marihuana: Hearing before the Subcommittee of the Committee on Finance, United States Senate, Seventy-Fifth Congress First Session on H.R. 6906. (1937b). Washington: United States Government Printing Office.

Tittle, Charles R. (1994). "The Theoretical Bases for Inequality in Formal Social Control." Pp. 21-52 in Inequality, Crime, and Social Control, edited by George S. Bridges and Martha A. Myers. Boulder: Westview Press.

Tonry, Michael. (1995). Malign Neglect: Race, Crime and Punishment in America. New York: Oxford University Press.

Trevino, A. Javier. (1996). The Sociology of Law: Classical and Contemporary Perspective. New York: St. Martin's Press.

Tsai, Shih-shan Henry. (1986). The Chinese Experience in America. Bloomington, IN: Indiana University Press.

Turk, Austin T. (1976). "Law as a Weapon in Social Conflict." Social Problems 23(2):276-91.

Uggen, Christopher & Manza, Jeff. (2002). "Democratic Contraction? Political Consequences of Felon Disenfranchisement in the United States." American Sociological Review 67: 777-803.

United States Constitution.

United States Department of Justice. (2008). http://www.usdoj.gov

United States Drug Enforcement Administration (2010), http://www.usdoj.gov/dea

United Nations Office of Drugs & Crime. (2008). http://www.unodc.org

Williams, Bruce B. (1987). Black Workers in an Industrial Suburb: The Struggle Against Discrimination. New Brunswick, NJ: Rutgers University Press.

Wilson, William J. (1973). Power, Racism and Privilege: Race Relations in Theoretical and Sociohistorical Perspectives. New York: Macmillian.

----- (1978). The Declining Significance of Race: Blacks and Changing American Institutions. Chicago: University of Chicago Press.

Wright, Hamilton. (2002). "The Shanghai Commission's Recommendations on Cocaine: Report on the International Opium Commission and on the Opium Problem as Seen Within the United States." In Drugs in America: A Documentary History, edited by David F. Musto, pp. 368-379. New York: New York University Press.

Wright, Hamilton. (1910). "Report on the International Opium Commission and on the Opium Problem as seen within the United States and its Possessions." Senate Document No. 377. Government Printing Office.

Yinger, John. (1995). Closed Doors, Opportunities Lost: The Continuing Costs of Housing Discrimination. New York: Russell Sage Foundation.

Index